MEAD AND
HONEY WINES

A Comprehensive Guide

Other publications by Michael Badger:

Heather Honey: A Comprehensive Guide
How to Use a Horsley Board for Swarm Control
The Morris Board Method of Queen Rearing

MEAD AND HONEY WINES
A Comprehensive Guide

MICHAEL BADGER, MBE

Illustrations by
Michael Badger, David Lumb RIBA,
Erica Osborn and Damien Timms

Wicwas Press

Published 2018 under licence by
Wicwas Press LLC
1620 Miller Road, Kalamazoo, MI 49001 USA

www.wicwas.com

ISBN paperback book: 978-1-878075-52-9

Design by Tim Jollands

Printed and bound in the United States of America

DEDICATION

Dedicated to my late departed mead- and beer-making peers,
SW (Andy) Andrews and my father, Tim, Charley Hopwood, Charles
S Bell and Dennis Rouston, who were also imbibers
of the nectar of man and mead.

Best in Show for a bottle of Sweet Mead at the Great Yorkshire Show: laid-in
bottle 1981 by the author in readiness for the birth of his son in August 1982
[Caroline Badger]

Part royalties from the sales of this book will be donated in
equal parts to the charity Bees Abroad and those of the
Worshipful Company of Wax Chandlers of London.

THE AUTHOR

Michael Badger MBE

The author in deep concentration "nosing" the bouquet of a splendid
dessert wine at the 2016 Institute of Northern Ireland Beekeepers' Annual Honey
Show, Lough Neagh Discovery Centre, Oxford Island, Craigavon [Edward Winter]

CONTENTS

PREFACE

Peter Tomkins
Master, Worshipful Company of Wax Chandlers of London

As Master of the Worshipful Company of Wax Chandlers, I am delighted to welcome Michael Badger's comprehensive survey of the history and practice of mead making. Our historic trade guild dates back to the 14th century, together with a charter granted to us in 1484 by King Richard III. We are number 20 out of more than 100 City of London livery companies and especially support the wax industry – ancient and modern – and the craft of beekeeping which includes the production of wax candles.

Beekeeping brings us access to the finest of all waxes and thus the candles which traditionally graced the tables of the rich and lit the worship of the people. We continue, as we have ever done, to support wax-making and use in all its many forms. The high point for our company was probably during the later Middle Ages

Peter Tomkins – Master, Worshipful Company of Wax Chandlers of London
[Georgina Brown, Clerk to the Company]

when demand for candles for lighting in churches in memory of the dead was high. The low point was when Henry VIII and the Protestant Reformation led to the abolition of candles in churches!

Beekeepers also, of course, gave us honey, the finest of sweeteners, and there is little doubt that one of the earliest of human alcoholic drinks would have been the fermentation of diluted honey, probably long before the oldest extant pictorial records of primitive man creating or drinking it.

Our history goes back only 650 years, a fraction of the time since people first collected and consumed the honey from the hives that hunter-gatherers would have taken from the woods. It is our pleasure today to support young people as they pursue the development of their skills through education and training as apprentices in the beekeeping world. A book of this substance will be a great assistance to so many people in their studies. It is our hope that the many stories contained within it will inspire more people to take up and pursue this ancient and worthwhile craft – and that it will enhance the enjoyment of the many varieties of the beverage itself. As we would say in our livery company, may the drinking of mead flourish root and branch, coupled with the name of this book's author, Michael Badger.

FOREWORD

Ken Schramm

MICHAEL YOUNG MBE

I t is a rare treat to be given the chance to lead off such a wonderful work as Michael has crafted here.

Mead's grip on our imagination spans the thousands of years of its incredible history. People have made honey-based alcoholic beverages in virtually every corner of the earth. Great Britain has had a romance with mead going back centuries, but mead's appeal has entrenched it into the cultures of Eastern Europe, Asia and Africa. With the Proto-Indo-European word "madhu" meaning both "mead" and "honey", it would appear that we were intoxicated both by honey's sweetness and by its potential for intoxication itself. New World natives were pressing their miniscule supplies of honey – from tiny, stingless *Meliponini* honeybees – into the fermentation of alcoholic beverages when the first Europeans arrived in the middle of the last millennium. Even without the abundance of the European honeybee, mead was an important part of their lives, rituals and religion.

It has been riveting to watch as modern historical study and archaeological technique have solidified our knowledge of the pivotal role of honey and mead in so many different cultures over nearly 100 centuries. From the honey gatherers pictured in the cave art of Bicorp, Spain, to the 2,500-year-old mead cauldron from the Celtic Chieftain's tomb in Hochdorf, Germany, and from the mixed honey drink in the Midas Tomb in Turkey to the fermented honey beverage chronicled in 9,000-year-old pottery shards from Jiahu, China, honey and mead have revealed themselves to be fundamental to each of those societies. Science, curiosity and human innovation have given us the tools to pull back the curtain on our long history of fermentation. The further back we are able to reach, the more we confirm that humans have been drawn to honey and mead.

Many contend that mead's greatest hour has come and gone, and that it is experiencing a faddish "renaissance" of interest from beverage enthusiasts. For all of mead's formidable history, though, I am genuinely convinced that we are living now in the Golden Age of Mead. There are too many powerful reasons why mead is now greater than it has ever been. Mead makers have access to magnificent honeys from around the world at the click of a web link. We can easily purchase fruits, either fresh or frozen, as well as a treasure trove of spices and yeast strains that would have mead makers of even 20 years ago – let alone eight hundred or eight thousand – green with envy. We have access to information on how to craft our spectacular beverage through proven fermentation and recipe formulation techniques. Our mazer cup runneth over with splendid opportunities. And the drinking public, when confronted with the deliciousness that is mead today, is being bowled over by how good mead really is.

Michael's first-hand knowledge of honey, mead and beekeeping is an invaluable foundation for the book he has written here. His expertise is a doorway into exquisite taste experiences unavailable to those stumbling, unaware, through their existence. Here, then, is Michael Badger's invitation to become one of the enlightened. For those who know mead, and especially well-made mead, it has become a stable, regular part of our lives. It is on our dinner table with roast pork. It is with us in the summer, in the garden, with friends and family. It is on our fishing trips and a part of our holiday celebrations. Mead is not a novelty for us; it has become, like good food, beer and wine, a staple of our lives.

This is not a book to be read and set aside. This is a reference text to keep at your elbow and refer to over and over. At Schramm's Mead, we revel in hearing customers blurt out, "Wow! This may be the best thing I've ever tasted", at their first sip of mead. With time, care, devotion to great ingredients and Michael's capable tutelage, you should be hearing that exclamation from friends and acquaintances in the very near future.

Ken Schramm
Schramm's Mead – www.schrammsmead.com
327 West Nine Mile Road, Ferndale, Michigan, MI, 48220, USA

ACKNOWLEDGEMENTS

I would like to express my thanks and appreciation to Peter Lewis and Michael Young, MBE, for their help and assistance in the production of this guide to mead and honey wine production; Gerald (Gerry) Collins, NDB, for providing many photographs of honeys; Ken Schramm, Ferndale, Michigan, USA, for advice on mead produced "over the pond", his thoughts on the use of nutrient additions, and his most welcoming foreword; Kim Flottum for kindly providing a prologue and giving publicity to this book in the USA; Ivor Flatman for technical assistance on terms and meanings; Professor William (Bill) Sutherland, Miriam Rothschild Professor of Conservation Biology, University of Cambridge, for reviewing the environmental aspects; Bill Cadmore for reviewing the biological details in the text; Norman Carreck for permission to use illustrations of bees and flowers from *Pollen Loads of the Honey Bee* by Dorothy Hodges, the cover of Dr Eva Crane's magisterial work *"Honey, A Comprehensive Survey"*, each published by the International Bee Research Association in 1974; William H. Kern Jr. Associate Professor, Urban Entomology; Fort Lauderdale Research and Education Center, African Honey Bee Extension & Education Program, University of Florida for advice and the use of a photograph of African honeybee, *Apis mellifera scutelatta* Lepeletier; ibrew, Parkwood, Queensland, Australia, for permission to use its sketch of the principle of the use of a vinometer; Vigo Ltd for permission to use its illustration of the stainless steel bottle syphon filler; Rochester Area Home Winemakers, New York, for giving me the incentive to research types of mead and honey wines; DK Publishing for the use of pictures of wines for the assessment of mead and honey wine – publication ISBN 978-0-7894-9685-0: *101 Essential Tips: Wine*; the helpfulness of Paul Trigwell, Tanglewood Wine Accessories, Weybridge, Surrey, for permission to use details and photographs of wine racks and wine cellars; my thanks to Dr Vlasta Pilozota and Dr Nela Nedic Tiban – their treatise August / September 2009 – Advances in Honey Adulteration Detection – and also to the FoodSafety magazine for the excellent narrative on this subject; I am indebted to kegging procedures and photographs by Dan Daugherty, Cidersage, Colorado, for his willingness and helpfulness in allowing these to be used; Coravin™ for their helpfulness with details of Model Two Wine System; David Lumb RIBA, Erica Osborn and Damien Timms for providing sketches of the honeybee's glandular system, digestive system and man's olfactory senses: thanks go to the Hallewell-Sutcliffe family trust for financial support in the production of this book; my wife, Hilary, and children, Caroline, Joanne and Andrew, for their unstinting support in the production of this major work on mead and honey wine.

Michael Badger
17 April 2017

An Ode to the Mead and Honey Wine Producer

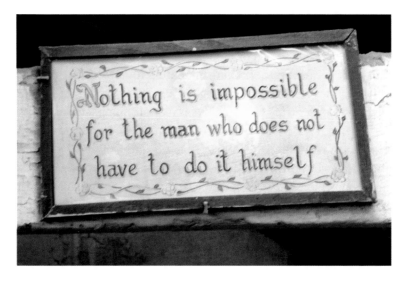

A sign in the workshops at the Whitechapel Bell Foundry, Whitechapel Road, London EC1 1DY [Erica Osborn]

INTRODUCTION

M*ead and Honey Wines: A Comprehensive Guide* is the second book of a possible quartet of subjects in a series of comprehensive guides concerning honey. The first, *Heather Honey*, has been well received; hopefully this one will, too. The remaining two will be titled *Honey Beers* and *Cooking with Honey*, for possible issue within the current decade.

There are many publications on the subject of mead making, with the majority of the literature becoming dated because of the rapid advancement of the types of yeasts and nutrients introduced in the past 20 years that help the mead vintner produce better-quality wine than ever before.

For my part, in this book I wish to reach out to the increasing wider audience of mead and honey wine producers, helping them to understand the many facets concerning honey and its elaboration from nectar to the finished article. I want to give the non-beekeeper a better understanding of the honeys available, their type and constituents, to ensure they can obtain the correct honey for the wine they wish to produce. Whilst it is hoped to have a broader readership, present-day and future vintners will, I am sure, find my exposition fascinating: hopefully it will arouse in those who are indeed well qualified in mead making both nostalgic and no doubt happy memories of times past and present. I am conscious, too, of the adage of those rushing into taking up making meads and honey wines – "All the gear, but no idea" – hence, for those that embark on this fascinating pastime, I am hoping my treatise will be a real aid to being successful in their endeavours.

The book has been written to meet the needs of mead makers in the UK and the USA and Canada, but not forgetting our mead-making compatriots of Australasia. I have, where applicable, separated the practices and thoughts applicable to mead making in the UK and USA. For the purposes of meeting the criteria of both the National Guild of Wine and Beer Judges (NGWBJ) of the UK, and likewise the Beer Judge Certification Program (BJCP) in the USA, there are specific diversions in approach to the criteria of mead and honey wine in terms of both its production and its use in competition. Therefore I have gone out of my way to give the reader a guide to meet all the needs of its production to ensure the correct criteria are met.

My mentors instilled upon me, as with all subjects of life that I had to "test the rungs of the ladder before I could climb it": this maxim is well suited to those wishing to produce mead and honey wines. Nevertheless, the mead maker needs to be fully aware of the pitfalls that may beset him when using different types of honey and how its origin could so easily spoil a good sample of mead and honey wine. I have made dedications to the late SW (Andy) Andrews and the late Dennis Rouston, to whom I owe a debt of sincere gratitude for their unstinting help and support in my tottering steps towards understanding meadery activities: their words of wisdom are now hopefully being passed on to a new and rising fellowship of mead makers.

Sad that it is, for many years the art of home wine making (other than beers) has been in gradual decline, due in part to changes in lifestyles, coupled with the availability of good wines at moderate prices. However, interest in mead is experiencing a renaissance – and long may it continue. Any interest that I can generate in mead and honey wine making that will ensure its production continues for generations to come is not lost. I feel it pleasurable to have been a mead maker, and latterly a honey beer brewer. If I can pass on my ideas to others it will be a good thing for all.

I have purposely not included too many photographs showing all the physical work of making the meads and wines, as I felt it not necessary on the premise that it might be somewhat self-explanatory to the reader of what is required. With this in mind, the reader will find at the beginning of each chapter, the subject's contents are itemised and page numbered which obviates the need for a detailed index. In addition, the extensive appendices cover a wide-church of information and detail. Nevertheless, writing a book of this magnitude is fraught with difficulties trying to determine what the reader might expect; it is further complicated not knowing what information is needed or required and to what depth, the level of information is required. I trust the reviewers of my treatise will take this into account.

It is my sincere hope that this book will enable you to derive the same sense of fun and enthusiasm for this pastime that I have experienced, and that it will provide the means for you to produce mead and honey wine of quality, merit and satisfaction.

Michael Badger
17 April 2017

USE OF TERMS, INCLUDING MEASUREMENTS AND WEIGHTS

For the ease of explanation, the terms of gender are ignored; therefore "his or he" equally applies to "her or she".

The term *juice concentrate* applies to commercially grown concentrated wine unless specified otherwise.

The term *mead maker* applies equally to a maker of honey wines.

The term *wine* applies equally to meads, country and honey wines.

The term *vintner* is used for mead maker and honey wine maker.

The term *cellar-craft* is used to denote the storage and maintenance of the completed wine.

The term *sterilisation* used singularly denotes all aspects of cleanliness, sanitisation, disinfecting and sterilisation.

To avoid duplication of technical words in the text, the term *liquor* will be used singularly to avoid over complication of the common theme for meads and honey wine, unless there is an express need for differentiation.

MEAD TYPES
AND HONEY WINES

HISTRIONICS

There is much written about the origin of mead and honey wines being the first alcoholic drink known to man: much of this can be more legend than actuality. Nevertheless, mead does indeed have a long history, as alluded to by Ken Schramm in his Foreword. Whilst researching my previous work on heather honey, Professor William (Bill) Sutherland reinforced a view extolled by the late Dr Oliver Rackham (former research fellow at the Botany Department, Cambridge) that man's liking for a honey-based beverage may so easily have arisen through early mankind (as a hunter-gatherer) finding discarded honeycomb from marauding bears lying on saucer-type leaves on the jungle floor. Regular rainfall combined with the naturally high temperature turned the vestiges of honey into a fermented liquid that he readily imbibed: the liquid to his liking was probably sought. Such a theory, albeit not legend, can be taken uncritically as more than feasible, especially as these early peoples relied on their wits to survive. To digress, it is believed that early man found that the animals killed in ferocious bush fires were very palatable compared to raw flesh that he cooked all meat, and by doing so killed off any parasites in the meat: so easily can fact be nearer the truth than fiction.

I attended in 2006 the mead show at Boulder and listened to a lecture by Mark Beran of Medovina, Niwot, Boulder County, Colorado. Mark gave an interesting synopsis of the origins of mead traced back to the African bush 40,000 years BC The wild honeybees were well established in the heartlands of Central Africa, and with the many woodland areas of buffalo thorn (*Ziziphus mucronata*), baobab (*Adansonia digitata*), jackalberry (*Diospyros mespiliformis*), bushwillow (*Combretum apiculatum*), the elephants roamed across the vast plains as they do to this day. The extreme weather patterns of torrential rains and drought saw the elephants in times of food scarcity uproot the trees or pull the

An African honeybee, *Apis mellifera scutelatta* Lepeletier,
colony between buttress roots of a tree. [Photograph by
W. H. Kern, Jr., University of Florida (with permission)]

large branches from the trees, creating many rotting hollows; over time, the wild bees would swarm into the boles.

Creating a natural cycle in the dry season, the bees would nest in these hollows, and during the wet season the hollows would fill with water. Water, plus honey with wild osmotolerant yeast present, the naturally high temperature on the vast open plains set the environmental conditions for a fermented drink to come into being. These early peoples gathered not only honey, but also this early form of mead. As these early peoples migrated away from Eastern Africa, believed to be the cradle of human evolution following the intensive palaeoanthropological researches of Louis and Mary Leakey at Olduvai Gorge, Tanzania, they no doubt took their beekeeping and mead-making techniques with them.

Archaeological investigations in northern China found pottery vessels dating from 9000-6500 BC discovered showing chemical signs consistent with the presence of honey, rice and many organic compounds supplementary to fermentation.

The original surviving description of mead is believed to be portrayed in the hymns of the Rigveda, part of the sacred books of the ancient Vedic religion (later Hinduism) around 1700-1100 BC. In the period known as the Golden Age of Ancient Greece, mead was said to be the favoured drink. It is believed that Aristotle (384-322 BC) discussed mead in his *Meteorologica*, while Pliny the Elder, a Roman naturalist and author (AD 23-79; Gaius Plinius Secundus), termed mead **militates** in his majestic work *Naturalis Historia* by differentiating wine sweetened with honey or "honey wine" from mead.

So with the passage of time, we arrive at present-day mead production.

DISTINCTIVE MERITS OF MEAD AND HONEY WINES

The alcoholic content of these wines may range from about 8 per cent alcohol by volume (ABV) to more than 20 per cent. The defining characteristic of meads and honey wines is that the majority of the beverage's fermentable sugar is derived from honey. It may be produced as still, carbonated or naturally sparkling; and it may be dry, semi-sweet or sweet.

NOTE:
The trained palate is the only real practical arbiter in determining the level of sweetness of a wine, other than precision bench analytical methods, which in reality are not a practical methodology to be considered for the hobbyist vintner. It should be clearly understood that the use of the hydrometer is not the true method of determination of sweetness due to the amount of salts / solids present in a given sample of wine. The presence of these items can influence quite readily and incorrectly the amount of sugar present in the wine. Taste really is the only guide to the sweetness of a wine.

It needs to be made clear that the specific gravity (SG) of a wine when related to the process of fermentation is that, as the sugar is converted to alcohol, its specific gravity will decrease. Taking the SG of pure water, the hydrometer will give a reading of 1.000

– there may need to be an allowance for minor variations due to both altitude and temperature. When the mead vintner adds honey or other soluble solids, the SG will increase: this arises because a liquid containing sugar is denser than plain water; therefore, in a dry wine the SG may well be 0.990, as there is no sugar present, and alcohol is less dense than plain water.

Sweeter mead and honey wine variants are inclined to have an increase in viscosity (body) through the remaining residual sugar in the finished mead; in addition, this is influenced by initial strength with increased alcohol.

Mead Types produced in the United Kingdom under the rules of the National Guild of Wine and Beer Judges (NGWBJ) can be summarised as follows – bearing in mind the summation given previously above:

Dry	As the name implies – Specific Gravity 0.990-1.000
Sweet	As the name implies – Specific Gravity 1.009-1.020
Sack	Heavy sweet meads are generally served as a dessert wine – Specific Gravity 1.021+. This type of wine is very much like a Sauternes wine (a sweet wine from the Sauternais region of the Graves section in Bordeaux, France. Interestingly, Sauternes wines are produced from Semillon, Sauvignon blanc and Muscadelle grapes affected by *Botrytis cinerea*, a generic necrotrophic fungus that affects many plant species, most notably wine grapes). This mead type is made with more honey than is typically used, hence its sweetness and high alcohol level. The finished product contains a higher than average ethanol concentration (meads at or above 14 per cent ABV are generally considered to be of sack strength), and often retains a high specific gravity and elevated levels of sweetness, although dry sack meads (which have no residual sweetness) can be produced. According to one theory, the name derives from the fortified dessert sherry wine (which is sometimes sweetened after fermentation) that, in England, once bore the nickname "sack". Another theory is that the term is a phonetic reduction of "sake", the name of a Japanese beverage that was introduced to the West by Spanish and Portuguese traders.

Pyment	Made from pure grape juice, often known as "white mead".
Melomel	Made from honey and any fruit or fruit juice other than grape and apple. Depending on the fruit base used, certain melomels may also be known by more specific names, possibly from the Greek melomeli, literally "apple honey" or "tree fruit honey".
Cyser	Made with pure apple juice.
Metheglin	Pyment mead flavoured with spices; traditional mead with herbs or spices added. Some of the most common metheglin spice additives are ginger, tea, orange peel, nutmeg, coriander, cinnamon, cloves and vanilla. Its name indicates that many metheglins were originally employed as folk medicines. The Welsh word for "mead" is *medd*, and the word "metheglin" derives from *meddyglyn*, a compound of *meddyg*, "healing", and *llyn*, "liquor".
Hippocras	A pyment mead with only spices added and no herbs.
Country wines	The use of vegetables to make melomel-type wines using honey and/or cane sugar.

Mead Wines produced in the United States of America and Canada under the rules of the Beer Judge Certification Program (BJCP) can be summarised as follows –

Traditional Meads	
Dry	As the name implies – Specific Gravity 0.990-1.000
Semi-Sweet	As the name implies – Specific Gravity 1.001-1.009
Sweet	As the name implies – Specific Gravity 1.010-1.020
Sack	Heavy sweet meads are generally served as a dessert wine – Specific Gravity 1021+.
Fruit Meads	The rule is that the fruit and the honey need to be apparent but not to dictate the flavour.
Cyser (Apple Mead)	Made with pure apple juice.
Pyment (Grape Mead)	A melomel made with grapes, commonly grape juice.
Berry Mead	A melomel made from berries with seeds excluding stones, i.e. raspberries, elderflowers, blackberries, etc. These may be mixed berries.

Stone Fruit Mead	A melomel made from stone fruits; i.e. apricot, peaches, etc., that contain a large pit or stone. They may be mixed stone fruits, too.
Melomel	Fruit mead that is other than the fruit meads mentioned above.
Spiced Mead	Mead from spice, fruit, herb or vegetable.
Fruit and Spice Mead	
Spice, Herb or Vegetable Mead	In addition to traditional spices, the BJCP taxonomy is accepted to include the term spices. In the situation of spices only, this is termed metheglin.
Speciality Mead	A US method of mead using grains, but is not a honey beer.
Braggot	A US method of mead using grains, but is not a honey beer.
Historical Mead	Meads that are not readily categorised
Experimental Mead	Mead that does not ally itself to any other mead not defined above that may be all-encompassing

OTHER MEAD TYPES KNOWN THROUGHOUT THE WORLD

Hydromel Its name is derived from the Greek *hydromeli*, literally "water-honey". It is also the French term for mead, *hydromel*. It is produced in the Catalan district of Spain, Catalan *hidromel*, and referred to also as *aiguamel* (Galician *aiguamel*); in Portugal, *hidromel*; Italy, *idromele*: in essence it is regarded as an inferior mead, and as the name implies (*hydro*) it is a watered-down low-alcohol mead.

Great Mead A lesser-known term given to meads of any style that are known to have been allowed to age over at least seven years.

Short Mead Also colloquially known as "quick mead". A type of mead recipe meant to age quickly and for immediate consumption. Because of the techniques used in its creation, "short mead" exhibits some qualities found in cider (or even light ale): primarily, it is effervescent, often with a taste of cider. It can also be champagne-like.

Show Mead A term which has come to mean "plain" mead. This is mead which has honey and water as a base, with no fruits, spices or extra flavourings added during or after the fermentation period. Since honey alone often does not provide enough nourishment for the yeast to complete its life cycle, mead that is devoid of fruit (to add further sugars, etc.) will sometimes require the use of a special yeast nutrient, acids and other enzymes to produce an acceptable finished product.

WHAT THE VINTNER IS STRIVING FOR

ASSESSING THE VIRTUES OF MEAD AND HONEY WINES

The tyro mead and country wine vintner needs to be advised of what he should be aiming for in its production. Meads and honey wines uniqueness is through the use of honey as its base as a sweetening agent as opposed to sucrose. In the interests of tact, and the avoidance of becoming patronising, this is my summation of the practices of mead and honey wine making which all wine producers should strive for in their quest for excellence for the perfect wine.

It is my belief, as a long-time vintner, that it essential for those embarking on mead production to be aware of the principles of an analysis of the wine they seek to produce, what they are striving for, and the liquor's true qualities and attributes to make it a wine of supreme quality exceeding the vintner's own expectations. If I may be permitted to digress, Richard Brooksbank, the Nottingham wine judge, judging mead at the 1993 Great Yorkshire Show, expressed the view that the meads (sweet and dry) he had tasted were of such high order that some of them were so well produced that they might well have been of the finest-aged Solera sherry wines: this statement exemplifies typically what the mead and country wine maker should strive and aim for in his wine making.

The easiest way of expressing these requirements to achieve such a finished wine is for the vintner to "wear the hat of a wine judge". By this, I mean you need to meet his criteria for the wine to be par excellence: using this critique will ensure you meet success, as it is an ideal yardstick to achieve excellence.

So what are these requirements that need to be fulfilled?

WORKING CRITERIA

The vintner needs to take account of the following when commencing a batch of wine:

- Colour
- Viscosity, legs or tears
- Bouquet
- Tasting
- Flavour
- Balance, weight and body
- Length

Colour

The colour of a wine (mead and honey wine) is an immediate give-away to a wine's qualities. So examine and study the wine in a natural light: artificial light affects its colour to the eye. A wine's hue, its intensity and colour depth, gives an indication of the maturity and age of the wine: more especially in red wines. Clarity is important to a young, fresh wine; it will in the main be brighter than older meads. Caution is needed as cloudiness may result from disturbed sediment; however, it may well suggest a fault in the wine, too.

With mead and honey wines their colour ranges across a wide spectrum of light colours: colourless, water-white to a deep colour. The honey base determines whether the mead will be light, straw-yellow (acacia) to lemon yellow (clover), yellow gold to old gold (ling heather), with the choice of yeast having some impact on the resultant wine, too.

Water-White The wine with a defined edge suggests a wine of quality despite its apparent watery colour, yet it is often clear and star-bright. In grape wines, the pale colour is an indication of its origin relating to a cool climate.

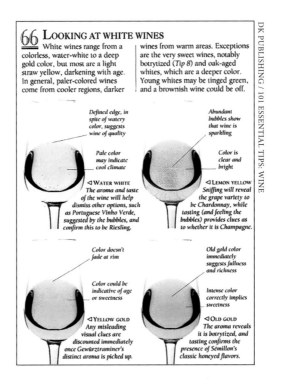

66 LOOKING AT WHITE WINES

White wines range from a colorless, water-white to a deep gold color, but most are a light straw yellow, darkening with age. In general, paler-colored wines come from cooler regions, darker wines from warm areas. Exceptions are the very sweet wines, notably botrytized (*Tip 8*) and oak-aged whites, which are a deeper color. Young whites may be tinged green, and a brownish wine could be off.

Defined edge, in spite of watery color, suggests wine of quality

Pale color may indicate cool climate

◁ **WATER WHITE**
The aroma and taste of the wine will help dismiss other options, such as Portuguese Vinho Verde, suggested by the bubbles, and confirm this to be Riesling.

Abundant bubbles show that wine is sparkling

Color is clear and bright

◁ **LEMON YELLOW**
Sniffing will reveal the grape variety to be Chardonnay, while tasting (and feeling the bubbles) provides clues as to whether it is Champagne.

Color doesn't fade at rim

Color could be indicative of age or sweetness

◁ **YELLOW GOLD**
Any misleading visual clues are discounted immediately once Gewürztraminer's distinct aroma is picked up.

Old gold color immediately suggests fullness and richness

Intense color correctly implies sweetness

◁ **OLD GOLD**
The aroma reveals it is botrytized, and tasting confirms the presence of Sémillon's classic honeyed flavors.

DK PUBLISHING / 101 ESSENTIAL TIPS: WINE

Assessing the light colours of melomel, metheglin, hippocras meads and other honey fruit wines

Lemon Yellow The colour is clear and star-bright. The abundance of bubbles is a sure sign that the wine is sparkling through the use of champagne yeast.

Yellow Gold Colour does not fade at the rim. This colour can be indicative of both age and sweetness or singularly of these two characteristics. In grape-based wines, the Gewürztraminer's strain quickly announces its aroma.

Old Gold The colour suggests fullness and richness. Its intense colour implies sweetness and alcoholic strength. In grape wines the aroma is indicative that it is botrytised, reflecting classic honey flavours, too.

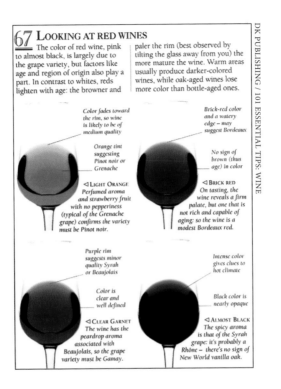

DK PUBLISHING / 101 ESSENTIAL TIPS: WINE

67 LOOKING AT RED WINES

The color of red wine, pink to almost black, is largely due to the grape variety, but factors like age and region of origin also play a part. In contrast to whites, reds lighten with age: the browner and paler the rim (best observed by tilting the glass away from you) the more mature the wine. Warm areas usually produce darker-colored wines, while oak-aged wines lose more color than bottle-aged ones.

Color fades toward the rim, so wine is likely to be of medium quality

Orange tint suggesting Pinot noir or Grenache

◁ LIGHT ORANGE
Perfumed aroma and strawberry fruit with no pepperiness (typical of the Grenache grape) confirms the variety must be Pinot noir.

Brick-red color and a watery edge – may suggest Bordeaux

No sign of brown (thus age) in color

◁ BRICK RED
On tasting, the wine reveals a firm palate, but one that is not rich and capable of aging; so the wine is a modest Bordeaux red.

Purple rim suggests minor quality Syrah or Beaujolais

Color is clear and well defined

◁ CLEAR GARNET
The wine has the peardrop aroma associated with Beaujolais, so the grape variety must be Gamay.

Intense color gives clues to hot climate

Black color is nearly opaque

◁ ALMOST BLACK
The spicy aroma is that of the Syrah grape: it's probably a Rhône – there's no sign of New World vanilla oak.

Assessing the red colour of melomel, metheglin, hippocras meads and other honey fruit wines

Honey Wines and Country Fruit Wines Colours

The colour of these wines varies from red and pink to almost black, arising from the origin of both the fruit and the honey used. As a comparison with white meads and honey wines, reds lighten with age: observation will reveal depth of colour by a specimen taken of the mead with the vintner tipping the tasting glass away from him, very often (but not always) reveals the browner and paler the rim, the maturity of the wine can be assured by this observation. In the laying down of grape-based wines in oak-aged barrels, they in fact lose more colour than bottle-aged wines.

Light Orange The wine colour is seen to diminish towards the rim of the tasting glass; the expert vintner would unhesitatingly suggest it to be of medium quality. Nevertheless, honey and fruit wines whose fruit base might be peach, apricot, raspberry or strawberry would totally disagree, as the bouquet and aroma would be revealed immediately. In a grape wine the orange tint might suggest Pinot noir or an equally excellent grape, Grenache.

Brick-Red This colour invariably comes with a watery edge, very often with no sign of brown demonstrating age in the colour. To the wine vintner this would indicate a Bordeaux wine. Brick-Red colour of a honey and fruit wine may well be attributed to either elderberry or red currant fruit base.

Clear Garnett This wine reveals a purple rim that has a colour that can be defined as clear and well distinct. The wine vintner might regard such a wine as a lesser Beaujolais or Syrah. For the honey and fruit wines, the fruit base might be of damson or plum fruit base.

Almost Black A concentrated, often intense colour whose black colour is almost impervious to opaque. For the honey and fruit wines the fruit base might be of black currant or loganberry or blackberry that would age well in a French oak barrel (see page 37) that would benefit from its vanilla presence that ages such wines to perfection. The wine vintner might regard such a wine as Burgundy or Rhône.

Viscosity, Legs or Tears

These characteristics are most important: it gives the vintner the knowledge of the strength of the wine by the "legs or tears" offered up by the wine as it adheres to the glass sides following the customary swirled-around procedure. The swirling action is a simple visible method which, if prominent traces are left on the glass, is a determinant that the wine is of a high sugar or alcohol content, or that of course it may be both. This method requires that the glass is completely clean and free of detritus. Some vintners use the term "legs", and others "tears": a pronounced, trailing, unbroken tear is a clear sign of a likely high alcohol content present.

Bouquet

Vintners use a specific wine glass for sampling wines by using the ISO tulip fluted glass: the use of such a glass makes it an essential requirement. The sense organs of smell react to the aromas given off through the practice of swirling the wine around the glass and the "nosing" effect of reaching the taster's nose. The purpose-designed tasting glass ensures the wine's unique smell is picked up by the wine taster.

In the arena of professional wine tasting there is a recognised distinction between "aromas" and "bouquet": in some respects there is a sort of superciliousness attached to these two methods of gauging a wine's smell. Whilst at the Napa Valley winery of Robert Mondavi, Oakville, California, they dispelled this as snobbishness. It was explained to me that in their winery values as a wine ages, whether in barrel or laid-in bottle, chemical reactions take place among acids, sugars, alcohols and phenolic compounds present

French oak wine barrels used throughout at Robert Mondavi winery, Napa Valley, California, USA [Hilary Badger]

in the wine. These reactions create new smells that are known as a wine's bouquet. For the purposes of wines, these can include honey in an aged Sauternes, or truffles in a Pinot noir. They believe the term "bouquet" can also be expanded to include the fragrances derived from fermentation and exposure to oak.

Burgundy wines are a good example as an expansion of the criteria for aroma / bouquet, the aromas of wines are subdivided into three categories – Primary, Secondary and Tertiary. In the situation of grape wines, *Primary aromas* are those specific to the grape variety itself. *Secondary aromas* are those derived from fermentation and oak ageing. *Tertiary aromas* are those that develop through bottled ageing.

The relatively new technique of micro-oxygenation perfected in the early 1990s affects the wine with an aromatic bouquet, its colour, mouth feel and most importantly its phenolic content. When tasting a wine we smell the aromas shaped and produced during fermentation in combination with the taste and the physical elements of the grape or, in the case of mead, the honey. It is not unusual for persons who smell a wine to think they will like it; however, when tasting the wine in their mouths they might well say *Yuk!* This arises not because they don't like the wine; it is because the brain was expecting different stimuli in the mouth. This synopsis is based on the aromatics of the wine arising when the brain is deluded from what was expected, thereby telling the body to discard it.

From an early age our brains become associated with a large, specific aromatic esters with either visual or taste / tactile sensations. A fermented wine is known to create over 200 aromatic esters that the brain becomes associated with both visual and taste / tactile senses. Understandably this causes confusion at first, with the brain trying to adjust to the new stimuli.

Tasting and Flavour

Those embarking on mead making and wishing to become good practitioners of tasting meads and honey wines will need to have a better understanding of the taste and flavour of meads and honey wines. Essentially there will be a need to retrain your olfactory senses. The olfactory system, or sense of smell, is that part of the sensory system used for smell. The main function of the olfactory system is to detect airborne elements, while the accessory system senses fluid-phase stimuli. This retraining starts by redefining the relationships of aroma, taste and flavour. The interrelationship of aroma vs. taste vs. flavour needs to be properly understood. Granted, these three words are inclined to be used interchangeably: in essence they mean very different things to our senses, requiring a better understanding of the responsive components in food and wine. So what do aroma, taste and flavour represent?

Aroma Denotes a definite aromatic multifaceted compound with a specific fragrance that can be identified by smelling. Raspberries, tea and coffee and meats all have specific aromatic compounds that allow us to identify them solely by their smell without seeing them physically.

Taste The tongue is the primary organ of taste and feel texture. It senses the four sensitivities – sweet, sour, salt and bitter. In addition, there are two disputed tastes: "umami" (i.e. deliciousness) and "metallic". But it's challenging as to whether or not either of them constitute a true taste, or are just a mixture of textures and tastes. Furthermore, it can feel heat from alcohol, astringency from tannin, bitterness from hops.

Flavour Is the brain's association between what it smells through the nose, tastes with the tongue, and feels in the mouth. Flavour is regarded by some authorities as "pleasurable", a sense involving smell, texture and anticipation / expectation. In some circles the term "Hedonic" is a common expression by wine aficionados.

Common flavours in mead are the minty taste from lime-based tree honey (*Tilia vulgaris*), the smooth, full but light vanilla flavour comes out from acacia tree honey (*Fabaceae* genus), or the full, strong flavour of ling heather honey (*Calluna vulgaris*), whose flavour can vary to a smoky taste reminiscent of the finest malt whiskies of the Scottish Highlands, due to the upland moorland soils.

Balance, Weight and Body

Mead fermented to perfection is ideally in balance with its alcohol, acid, tannins and its base honey. Elsewhere in the text emphasis has been given to the importance of the correct acidity. A shortfall in acid produces a dull wine, expressed as flat and short; conversely, acid in excess produces a wine that is sharp and a raw texture to the palate. Overindulgence in tannins gives a wine an excess of bitterness: the correct amount of tannin enhances "bite" to finished meads and honey wines. The correct amounts of acidity and tannins reflect a wine which can be said to be both uplifting and refreshing with the flavour lingering on taste. The quality of balance is known to shift or alter with time: a characteristic that can be said to be a cliché-ridden "moving feast" through the ageing process of a laid-down wine. Alcohol is the main contributor to a wine's body: it is the alcohol that gives the distinguishing feature of viscosity contributing to the admixture, much regarded as "fruitiness", with the alcohol revealing the "mouth feel experience" when imbibed in the tasting. It is often regarded that a full-bodied wine is of a high alcohol content, revealing its fruitiness, whereas a light-bodied wine is said to be "crisp", supported by a low alcohol content.

Length

This a term that is used to emphasise the characteristic of a wine in respect of its flavour. Simplistically it is where the wine's flavour remains in the mouth after swallowing: this time period is called "long" or "length". Both strength and persistence of flavour reflect the quality of the wine, as both aroma and flavour linger in the mouth after it has been swallowed. This effect is a quality referred to as "aftertaste". The characteristic of quality and pleasure in aftertaste is the feature of how long its taste lasts, referred to as "finish". Understandably a poor finish to a wine will inevitably affect how it ages.

The "Trusty" Sense of Smell and Taste

The emphasis on taste and smell when tasting a wine is mentioned in the judging of mead and honey wine and vinegar – *"Flavour and Taste"* page 31. The object is to take a judicious mouthful of the wine, avoiding the impulse to swallow it. You should immediately roll the wine around the mouth, exposing the wine to the many taste buds on the whole of the tongue, and correspondingly breathe in over the wine, releasing all of the wine's unique flavours (good or bad). Similarly the taster assesses the alcohol strength, acidity, flavour and sweetness or, conversely, dryness.

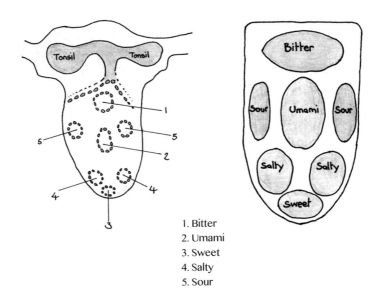

1. Bitter
2. Umami
3. Sweet
4. Salty
5. Sour

The human tongue and the areas that disclose the physical characters of the mead when sampled [David Lumb]

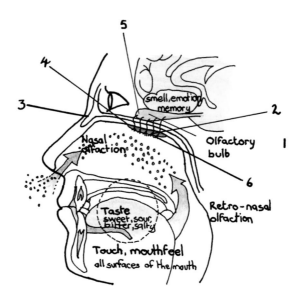

The olfactory nerve endings and sensors to the human brain [David Lumb]

1.	Olfactory Bulb	This is the structure that receives neural inputs of odours and smells where information is processed and assimilated.
2.	Mitral Cells	From these cells, messages are transmitted to the brain with messages sent onto other parts of the olfactory nerve centre for assimilation and integration by other receptors at olfactory cortex.
3.	Bone	Located at upper part of mouth cavity area.
4.	Olfactory Epithelium	Specialised tissue within nasal cavity whose principal function is to define smell.
5.	Glomerus	These are important receptor way stations for the pathways from the nose to the olfactory cortex within the brain.
6.	Olfactory Receptor Neurons	Their function is to transfer information to the brain and other working stimuli for taste and smell.

Finally, for the mead vintner, whether checking his wares for his own consumption, or a tasting session or exhibition, it is essential that a few "do's and don'ts" are adhered to, namely as listed below, although in no order of priority other than to use a well-lit room free of odours and distractions as you need to use your senses of sight, smell and taste and, above all, avoid your heart overruling your head!

- Make notes of all the individual meads sampled, their impressions and virtues, good and bad
- Do not eat any food immediately before or during tasting
- Avoid using any form of perfume or scented applications, as they may easily mask sensitive bouquets of your meads

Use correct tasting glasses that have the correct bowl size and the tulip effect of a narrow mouth to arrest and concentrate the aroma / bouquet (see page 231).

Finally

The new mead vintner's sole aim is to ensure that, whether for exhibition or consumption, they are fully aware of the wine's true characteristics, and that their virtues are met in their methods of production.

PART ONE

MEAD IN GENERAL

OPPOSITE

The author dividing out additives for inclusion to must

[Charlotte Lewis]

GENERALLY

The production of mead and honey wines is, in reality, about trial and error until you perfect a type of liquor which is to your liking. This perfection comes about by using a selection of the finest honeys and ingredients available to you. Therefore it is essential that you keep detailed records of each batch of liquor produced. These accounts allow the characteristics and points of the liquor to be assessed, both critically and positively, so that the mead maker can consider these when making another batch of the delightfully produced liquor. Conversely he will be able to avoid making a batch of mead that is below par. Good record keeping is virtuous and makes for a good vintner.

INGREDIENTS THAT MAKE UP MEAD AND HONEY WINES

By definition, the basic ingredients that make up mead and honey wines are each as important as the other, with no particular ingredient being superior or deemed more important or vital than the other. The constituents are:

- honey
- water
- yeast
- tannin

Acids and supplements (or compounds) and sometimes other substances may be added by the vintner to enhance the final outcome of the finished mead (see page 96 – Adding Additional Nutrients "Staggered Nutrient Additions (SNA)").

Additionally, to make specialist mead and honey wines, ingredients are often added by vintners, especially to country-type meads. Nevertheless, it has to be recorded that such superfluities will make straight mead (dry or sweet) into a melomel, or a fruit or a specialist-type country wine. Such wines need to be chosen carefully for exhibition or show purposes.

INGREDIENTS, PROCESS AND PRODUCTION

To understand the process and production of wine, there are basically ten steps in either the hot or the cold method for mead and honey wine production. In summary these are:

- Clean, sanitise and sterilise *all* the equipment to be used (see page 74 – The Importance of Cleaning and Disinfecting)
- It is essential that the honey, fruit, liquids, vegetables that make up the must will require some mechanism for pasteurisation to ensure wild yeast and other contaminants are kept at bay

- cool or chill the must; my counterparts in the USA use very chilled water stored in the refrigerator to add to the must
- additions of acids and compounds to the must to feed the yeast in its quest of natural growth and multiplication
- prepare a starter bottle or rehydrate the yeast
- add to (or pitch) the yeast to the must at the correct temperature, ensuring the must is maintained in a stable environment until the fermentation is completed
- add oxygen to the must or condition it by oxygenating the must
- once fermentation is completed to the desired specific gravity (SG), halt the fermentation and rack the must into a new sterilised fermentation container
- rack the mead once appreciable amounts of sediment or "lees" are seen in the base of the maturing container
- bottle after a year or more.

For sweet and dessert-type wines, honey is added to the must at about SG1120 maximum with additional honey added incrementally in small amounts of between 56 g to 112 g (2 to 4 oz). This method is the surest way of not overwhelming the yeast to work in high sugar concentrations from the onset, thereby minimising the risk of a "sticking" fermentation.

It is recommended that you fully understand all of these stages of production before going headlong into making your first mead wine. It is essential to make notes of your mead-making procedures when making wine batches. Above all, patience is needed, complete with thorough cleanliness and sterilisation of all equipment being used.

To produce meads and honey wines of quality requires the mead maker to understand that the finished wine will only become first-rate if the desired components are used in their correct proportions.

The Honey

The subject of honey is exceedingly complex. This topic is discussed in much greater detail in Part Eight – Floral Species, Nectar and Honey. The honey to be used needs to fulfil the following criteria:

- Use locally produced honey, don't skimp on quality
- Honey is one of the principal ingredients playing a collaborative role with other ingredients
- Aroma and flavour work with other ingredients to underpin the outcome of the finished wine
- Use a honey with varietal characters that will dictate the final wine finish
- Certain honeys (ling heather) add complexity and features to the wine.

The Water

Water quality is an essential requirement: water from the national water supply network is known to contain chemical additions of both fluoride and chlorine injected directly into the distribution systems. Water from upper moorland catchment areas is known to be treated with iron-free aluminium sulphate to create a primary coagulant for the removal of the reddish, peaty colour from the water as it leaves the fell. All these additions to the water might have a bearing on the water quality used for wine production. It is advocated to draw off the water to be used at least 24 hours for these unwelcome additions to have evaporated and dispersed.

Mains Water Supply Generally, water from the public water supply contains all the trace elements necessary for good winemaking, although some areas of the national water system may be lacking in magnesium sulphate. This deficiency can be rectified easily by the addition of a pinch of Epsom salts (magnesium sulphate) per gallon of water.

Well or Borehole Water In locations that rely on well or borehole water, care needs to be taken as the water supply can become contaminated with pathogens and chemicals. The possibility of nearby septic tanks leaking into the watercourse is a major concern. Boiling the water for at least two minutes should kill off any micro-organisms, or a reverse osmosis filtration system can be installed. Such equipment should be maintained regularly.

A new concern is environmental contamination from fracking operations, methane infiltration and soil salination.

Rainwater This is often used by mead makers. It should be from a sound source, the run-off from the conservatory or greenhouse roof being ideal. Never use rainwater from roofs constructed of asbestos or felt, as additional impurities leech from such materials which will undoubtedly affect the final flavour of the mead wine. The addition of a pinch of Epsom salts (magnesium sulphate) is essential.

Distilled and Spring Mineral Water These water types are not recommended for winemaking because they lack natural nutrients, as these are removed by filtering in the bottling plant. Such water often sees the must "stick" very quickly. Spring Mineral water is used extensively by beer makers; beer is ideally brewed from this blend of water as it is invariably soft and free of both Temporary hardness (dissolved calcium hydrogen carbonate) and Permanent hardness (dissolved calcium sulfate)

The Acids

The addition of specific acids is an essential requirement for making quality meads. Using the correct acids aids both fermentation and the finalisation of the flavour of the finished wine. Fermentations can be spoiled by the lack of acids in the must. The mead will also "lag" if certain acids are not used during the fermentation period. The absence of acid will introduce off-flavours which will invariably spoil the finished wine. Meads and honey wines found lacking the correct acids will acquire a taste reminiscent of medicinal cough mixture.

The acids commonly used in mead and honey winemaking are used in different proportions from those in other wine types. This equally applies when making "melomel" (fruit-based mead). It is essential not to add too much of other acids as these will certainly influence the final flavour, more often for bad rather than for good. Care needs to be taken with modern yeasts: they are not suited to the overuse of acids. Mead and honey wine makers, especially those new to the craft, need to take care when reading old books on the subject of mead production. Using additions stated in old literature should be made with extreme care to the point of not using them at all; adding incorrect additives may well interfere with the natural balance of the must. A typical example is the use of outdated ammonium phosphate as a yeast nutrient.

A number of recipes recommend the use of citric acid or the juice of lemons. The chemical form is in my opinion preferable to using fresh lemons as the quality of these fruits can vary. The harvested lemons are unlikely to be from the same tree, and the amount of citric acid they produce will be at variance – a very moot point that should be heeded.

The Nutrients

Nutrients aid and assist the yeast to do its job to perfection. The correct amounts of nutrients need to be added to feed the must, thereby assisting the yeast to grow and multiply. The most important nutrient is diammonium phosphate (DAP); it is the mainstay of nutrients for current wine production technology. The modern-day nutrients have a complete dietary supplement for the growing budding yeast; these include minerals of zinc, manganese, magnesium and many others.

There are three recommended yeast nutrients in common use, namely:

- "Gervin Minavit"
- "Fermaid K"
- "Go-Ferm"

These nutrients have been developed specifically for mead production, together with the addition of the ingredients listed below, at per gallon (Imp):

- half a tablet of thiamine (vitamin B1, 1 mg) per gallon (Imp)
- one tablet of ascorbic acid (vitamin C).

The use of a proprietary yeast nutrient will ensure that the correct acids are present in the must, and will see that fermentation gets underway to a good start, creating a vigorous fermentation and ensuring that the yeast grows promptly and multiplies quickly. Failure to get the fermentation underway promptly will often result in a very poor wine.

The Use of Tannin

Tannin is a key ingredient contributing to a wine's structure and taste. It is a key component of age-worthy wines. Tannins are extracted mainly from grape skins during the maceration process in red winemaking, or from oak wood during barrel-ageing of white and red wines. The lesser-known application of tannin is in the fining operation. Although tannin is not classified as a fining agent, clarification is often dependent on the presence of tannins and requires it to be added (in the form of oak bark powder or cold, non-scented, strong tea).

For fining low-tannin wines with gelatin, tannin powder is added at a rate of 10-30 g/hl of wine. Prepare the tannin by dissolving the powder substance mixed within the permitted acids and nutrients. Tannin added directly to the must will float on the surface, becoming difficult to incorporate. A simple procedure is to use a discarded removable capped chemical container, add all the chemicals to it, plus the tannin powder. Close the lid and shake the contents vigorously: this will see the tannin powder incorporated within the bulk of the chemical additions; the contents are added to the must that assists the tannin's incorporation.

A simpler method is to use strong, cold tea directly from the teapot, straining out the tea leaves. Use one dessertspoonful to the gallon for dry meads, and two or three spoonfuls for sweet mead. Stir this into the must when the nutrients are added. Tannin is an important ingredient of mead, especially show meads. It is the one ingredient that brings all the tastes together on the palate for a full-bodied overall flavour, what wine buffs call "a good finish". Without tannin, the mead will be flat. Conversely, if you add too much tannin, you end up with a very over-dry mouthfeel, especially behind the bottom lip.

PERMITTED ADDITIVES TO THE "MUST" FOR COMPETITION AND EXHIBITION WINES

The majority of mead makers prefer not to add any chemicals or additives; they prefer to stick to natural means as far as the techniques allow. However, it needs to be emphasised that to make perfect meads and honey wines, chemical additions make for a positive finished wine.

Many mead makers add a number of concoctions to their meads and honey wines. Such additions make these wines *not* a true mead in the strictest sense of the word, but a melomel or country wine; whilst wholesome and delightful to imbibe, they are not a true mead.

A true mead is made up of water, permitted acids to feed the yeast, yeast nutrients to feed the yeast throughout its development stage, and, finally, the addition of tannin.

Note the following points:

- Once fruit of any kind is added to the must it becomes a melomel-type mead. Firm favourites with mead makers are sultanas, raisins, bananas and many other fruits.

- The addition of spices and herbs to the must makes this wine a metheglin or hippocras.
- The addition of pure grape juice to the must makes the wine a pyment type of mead.
- The addition of apple juice to the *must* makes the wine a cyser type of mead.
- The addition of hops adds bite to any mead, but is *not* a permitted additive for a true mead type for exhibition purposes unless the rules permit their use.

WINE KITS

Those new to mead making might easily be tempted into trying wine kits as a way of getting into mead making proper. 'Tis true there are many, many good wine kits on offer at the typical home brew shop. The majority of established home brew shops offer a wide range of wine and beer making artefacts for the vintner, including grape wine kits which offer wide variety of grape juices, ideal for making superior pyments. My preference is to use solely the fruit additions, especially the grape skins for use with red melomels: these add real character to fermenting mead. The yeasts and other ingredients are discarded, as I find them inferior to my own selected components. When purchasing wine kits the fruit juice is generally a concentrate from a wide variety of sources from raspberry to elderberry. My liking is to purchase those kits which are all fruit with *no added sugar*. As an afterthought, I try to patronise my local home brew shop as, if you do not use them, you will lose them: a situation that does not bode well for the future of winemaking.

THE DOMINANT ACIDS, PECTIN LEVELS, WATER AND SUGAR CONTENT COMMON TO FRUIT

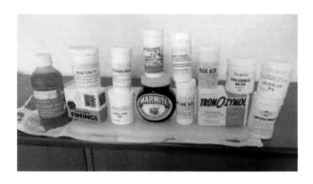

Acids and additives for Mead and Honey Wine
Production [Michael Badger]

Water, Sugar, Acid, and Pectin Common to Fruit (USDA
Database)

Fruit	Water %	Sugar %	Dominant Acids	Pectin Level
Apple	88.24	9.62	Malic	High
Apricot, dried**	30.05**	53.25**	Malic**	N/A**
Apricot	86.35	9.24	Malic	Low
Bananas	74.91	12.23	Malic and Citric	N/A
Blackberry	88.15	4.88	Malic	Low
Blueberry	84.21	9.96	Citric	Medium
Cantaloupe melon	90.15	7.86	N/A	Low
Cherries, sour	86.12	8.49	Malic	Medium
Cherries, sweet	82.25	12.82	N/A	Medium
Cranberry juice	87.13	12.10	Citric Malic	High
Currants, black	81.96	N/A	Citric	High
Currants, red and white	83.95	7.37	Citric	High

NB: ** Non-USDA fact sheet

Dates, dried**	30.10**	65.00	Malic	N/A
Elderberry	79.80	N/A	Citric	Low
Figs, dried	30.05	47.92	Malic	N/A
Figs, raw	79.11	16.26	Malic	N/A
Gooseberries	87.87	N/A	Citric	High
Grapefruit juice, white	90.00	9.10	Citric	N/A
Grapes, muscadine	84.29	N/A	Tartaric and Malic	N/A
Guavas	80.80	8.92	N/A	High
Honeydew melon	89.92	8.12	N/A	Low
Kiwi	83.07	8.99	Citric	N/A
Lemon juice	92.31	2.52	Citric	N/A
Lime juice	90.79	1.69	Citric	High
Loganberry	84.61	7.70	Malic and Citric	N/A
Mango	83.46	13.66	N/A	N/A
Mulberry	87.68	8.10	N/A	N/A
Nectarine	87.59	7.89	Malic	Low
Orange juice	88.30	8.40	Citric	High
Papayas	88.06	7.82	N/A	N/A
Peaches	88.87	8.39	Malic	N/A
Pineapple juice	86.37	9.98	Citric	Low
Pineapple, raw	86.00	9.85	Citric	Low
Plum	87.23	9.92	Malic	High
Pomegranate juice	85.95	12.65	N/A	Low
Pomegranates	77.93	13.67	N/A	Low
Prickly pear	87.55	N/A	N/A	Low
Prunes **	32.50	38.00	Malic	N/A
Raisins**	30.50**	59.08**	Malic	N/A
Raspberry	85.75	4.42	Citric	Medium
Rhubarb	93.61	1.10	Malic and Oxalic	Medium
Strawberry	90.95	4.89	Citric	Low
Tangerine juice	88.90	9.90	Citric	N/A
Watermelon	91.45	6.20	N/A	Low

NB: ** Non-USDA fact sheet

TO SUMMARISE ON ACIDS

GENERALLY

I remember listening to Ken Schramm mentioning in a talk on mead making at the 2007 Eastern Apicultural Society Conference, University of Delaware, USA, that "acids impart the tart twang on one's tongue that balances the residual sugar in your mead". Ken is no slouch when it comes to making mead and honey wine, and he has kindly offered the following narrative on acids, their uses and inclusion in the fermentation of mead and honey wine.

To recap, the addition of acids can provide the balance needed to enhance the flavour of the mead. Even excellent dry meads can benefit from the added complexity that acidity brings. Acidity helps mead pair more deliciously with different foods. There are, however, differing schools of thought on how and when acids should be added to a mead or the must.

In the 1960s, Dr Roger Morse and Dr Keith Steinkraus, of Cornell University, Ithaca, New York, set out to learn how to perform strong and trouble-free mead fermentations. Their research centred on the nutritional needs of yeast. Furthermore, they examined the effects of pH on the duration and quality of honey fermentations. Their collaborative work, 'Wines from the Fermentation of Honey', was published in Dr Eva Crane's *Honey: A Comprehensive Survey*, in 1975. Subsequently, Dr Morse published additional information in his magisterial work, *Making Mead (Honey Wine): History, Recipes, Methods and Equipment*, in 1992. The findings of Dr Morse and Dr Steinkraus revolutionised the process of mead fermentation in the USA.

It needs to be observed and understood that different yeast strains will perform best under different pH ranges. Wine strains will ferment better than beer strains in a medium with lower pH. All strains, however, will struggle to ferment effectively when the pH level drops below around 2.9. The fermentation may go from a steady activity that should finish in two or three weeks, to something taking several months (not uncommon when using high-quality ling honey of the British Isles).

All of these phenomena are geared to the quality of the honey used, whether it has been heated at the extraction/processing time, or its general quality when used in the must.

Equally concerning is the prospect of the stressed yeast not fermenting the sugars correctly into ethanol, but rather fermenting them into fusel alcohols whose end product results in a bad taste and can produce nasty hangovers to the imbiber of such liquor.

The pH scale from 0 to 14 reflects the relationship between the amount of acid (the amount of positively charged ions) in solution and the amount of alkaline compounds (substances which contribute negatively charged ions), thus providing a buffer to those H+ ions. Acidic substances have low pH – a pH of 7 is neutral – and alkaline substances have high pH.

Managing pH is of great importance in making traditional or show-style meads. Most honeys have pH readings of between 3.2 and 4.2, and the pH remains pretty much static when the honey is diluted with water. This instigates mead musts with low pH from the start. In wines and beers, both acidic and alkaline compounds are present and in much larger quantities, meaning that, in fermenting beer or wine, additional small amounts of acid or alkaline compounds will change the pH very slightly. In meads, however, both acidic and alkaline compounds are present in only very small quantities. This means that the addition of small amounts of acid can cause a much larger drop in the pH.

This effect is further compounded by the fact that the yeast uses many of the buffering compounds as life-giving nutrients for cell growth and metabolism. When these amalgams are consumed by the growing yeast population, their growth and expansion in numbers ensure that the buffers are no longer available to counter the acids in the must: in effect, they are no longer neutralised. The progressive consumption of these nutrients ensures that the pH of fermenting meads generally drops continually from the beginning of fermentation to its completion. It is very easy for the pH in a fermenting mead to drop enough to slow the yeast down dramatically, or to stop fermentation altogether. A pH meter can be a very useful tool for monitoring pH (see page 151).

The pH of a fermenting mead must that has become too acidic can be raised by adding potassium bicarbonate. This has the added positive characteristic of contributing potassium to the must. Potassium is a much-required nutrient for the yeast's development; it is often present at levels below those which the yeast prefers, especially in honeys of lighter colour. The addition of potassium bicarbonate needs to be undertaken with absolute precision.

ADDING ACIDS – AN ALTERNATIVE METHOD

In recent years, a practice used in the USA is to add the acids after fermentation is completed and finished.

As an experienced vintner, Ken Schramm adds the acids to the required taste just before bottling or packing the mead. There are as many ways to accomplish this as there are mead makers, but the critical aspect is to make the addition predictable and repeatable.

The acids that mead makers can use individually include citric, malic, tartaric and lactic, or as a blend of citric, malic and tartaric. Each of these acids has its own flavour profile and 'punch' of tart or sour impact. Early on in your mead making, you may just want to use an acid blend but, as you progress, it is valuable option to taste each mead type produced individually to learn its characteristics. You can use that knowledge to tailor the mead to your desires by producing a beverage at the first stages with acids or after fermentation or, as Ken Schramm does, by adding the acids prior to the bottle stage.

The novice mead maker should be very careful about such procedures: taking advice from a mead sage is essential. Don't ruin in five minutes what may have taken five months to become a first-rate wine.

A SIMPLE PROCEDURE FOR ADDING THE ACIDS TO A COMPLETED FERMENTATION

To undertake this procedure you should have an acid testing kit from the basic to a highly sophisticated instrument, accurate weighing scales or balance, and notepad and pencil for recording your additions to the wine.

Simple acid testing Kit [Erica Osborn]

A simple method for adding the ingredients to the finished wine is to:

- Dissolve a gram or two into 20 ml of distilled water. It is essential to sanitise and sterilise anything that will come into contact with these ingredients: the spoons and measuring cup, etc.
- Stir the ingredients to ensure they are fully dissolved, and add to the mead following transfer at the laid-in bottle stage of the fermented-out wine. Stir in carefully and taste the mead.
- You can repeat the process until you hit the level of acid character you prefer. For larger batches of five gallons or

more, you can increase the amount of acid per addition.

- Consistency and accurate measurement are essential. It may seem time-consuming to repeat this many times, but once the acid is added, it cannot be taken back out, so the outlay of time in getting this right is well worth it.
- Good, written-up documentation will provide a frame of reference for additions in future batches.
- Above all, take care in what additions you make to a must or a fermented-out wine.

BASE HONEY AND ACIDS

Many, many acids found in the base honey cannot be purchased at wine home brew supply shops, so the mead maker has to make do with what is available.

- **Gluconic acid** is the primary acid found in honey: it occurs naturally in fruit, honey and wine. As a food additive (E574), it is an acidity regulator. It is also used in cleaning products. It dissolves mineral deposits, especially in alkaline solutions.

In the UK, mead and honey wine producers use four of the most common acids available in dry matter form:

- **Ascorbic acid (vitamin C)** This is favoured as an antioxidant that inhibits the oxidation of other molecules because it is less acerbic than the other acids available for use as antioxidants.

- **Citric acid** As its name implies, this occurs naturally in citrus fruits. In biochemistry, it is an intermediate in the citric acid cycle which occurs in the metabolism of all aerobic organisms.

- **Tartaric acid** This is a white crystalline organic acid that occurs naturally in many plants, most notably in grapes. Its salt, potassium bitartrate, is commonly known as cream of tartar. It is developed naturally in the process of winemaking.

- **Malic acid** This is an organic compound with the molecular formula $C_4H_6O_5$. It is a dicarboxylic acid that is made by all living organisms. Its presence contributes to the pleasantly sour taste of fruits. It is used as a food additive, regarded by many wine makers as adding a harsh taste to the wine if overcompensated for during the fermentation phase. It should be used with care.

Some vintners add thiamine (vitamin B1) at the commencement of the fermentation.

The use of these acids needs care; it is so easy to upset the pH (acidity) if used at the beginning of the fermentation process. The use of a simple acid wine testing kit can be most useful at the start of the fermentation; these are available, with detailed instructions, from winemaking suppliers.

Should the pH be found to be incorrect after the fermentation has ceased, the experienced wine maker will deploy acids or alkalis at the "laying down in-bottle" stage.

OTHER SUBSTANCES ADDED TO THE "MUST" BY MEAD VINTNERS TO ASSIST YEAST PRODUCTION

GENERALLY

The use of fruit and other organic substances are not permitted in certain exhibition wines, so beware: as mentioned elsewhere, the addition of such fruits turns plain mead into a melomel honey wine. These additions include many vine fruits: sultanas, raisins, bananas, herbs, spices and hops.

Sultanas

These seedless dried grapes are washed and any stalks removed. The Californian golden "Thompson Seedless" variety is the best quality; these should be halved and added to the must. In its reproductive "budding" phase, the yeast feeds on the natural sugars present in the sultanas. The addition of sultanas helps to give melomel freshness to the finished wine.

Raisins

These seedless dried grapes are washed and any stalks removed. The use of raisins adds body to the finished wine. Like sultanas, they are halved and added to the must. The comment for sultanas applies equally to raisins.

Bananas

The fruit used should be as over-ripe as possible: the riper they are, the more sugar is available for the yeast to feed upon. The bananas are removed from their skins, diced and added to the must. Bananas give body to a honey wine.

Herbs and Spices

These may be cinnamon, cardamom pods, dried cranberries, orange and lemon peel, pimento berries, star anise, bay leaf, mace, nutmeg, rosemary, coriander, aniseed, elderflower, juniper, and many more.

They need to be used sparingly, otherwise their use will affect the taste of the wine, making it overbearing and far from appetising. The spices and herbs are added to a completed wine. It is racked into a clean, one-gallon demijohn. A small muslin bag is made up, from which the spices or herbs cannot leak. The bag is suspended in the wine on a strong thread. The demijohn is sealed to keep out oxygen and vinegar flies. The wine should be tasted after three days to gauge the flavour. An additional day may be needed, but when the desired flavour is attained, the bag is carefully removed, avoiding any spillage of the contents into the wine.

Bergamot

Known as bee balm, Eastern bee balm, bergamot, wild Oswego tea, horsemint and monarda, it is a member of the mint family of flowers. The leaves and blossoms are harvested, having been sanitised with alcohol, preferably vodka. The blossoms and petals and the vodka are added to the mead: albeit only a nominal amount is needed to impart a noticeable floral and minty addition to the mead. Should this be added to plain mead as a means to enhance flavour, a knowledgeable mead judge (and a producer of meads) will pick up this immediately at the tasting stage.

Rose petals

The use of edible rose petals from blossom tea roses from your own gardens are recommended that will be generally free from treatment with toxic insecticides, fed with food-grade rose water. Above all, avoid flowers purchased at a flower market stall or sweepings, as they may well be toxic. Sanitised as above.

Flowers

Flowers of many kinds can be used provided they are non-toxic to humans. Commonly chosen are the tea blends of chamomile, hibiscus, jasmine, lavender and rose, to name but a few, sanitised as above.

Wood

The use of woodchips to enhance or change the flavour and taste of a perfected mead is not a method to be undertaken lightly, as the effects of their use can so easily spoil an excellent beverage. The use of oak barrels for storing wine is a centuries-old tradition: it has stood the test of time through the techniques and skills being handed down through the generations of vintners. A common method is to use oak woodchips about 15 mm (½ inch) in length, whose purpose is to impart different features to the maturing wine. The woodchips are referred to having a toast level of heavy, medium plus, medium, and light. The use of wood is itself an art, as its introduction is to avoid an overbearing wood flavour. Such material adds specific qualities that include tannins, aromas and, above all, flavours that might not be welcomed. These arise because each of the oak species can impart its own characteristics to the mead. These oaks may be French, American, English or Hungarian, the French oak being the preferred type in the wine industry. Following my visit in 2016 to the Sonoma and Napa Valley wine districts of California, several wineries have tried Spanish cedarwood with mixed results; possibly time will tell whether this timber will be used in greater amounts. The use of oak chips requires their sanitisation, with total immersion in vodka for about five minutes maximum. Once the woodchips are added to the must it requires constant checking by sampling the mead to ensure the maturing liquor is reaching the required maturation point; this is accomplished by a wine thief (pipette) to obtain a sample of the maturing mead. The experts usually decant the maturing mead from the woodchips in advance of the required flavour levels into a fresh vessel. Once this is done there is the option to add a concentrated amount of saved tincture to finalise the desired flavour.

Ginger

The addition of this flowering plant adds bite to the mead. The simplest way to add to the must is to slice the raw tuber into slithers and place in a sanitised mesh bag placed directly into the fermentation vessel, checking daily by sampling the liquor to see if the desired level of taste has been reached. This can be achieved in a few days, so vigilance is needed sampling the wine daily.

Mint
Like ginger, this is used sparingly, more or less under the same constraints. Fresh or dried mint can be used.

Chocolate
The addition of chocolate to a fermenting mead is best achieved by the use of cacao (cocoa) nibs made from pure cacao beans straight out of the tropical cacao fruit. Cacao was a culinary treasure to Mesoamericans hyped as the "food of the gods" for its superior nutritional profile and exceptional flavour. The cacao nibs are added to the must once the initial fermentation has subsided, due to the promoted foaming that will occur. Once the fermentation is nearing completion, a floating scum of cocoa fat (butter) will be evident that needs to be left behind at the first racking.

Hot Peppers
The chilli pepper is the fruit of plants from the genus *Capsicum*. The progenitors of their use recommend dried peppers, as this minimises the number of vegetal parts of the plant; these are not welcome as they add characteristics that mask the desired ones. Like ginger, their use should be strictly controlled as their pungency will definitely overwhelm the wine. It is better to be modest in usage and, if desired, regulate additions later in the fermentation process.

Coffee
Experience has shown that the best coffee meads arise when using cold-pressed coffee, as this avoids the harshness of heated coffee grains. Three tablespoons per 1 gallon of coffee is placed within a small muslin bag, secured to avoid leakage to fermented-out cleared wine, very much on the principle of metheglin-type meads. The coffee needs to be removed at about three days, with sampling taken after the second day to decide the exactness of the coffee to the finished mead.

HOPS AND THEIR USE
FOR MEADS AND HONEY WINES

[**Note**] The addition of hops to show meads and honey wines should not be made ad-lib. Record any addition of hops to the must, as the show rules may preclude their use.

Hops are the flowers (known as cones or strobiles in the USA) of the hop plant, *Humulus lupulus*. They are used primarily as a flavouring and stabilising agent, their antibacterial properties favouring the brewer's yeast, making them ideal for brewing beer. However, they are used frequently by experienced wine producers for the production of mead and honey wine. The addition of hops to wine imparts a bitter, tangy flavour. Mead makers who have experience in producing mead and honey wine use them to add "bite" to the mead.

Hops are used for various purposes in other beverages and herbal medicine. They are native to the temperate regions of Europe, Asia, the USA and Canada. Hops are dioecious, having separate male and female plants, with only the female vines producing the cones. The leaves resemble grape leaves, and the cones look vaguely like pine cones in shape. They are light green, thin and papery. At the base of the petals are the yellow lupulin glands which contain the essential oils and resins that are required to add the necessary

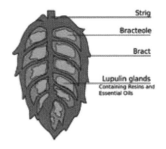

Hop Strobile [By Herr Schnapps – Own work, Public Domain]

flavour. If I may be permitted to digress, in the years preceding the Second World War, the hop harvest was gathered by migrating peoples from the major cities as a means of a holiday and a break for the children, the hop-pickers being paid a meagre sum of money for their labours. This was an annual affair for working people of the East End of London who went to the Kent hop fields, and for the peoples from Birmingham who travelled to the Vale of Evesham, Worcestershire. Our mead-making colleague, Michael Young, remembers such holidays at Pershore, Worcestershire, in the 1950s. These forays to the countryside were an ideal way of giving young children the essential vitamin D.

Historically, hops act as a natural preservative for beer and ales; they were added directly to the cask after fermentation was completed. India Pale Ale (IPA) was developed at the turn of the 18th century when British brewers added extra hops to the barrels when shipping their strong ale to the outposts of the British Empire, as travel was generally slow. The voyage to India taking several months, understandably, over the long journey and the time involved, the addition of hops gave the beer an acquired natural-added flavour and taste that became known as India Pale Ale (IPA).

The addition of hops provides balance and natural bitterness when introduced to the liquor. They balance the sweetness, providing a refreshing finish to the production of the wine. The alpha acids bring out the main bittering agent that makes the liquor take on the essential flavour required to assist the mead to maturity. These unique compounds are released, dissolving when the water is boiled. There are many varieties of hops used today, generally divided into two general categories, bittering and aroma.

- Bittering hops are high in alpha acids, about 9 per cent by weight.
- Aroma hops are usually lower, around 4 per cent, contributing a more desirable aroma and flavour to the liquor.

Hop-picker families in Worcestershire – Michael Young the babe in arms [Michael Young Collection]

The addition of hops is recommended only for sweet, dessert and sack meads.

The methodology is simple: you must observe the sanitisation and sterilisation rules at all times.

- Boil 2 pints (Imp), 2.4 pints (US), of plain water.
- Add ¼ oz (7 g) of hops to the boiling water.
- Allow to boil for a maximum of 10 minutes.
- When the liquor reaches a temperature of 21 °C (70 °F),
  add to the must when the main components are awaiting the
  addition of the yeast.

It is recommended to use only aroma hops in meads, as bittering hop types, as the name implies, impart bitterness to the mead due to the high alpha acids present.

Bittering, Dual-Purpose and Aroma Hop Varieties

There are many varieties available and used by master brewers. My preference is for the recently introduced American varieties.

Name	Origin	Profile	Usage
Amarillo	Washington's Virgil Gamache Farms, USA.	A popular hop, prized for its distinctive aroma. Amarillo possesses a distinct quality of "orangeness". With the highest myrcene content of any hop variety, Amarillo can come off as pungent with a grapefruit texture at times, a hop taste very much like biting into a tangerine.	Dual-Purpose: Bittering Strong Ales and flavouring. India Pale Ale.
Citrus	Hop Breeding Co., Ltd, USA.	Released in 2009 in the Sierra Nevada. Championed by the Kern River Brewing Company, USA.	Bittering Strong Ales and flavouring. India Pale Ale.
Mosiac™	Mosaic brand HBC 369 cv	A daughter of the Simcoe® Brand YCR 14 cv hop variety and a Nugget derived male. It has high alpha acids and tropical, blueberry, tangerine, floral, and earthy aroma	Used for flavouring India Pale Ales
Simcoe	Created by Charles E. Zimmermann, developed by Select Botanicals Group, and released in 2000 through Washington's Yakima Chief Ranch, USA.	Pungent with a woody, musky, citrus-like taste and flavour.	Bittering Strong Ales and flavouring.

Summit	Bred by the American Dwarf Hop Association and released in 2003, Summit™, USA.	Specific aromas include pepper, incense, anise, orange, pink grapefruit and tangerine.	Used as a bittering hop, but does have earthy aromatic characteristics.

Other Bittering, Dual-Purpose and Aroma Hop Varieties

Brewers Gold	UK and USA	Blackcurrant, spicy aroma and fruity.	Used as a bittering hop.
Cascade	USA	Strong, spicy with floral varietals, citrus aroma.	Aroma hop for American Pale Ales for bittering and finish.
Challenger	UK	Medium flavour with spicy aroma.	Dual-Purpose: Bittering Strong Ales and flavouring. India Pale Ale.
Fuggles	UK and USA	Soft and mild floral aroma.	Aroma hop for American Pale Ales for bittering and finish.
Northdown	UK	Lovely aroma.	Dual-Purpose: Bittering Strong Ales and flavouring. India Pale Ale.
Nugget	USA	Herbal, heavy and spicy.	Used as a bittering hop.
Target	UK	Strong, mixed herbal and floral aroma.	Dual-Purpose: Bittering Strong Ales and flavouring. India Pale Ale.
Warrior	UK	Mild aroma, similar to Cascade.	Used as a clean bittering hop.

Conclusion

Meads and honey wine production can be both exciting and interesting, more specially using an assortment of additions. The finished wines are ideal for blending purposes (see page 155).

PART TWO

METHODS AND PRACTICES
FOR MEAD PRODUCTION

OPPOSITE

An open jar of ling honey – note the strike mark showing the thixotropic properties   73
[Brian Nellist]

THE IMPORTANCE OF CLEANING AND DISINFECTING

In all recipes, the vintner has to take heed of cleanliness, disinfecting, sanitation and sterilisation of all work surfaces, places of work and equipment used.

Due to the presence within the must of nutrients, trace elements and honey, the production of meads and honey wines is ideal for the growth of bacteria, moulds, wild yeasts and other undesirable pathogens that will imperil the wine if not contained.

However, the vintner should not overlook that cleaners, sanitisers and disinfectants are naturally hazardous in their concentrated form, leading to unpleasant consequences if mishandled or misused. The majority of disinfectants are modelled on a bleach of some kind, generally chlorine, making them highly toxic that will damage more or less any surface they come into contact with. The vintner should wear proper eye protection and protective gloves when handling these compounds, whether diluted or in neat solution: hands and fingers are excessively sensitive to exposure and should be washed in clean water and dried, applying hand cream to delicate and damaged skin. Furthermore, dealing with these chemicals should be undertaken in well-ventilated areas, avoiding inhaling any dust when handled. The majority of cleaning chemicals in a diluted format are relatively safe if applied and used correctly, but eyes and the skin can be irritated through splashing, so care is always needed with their use.

Under no circumstances blend or mix different chemicals together for whatever reason, as the resultant concoction may be rendered ineffective. More importantly, unwittingly combining certain chemicals of an ammonia base with those of a chlorine base will *produce toxic gases harmful to man*. It is essential to read the safety information of the chemical, especially if you are using aluminium equipment, as this metal is damaged by the use of the majority of cleaning aids.

THE OBJECT OF SANITISATION

It is to reduce all bacteria and other contaminants to insignificant levels, as near zero as possible. The terms "clean", "sanitise" and "sterilise" are often used interchangeably, but in reality should never be so. Items may be clean but not sanitised, and vice versa. Here are the definitions:

- Clean – to be free from dirt, stain or foreign matter
- Sanitise – to kill/reduce spoiling micro-organisms to negligible levels
- Sterilise – to eliminate all forms of life, especially micro-organisms, by either chemical or physical means.

Therefore, it is so vital that the new vintner should never overlook or, for that matter, take chances on, sanitation and sterilisation.

CLEANLINESS

Cleanliness is of foremost concern to the vintner. Good growing conditions for the yeast spores also provide good growing conditions for the other undesirable micro-organisms, especially wild yeast and bacteria. Cleanliness has to be maintained throughout every stage of the process of wine production. This is so vital that the new vintner should never overlook or, for that matter, take chances on sanitation and sterilisation.

Cleaning compound [Michael Badger]

75

SANITISATION

This is the process of removing all the dirt and grime from any surface, thereby removing all the situations that can harbour bacteria. Cleaning is usually done with a detergent and physical effort. None of the sanitising agents used by vintners are capable of eliminating all bacterial spores and viruses. The majority of chemical agents they use will clean and sanitise but not sterilise. Instead of worrying about sterilisation, vintners can be satisfied if they consistently reduce contaminants to negligible levels: this is about the best that they can do. All sanitisers are meant to be used on clean surfaces. A sanitiser's ability to kill micro-organisms is understandably reduced by the presence of dirt, grime or any unwanted organic material. Organic deposits can harbour bacteria and shield the surface from being reached by the sanitiser. So you need to make sure the surface of the item to be sanitised is as clean as possible: it is the best the vintner can achieve.

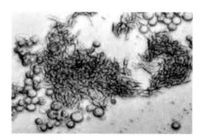

The yeast cells are the round objects, the worm-like objects are bacteria. 3000X [Author's Collection]

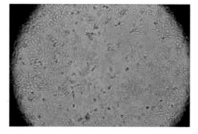

The yeast cells are the round objects, detailing other forms of bacteria. 3000X [Author's Collection]

STERILISATION

Types of Steriliser

Chlorine-based sterilisers – are the most popular products used in the home brew market, as they do not discharge irritating fumes and gases, making them ideal for blending with cleaning agents.

Sodium metabisulfite – is a traditional steriliser that generates sulphur dioxide gas when mixed with water. Although highly effective, there are hitches with using this product: the powder is harmful to skin, and the generated sulphur fumes produced when mixed with water should not be used by anyone with chest conditions such as asthma. Due to its hydrographic nature once opened, the powder fuses into a hard lump within a few days, making it difficult to use.

Active oxygen-based sterilisers – These are relatively new, acting in a similar way to chlorine sterilisers. It is claimed by manufacturers that these products do not need to be rinsed off: beware of unknown brands, as these may not contain detergents needed to clean residues off glass effectively.

Boiling water – the use of boiling water is not as trustworthy as chemical cleaning agents as it can shatter glass equipment. Its use is really limited to sterilising ladles or spoons.

A Suggested Modus of Sterilising

Use of Concentrate Steriliser

Using Star San concentrate; take a bucket with a lid of a capacity to hold 11.25 litres (2.5 Imp. gallons) of clean water; add 15 millilitres (0.5 fl oz) of Star San concentrate. Secure the lid and swirl the liquid around, ensuring all parts of the bucket are covered, including the inside lid. This bucket is the sanitising bucket, saved for the next operation. Star San is the ideal sanitiser, as it is fast-acting with no rinsing required after treatment.

Star San concentrate steriliser [Michael Badger]

Take a second bucket and use the contents to sanitise all the equipment to be used in the process of making the wine by filling this vessel with sufficient sanitising solution to cleanse all the equipment thoroughly. The equipment will include the following: hydrometer, trial jar, Pyrex jugs, thermometer, spoons, measuring cups, spatulas and any other items used, ensuring all surfaces are treated. The contact time should be at least 1½ minutes. The fermentation vessel after sanitising is often inverted to drain; however, the remnants of the sanitising solution will have no impact on the must.

Sanitising Bottles by Dishwasher with "Sanitise Cycle"
The higher specification modern automatic dishwashers have a sanitising cycle, an ideal method for sterilising bottles is to place the bottles, neck downwards, inside the dishwasher as compact as is possible to stop them toppling over during the washing cycle. Set the cycle to "sanitise", using no chemical additives or rinse aids. When the cycle is completed, the bottles will be both hot and sanitised.

SOME GENERAL CONSIDERATIONS

VOLUMES

US Gallons

US Gallons – =	= fl oz	= litres	= Imperial Gallons
One US Gallon – =	=128	= 3.7853 litres	= 0.833 Imperial Gallons

Imperial Gallons

Imperial Gallons – =	= fl oz	= litres	= US Gallons
One Imperial Gallon – =	=160	= 4.5459 litres	= 1.20 Imperial Gallons

A simple reminder is that 5 Imperial gallons equal 6 US gallons.

GENERALITIES

- Fill the fermentation lock with glycerine to ensure the airlock never evaporates.
- It is good practice to wrap the fermenting vessel with a black plastic cover (double-wrapped black refuse bin liners are ideal) to exclude the light, as, in normal situations, the yeast develops in anaerobic conditions and total darkness.
- For recipes using pectolase and Rohamet P (a special multi-active enzyme that releases aromatic components bound to sugars present in the must, enhancing colour and flavour), refer to the manufacturer's detailed instructions for their use.
- The Specific Gravity (SG) of honey is 1.425: therefore you will need a "sweetness" ratio – 1 sugar = 1.25 of honey.

0.56 kg (1.25 lb) of honey for the equivalent in sugar of 0.454 kg (1 lb).

- Natural grape juice or grape concentrate should be procured from commercially grown wine grapes. Dessert grapes or grape juice from health shops are devoid of the essential efficient acids found in commercial wine grapes, and should not be used unless "recipe-specific" for country wines and meads. However, grape juice concentrate from wine kits is an ideal media.
- Aeration is good; oxidation is bad. It is important to understand the significance and importance of both.
  Aeration is the essential required addition of oxygen at the commencement of the fermentation to assist the yeast to multiply, grow and bud.
  Oxidisation is the avoidance of introducing oxygen once the fermentation is completed.

To avoid duplication and clarity in wording, the following is noted:

- The term "make-up starter mix" is as described on page 92.
- Water is deemed to have been evaporated of chlorine / fluoride, borehole or well water is boiled for two minutes as a means of sterlisation
- Rainwater or still water is devoid of magnesium sulphate (Epsom salts) deemed have included add 1.75 g (1/16th ounce) added to the gallon (Imp) rate
- Remove all stalks from fruits, as stalk remains will impoverish the wine
- To "halt fermentation" refers to adding 1 Campden tablet and one level teaspoon of potassium sorbate per gallon
- To "bottle" means lay down in-bottle generally when the wine is star-bright, usually free of lees and at least 12 months old.

HANDLING HONEY IN BULK OR OTHERWISE

The removal of honey from containers large and small can present difficulties, more especially if the honey is provided in bulk. This may present the mead vintner with some difficulty if they are not a practising beekeeper who is adept at handling honey under such situations. Bulk honey is generally strained by the beekeeper at the time of extraction from the honeycomb, and, depending upon the ratios present of glucose (dextrose) and fructose (laevulose), the honey in bulk under normal storage conditions will settle out to a granulated mass. When fully granulated a scum appears on the surface of the bulk honey called dextrose hydrate. The thickness can be as little as 3 mm ($^1/_{10}$ inch) or 15 mm ($^1/_2$ inch): the variance is due to the ratios present of the principal sugars. It is recommended to remove as much as is possible before processing to liquid, as this is the ideal medium for harbouring unwanted matter for the mead-making process.

Bulk storage of honey showing dextrose hydrate on the surface (note the depth of the substance): it should be removed prior to warming in a heating cabinet
[Michael Badger]

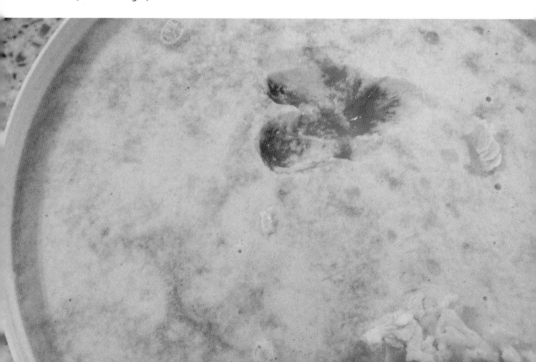

It needs to be realised that all honeys naturally harbour wild yeasts when extracted from the comb. These yeasts need to be destroyed by a simple method of pasteurisation to a temperature of 27 °C (80 °F) as a means of ensuring the bulk-stored honey will remain in pristine condition.

The use of a simple warming box

The pasteurisation process, if controlled correctly, should not raise hydroxymethylfurfural (HMF) beyond the accepted levels (see Appendix D). In the United Kingdom only, HMF is permitted at 80 mg/kg (under 20 mg/kg) UK Honey Regulations 1976. UK Trading Standards officials are known to use sophisticated equipment to check HMF levels within honey offered for sale. Destruction of the yeasts can be achieved by taking the bulk honey and gently heating it for one hour at 60 °C. Thereafter, the honey is stored in cool conditions. Food-grade plastic buckets with snap-on lids should be used, and, following the heating process, masking tape is pasted around the lid as an aid to prevent the honey taking in moisture due to its hygroscopic nature, naturally present in the atmosphere. Storage of honey at lower temperatures reduces the risk of fermentation. A simple warming box can be made using a well-insulated cabinet, suitably sized to hold the honey container and a heat source. While sophisticated purpose-made warming cabinets with accurate temperature control are available, a simple DIY cabinet can be made using a discarded refrigerator. The heat source can be a thermostatically controlled warming cable specifically made for warming honey, such as that made by Eco stat. The cabinet should be of sufficient size to accommodate two ten-litre buckets. The buckets will need to be situated on a slatted floor with the heating element placed below, but suspended

Honey warming cabinet [Alex Ellis]

above the floor of the cabinet to avoid contact with the cabinet structure to prevent damage and avoid risk of fire. A larger cabinet for an additional two buckets will require an additional 100W element to maintain the heat required. A heat sensor is placed about 150 mm above the heating element, although some degree of positioning may be required to establish the optimum temperature control. A small double-glazed observation port can be incorporated in the lid or door of the cabinet to enable a thermometer to be seen, thus avoiding loss of heat to read the temperature. A large bulk container 13 kg (29 lb) can take up to 8 hrs to liquefy the bulk honey mass if solid, or, if in a liquid state, half that time. Solid honey is best mushed up once it begins to liquefy.

Honey Warming Techniques for Bottled Honey

The inexperienced non-beekeeping mead vintner who is presented with honey found to be highly viscous to solid should on no account warm the bulk honey within a domestic oven, but resort to more subtle methods to liquefy the honey.

To expand upon this, if the honey is provided in glass containers, a simple way is to place the jars within a large saucepan with water filled up to the halfway mark; these jars need to be set upon thin, wooden slats (this allows the water to circulate when heated). The water is heated slowly and set at 55 °C (130 °F) and no more, and the honey will quickly turn to mush and part liquid; at this point the contents are carefully stirred to hasten the honey to settle out to clear.

The honey, when suitably liquefied, can be run into the "must container", using a spatula to extract the maximum, and then a little warm water can be used to dilute what is left and added to the must container. The same procedure applies to the warming of honey in bulk.

Cautionary Note

Liquid honey is by nature irascible, and makes no noise when overflowing: it should only be cleaned up when spilt with spatulas and the use of clean, cold water – never, never, hot water.

METHODS FOR PRODUCING MEADS AND HONEY WINES

Generally one of three are used to produce mead:

- **The hot method** – As the name implies, using heat to either pasteurise or bring the contents of the must to temperature. With the "hot method" the mead maker needs to be aware that overheating honey (to boiling point) is considered to drive off the essential ester varietals so essential to good mead making.
- **The cold method** – The addition of sulphites only to the must in the absence of heat or the using honey pre-pasteurised by the beekeeper.
- **The addition of acids after fermentation is completed** – As the title implies, the acids are added to the finished fermented wine at laid-in bottle stage whether the "hot or cold" methods have been employed to produce the finished wine. This is a system advocated most keenly in the USA and Canada.

SUGGESTED EQUIPMENT

Commonly Used Equipment for All Methods

Measuring cup – not enamel	Pyrex measuring jugs .75 litre and 1.5 litre capacity
Set of stainless steel measuring spoons	Acid measuring kit
Stainless steel saucepans for holding in excess of 1 gallon of must	Fermentation bins: those holding in excess of 1 gallon and others of 5 gallon of must
Stainless steel mixing spoons: large and small	Stainless steel teaspoons.
Large stainless steel mixing spoon	Scissors.
Plain and bored bungs	One gallon – demijohns
Airlocks and bung – standard type	Five-gallon carboys

Large food-grade fermentation bin with cover. 5-gallon capacity	Notepad + pencil + logbook
Trial jar – plastic or glass	Hydrometer
Kitchen weighing scales	Digital timer
Thermometer – Celsius or Fahrenheit – Electric or Physical	Funnels – large and small
1.5 m siphon tubing – UPVC 3/8 in or 8 mm internal diameter	Cleaning cloths
Water glasses	Wine bottles – clear, traditional non-screw cap
Bottle capper, plus caps for beer bottles	Beer bottles 330 or 500 ml
Floating thermometer Plastic cling film.	Plastic bottle filler Hand spray bottle for holding sanitising solution
Hand spray bottle for holding sanitising solution	Small-size auto-syphon
Bottling wand	Wine thief

Additional Equipment for Large Scale Wine Production.

Standard size auto-syphon	Plastic bottle filler
Purpose-made wine racks	Small set of scales for measuring minute quantities of ingredients
Large set of scales for measuring bulk quantities of ingredients	Purpose-made wine degasser for mounting into a variable-speed electric drill for periodic stirring of the must
A digital timer for tracking yeast rehydration timescales	Infrared thermometer and combined refractometer
Wine thief	Hand-operated refractor calibrated for honey sugars
An electronic pH push-button wine acid kit	A graduated calibrated measuring cylinder for blending wines
Floor mounted bottle corker for wine bottles	Medicine dropper
Beer bottle cap crimper-type bottle cap sealer	Purpose-built wine racks for storing and ageing wines

ESSENTIALS OF KEEPING ITEMISED RECORDS

All mead makers should keep notes and detailed records of the liquor they have produced by recording the original gravity (OG), the ingredients used, amounts and times in the production process, commencing with the original gravity (OG). Good record keeping is the right road to making good-quality wine. The mead maker needs to be able to repeat good batches and learn from the poor ones produced, and the best aid for this is record keeping. If you have a bad lot and want to ask another mead maker, whose experience will aid you, for their opinion, they will wish to know all the production details, the ingredients and amounts, how long you kept the must going, type of yeast and nutrients quantities used, how long it fermented, how the fermentation looked and proceeded, what the temperature was, etc. There are so many possible causes for a bad batch that you really need to keep a written pathway of everything undertaken, you can identify where it might have gone awry and gain the knowledge to fix it the next time. Good record keeping will help you succeed rather than fail.

A TYPICAL RECORD SHEET for MEAD or HONEY WINE PRODUCTION

Batch Name or Issue – 2017 /009	Wine Type – Dessert Sweet Show Mead
Date – 17-04-2017	Honey Source – Ling Heather
Water Source – Mains Supply	Water Treatment – Epsom salts – pinch
Batch Size – 1 gall. Demijohn	Method – Cold Process.
Opening Gravity – 1.120	Final Gravity – 1.021

Acids Used – Amount – Date Added

Tartaric	4 tsps	17/04/2017
Malic	$1/_8$ tsps	Ditto
Citric	1 tsps	Ditto
Ascorbic – $1/_8$ tsps	$1/_8$ tsps	Ditto
Tannin – Cold Tea.	5 table sps very strong	Ditto

Ingredients Used – Amount – Date Added

Vitamin B1	1 crushed tablet	17/04/2017
Rohamet P	Nil	N/A
Pectolase	Nil	N/A

Nutrient Mixture Used – Amount – Date Added

DAP	½ gr per gallon	18/04/2017
Fermaid K	3 gr per gallon	ditto
Go-Ferm	1 gr per gallon	ditto

Staggered Nutrient Additions – Amount – Date Added

DAP	½ gr per gallon	30/04/2017
Fermaid K	1 gr per gallon	19/04/2017
Ditto	1 gr per gallon	20/04/2017
Go-Ferm	1 gr per gallon	19/04/2017
Ditto	1 gr per gallon	20/04/2017

Yeast Type – Method of Addition – Date Added

Lalvin K1-V116	1 gr per gallon by starter bottle	17/04/2017
Notes:		

A RECOMMENDED METHOD FOR MEAD AND HONEY WINE PRODUCTION USING THE COLD METHOD

The Honey

A good source of quality honey is essential. If you are beekeeper using your own honey, you will have a good idea of where the honey came from, depending on the time of year it was collected.

The honey in my home apiary in late-May/early June could be sourced from sycamore (*Acer pseudoplatanus*), Norway maple (*Acer platanoides*), dandelion (*Taraxacum officinale*), horse and sweet chestnut (*Aesculus hippocastanum and castanea sativa*), plus garden flowers and the like. It is most likely to be a combination of all these floral sources. The honey should be in its liquid state. It ought to be free of extraneous wax and detritus that accumulate during the harvesting process, and free of honeydew and propolis. While harmless in themselves, these last two compounds are not welcome in mead and honey winemaking, and it is better to have neither in place that will interfere with the quality of the mead.

To expand upon the Mead Type

Dry mead, where all the fermentable sugars contained in the completed must need to have been used up by the yeast so that no sweetness remains. With sweet meads, some residual unfermented sugar will remain, hence the name. Therefore our aim is to have a dry wine with a specific gravity (SG) below 1.000 in the UK or below 1.009 under BJCP rules.

PRODUCING ONE GALLON OF DRY MEAD – COLD METHOD

Total Ingredients

4 litres plain water
1.36 kg (3 lb) floral honey
1 teaspoon tartaric acid
1/8 teaspoon malic acid
1/4 teaspoon grape tannin or 4
   tablespoons of strong, cold
   tea
1 teaspoon citric acid
1 teaspoon DAP
   (diammonium phosphate)
   Yeast Nutrient
Fermaid K – nutrient at

approximately 1 g per
gallon
DAP 1 g per gallon
Go-Ferm – Nutrient 1.25 g
   per 1 g of yeast
1 tablet thiamine (vitamin B1)
1 tablet ascorbic acid
   (vitamin C)
1 sachet general-purpose yeast
   (Gervin GV1 – Green Label
   or Lalvin 71B-1122)

For use at the end of the fermentation process
Campden tablets
Potassium sorbate

Method

Preparing the "Must"

Day One

Due to my inability to lift heavy containers, all my mead and honey wine production is now conducted with 1-gallon (Imp) demijohn fermenting vessels. Nevertheless, the procedures are the same whether 1 or 5 gallons are produced; the ingredients are divvied out proportionately. There are schools of thought suggesting that if the liquor is outstanding, you might well regret not making a larger batch: conversely, the opposite can so easily occur. What size of fermenter vessel you choose is a matter of preference to the vintner.

- Slowly heat the water to no more than 24 °C (75 °F) purely to assist the dissolving of the honey into the water.

Adding honey to the mixing vessel [Michael Badger]

- Add the honey slowly and begin stirring into the heated water to avoid "cold spots".
- Once the must reaches 24 °C (75 °F), remove from the heat.
- Despite having removed the dextrose hydrate (see page 81) on the surface of the bulk honey, there can be an appreciable amount of froth and scum produced in the warming of the honey: try to remove it.
- This method of warming honey is not detrimental to the honey esters and other desirable properties.
- However, these desirable properties could so easily be damaged or destroyed if much higher temperatures are adopted for sterilising the must.
- As a double-edged sword, the use of one crushed Campden tablet (potassium or sodium metabisulfite) can be added to complete the sterilisation of the must. The Campden tablet is crushed against the side of a sanitised 1-pint Pyrex jug,

Preparing the Campden tablet for adding to the must by crushing tablet between two spoons [Peter Lewis]

adding sufficient plain boiled-warm water at about blood-heat temperature; continue to stir the mixture until the crushed tablet is fully dissolved.
- When you are confident that the mixture is totally dissolved, add to the bulk must.

The must is left for 24 hours, stirring occasionally to ensure the must become fully sanitised; in addition, the stirring dissipates any sulphur fumes present.

Day Two

- It is essential that the Specific Gravity (SG) of the must is nearer to 1.115, but no greater than 1.120.
- Should you find the SG is over the desired limits, add cups of plain boiled water to the must, stirring continuously to

blend the water thoroughly. Once more using a sanitised hydrometer and trial glass, recheck the SG. Should the SG still be too high, repeat the procedure until you achieve the desired specific gravity.

- Conversely, should the must's SG be found to be below 1.115, using a sanitised cup, add small additional amounts of honey and incorporate into the must, stirring well. Repeat the procedure as described for ascertaining the required specific gravity.

Preparing the Yeast for use to add to the Must

There are various methods used by vintners: most vintners prefer to use the starter mix approach by making up a starter with the use of a starter bottle for incorporating rehydrated or liquid yeasts for adding to the main must.

A Typical Method for Making-Up a Starter-Mix by Prepairing a Starter Bottle

Items	Amount	Ingredients
1	Sterlised container	To hold all components
2	295 ml (10 fl oz).	Mains water
3.	Two tea spoons	Cane sugar
4	One teaspoon	Marmite, Yeast Extract
5	One pinch	Epsom Salts
6.	One Pinch	Citric Acid
7.	One Pinch	Ascorbic Acid
8.	One Sachet	Of the preferred yeast for the main fermentation

Bring to the boil the mains water, added cold into sterilised sauce pan. Add all ingredients (except yeast) whilst cooling to 21 °C (70 °F) and stirred all until fully dissolved; When at the cooled

A starter bottle ready for incorporation into the must to begin the primary fermentation [Michael Badger]

temperature sprinkle sachet of yeast on to surface. Cover vessel with clean cloth. Depending on the strain of yeast it should start to multiply with visible signs of bubbles arising on the surface: it is ready to add to the must.

NB. It should be noted that yeasts of different strains are apt to be either slower or quicker to multiply.

Primary Fermentation

Check the temperature of the must with a sterilised thermometer to ensure its temperature is above 17 (62 °F) but no more than 24 °C (75 °F).

Adding the Acids

1. Remove ½ litre (17.60 fl oz) of the must into a sanitised Pyrex jug.
2. Add to this liquid the following ingredients:
   1 level teaspoon tartaric acid
   ⅛ teaspoon malic acid
   ¼ teaspoon grape tannin or 4 tablespoons of strong, cold tea
   1 level teaspoon citric acid
   ½ teaspoon DAP (diammonium phosphate) yeast nutrient
   1 crushed tablet thiamine (vitamin B1)
   1 crushed tablet ascorbic acid (vitamin C).
3. Thoroughly mix into the liquid, ensuring they are fully dissolved, then add to the bulk must.

Oxygenate the must by stirring and sloshing the contents around to add as much oxygen into the must. This can be done either by hand or mechanical means known as degassing (see below).

Using mechanical means to incorporate the much-required oxygen and mix the contents thoroughly [Peter Lewis]

Adding the "Starter Mix" to the "Must"

- Add the prepared yeast starter mixture to the sterilised must (the bulk honey and water).
- Stir in the mixture with the object of incorporating as much oxygen as is possible. This can be achieved by hand or by mechanical means, slowly and deliberately.
- The fermenter should be kept in a warm place with the room temperature no more than 24 °C (75 °F). Stir the must every 8 hours; initially foam will occur but over time this will subside.
- The demijohn is best covered with black plastic, as the yeast works better in total darkness.

Demijohns shielded with black plastic sheeting [Peter Lewis]

ADDING ADDITIONAL NUTRIENTS – "STAGGERED NUTRIENT ADDITIONS (SNA)"

Generally

The notion is relatively straightforward, if the yeast doesn't deliver the essential trappings and environment to conduct a healthy, active fermentation, the final mead can be peppered with faults. To overcome this, mead nutrient additions can be added to yeast during fermentation in staggered proportions, and over time that will make for a profligate, healthy fermentation and diminish the chances of developing off-flavours through faulty fermentation pathways.

Why are Nutrients So Important?

Once yeast is added (pitched) into the mead must, it makes for a period of growth followed by the first stages of fermentation (see Part One – Mead in General – for a more detailed analysis). Growth of the yeast refers both to individual cells and the overall cell population. It is both vital and essential for individual yeast cells to have the proper nutrients available to aid and revitalise cell membranes to prepare them for cell division and budding.

Nutrients are required throughout the entire fermentation process: this is most essential and important, even after growth may have ceased to a conclusion. The yeast is needed to be healthy throughout fermentation; if not, then the state of the yeast deteriorates and could cause fermentation to cease prematurely. Should and when this happens, flaws and off-flavours arise in the final outcome of the mead.

It needs to be understood that a simple mixture of honey and water is almost lacking in all the essential micronutrients so essential for the yeast to flourish. To this end, the mead-maker adds additional compounds to the must thereby ensuring the yeast grows and budding takes place. As honey is devoid of the required amounts of these micronutrients for successful yeast growth and formation it is for the mead maker to add the types and amounts of these micronutrients to the must: the amounts added by the mead maker is in essence by trial and error. Over time the vintner becomes proficient with the use of such additions to the must, knowing more or less what amounts are added for each honey used, allied to any particular receipe or mead type.

The Importance of Nitrogen and Other Micro-Nutrients to the Fermentation

Nitrogen is particularly important throughout the fermentation process (see Part Four – The Requirements for Producing Meads and Honey Wines for a more detailed analysis). Nitrogen's importance is allied to the utilisation at the growth stage whilst the yeast is invigorating its cell membranes for budding and division during the metabolic stage when yeast is converting sugars into alcohol and CO_2. With the absence of appropriate levels of nitrogen, the fermentation can stall and be prolonged and may eventually be incomplete.

Nitrogen levels naturally present in honey vary from one variety to another. The presence of 150 mg/l of nitrogen in honey is an exception; in reality, levels present are very much lower. Mead practice recommends compensating for this shortfall, as the active yeast needs nitrogen levels in the range of 300-500 mg/l for superior fermentations. This is achieved with the must being complemented through enhanced nutrient additions.

Staggered Nutrient Additions (SNA) Concept

Traditionally, recipes call for all nutrients to be added at the time when the yeast is first added (pitched) into the must. This method provides the yeast with the essentials more or less immediately. However, the key (in my opinion) to a good fermentation is keeping the growing budding yeast content by providing all the desired nutrients throughout the entirety of the fermentation process. A number of established mead makers are shying away from adding all the nutrients at the beginning of the fermentation. This recent development has arisen through the advances in yeast technology these last twenty five years. The uses of modern yeasts very often see a proportion of the micronutrients not being used up before flocculating out begins. The additions in "toto" can be too much for the yeast to tolerate and consume at the onset, resulting in the must being overwhelmed; the growing yeast can only assimilate amounts relative to the rate of budding and reproduction the yeast can encounter at any one time with the nutrients not being consumed. For these reasons it is suggested to stagger the additions of nutrients during fermentation pathways.

Common Techniques' Adopted for
Staggered Nutrient Additions (SNA) Concepts

As explained previously, the process consists of nutrient doses with periods of off-gassing in between. The modus for an SNA schedule can be achieved by a number of techniques that involve the following:

- Determine the total amount of nutrients you want to provide the yeast.
- Then divide it up into multiple additions.
- Some mead vintners do multiple equal additions every other day.
- Others will gradually add smaller amounts at various intervals, depending on the progress of the fermentation.

An example of Staggered Nutrient Additions (SNA) schedule for producing a standard demijohn one gallon of mead:

Over three separate days add equal portions of the ingredients to the must:

- Prepared Fermaid K at approximately 1 g per gallon.
- Go-Ferm – nutrient 1.25 g per 1 g of yeast by shaking and stirring to incorporate into the must.
- 9 days later add the remaining ½ dose of DAP to the must (the first ½ dose of DAP was added at the initial start of the

fermentation process). This is best undertaken by taking 300 ml (11 fl oz) of the must into a sterilised Pyrex jug and slowly adding the DAP to the liquor; stir in studiously to ensure it is fully dissolved. The DAP may well quickly turn to efflorescence, hence the reasoning for adding to the must in this procedure. Once the incorporation is complete, add the contents to the bulk must, again in minority amounts to avoid excessive priming which will readily occur when added.

Staggered Nutrient Additions (SNA) schedule for a standard five-gallon batch of mead:

Day 1
- After making up a starter mix that included 5 g of Go-Ferm plus other additions of acids and nutrients.
- Add 4½ g Fermaid K.
- Add 2 g diammonium phosphate (DAP).

Days 2, 4, 6, 8 and 9
- Incorporate oxygen to the mead to degas by gently stirring, twirling the carboy carefully, or by mechanical means mentioned elsewhere in the text.

Left Jewellers weighing scales for ultimate accuracy when dolling out chemicals and compounds. [Peter Lewis]

Right Making up the ingredients within a plastic-capped container as an aid to mixing the contents thoroughly by shaking violently [Peter Lewis]

Days 3, 5, and 7
- Carefully add and gently stir 4½ g Fermaid K.
- Add 2 g diammonium phosphate (DAP).

Note: This is best undertaken by taking 300 ml (11 fl oz) of the must and adding the nutrients as mentioned earlier in the text to avoid excess efflorescence.

The primary fermentation may be very vigorous, especially if heather honey is used and the ambient temperature is warm. An active fermentation can very easily overflow through the fermentation lock, so, to avoid creating a sticky mess and impairing the quality of the finished mead, it is suggested that you reduce the initial volume of must in the demijohn and, once the fermentation subsides, add more of the honey and water by degrees until you reach to 10mm (3/8 inch) below the bung. Once the primary fermentation is working well (usually 36 hours), place the demijohn in a cool, dark place that has a minimum ambient temperature of 17 °C (62 °F).

Photograph of an overzealous fermenting mead, whose
base honey is ling heather [Michael Badger]

Secondary Fermentation

After about 28 days from adding the yeast starter mix to the must, the rate of bubbles through the airlock should have slowed to a mere trickle, on average one per minute.

- Transfer the fermenting liquor to a new, clean, sterilised demijohn jar by using a sterile, plastic racking hose and syphon off the must into the new demijohn vessel. Top up to the underside of the bung with cold, plain boiled water from a sanitised container.
- After a period of time the wine will be seen to clear, the clarifying process assisted by the dead or dying yeast cells dropping out of suspension, falling to the fermenting vessel floor. Placing the newly filled demijohn onto a cold concrete floor and a cool room assists the clearing process.

To aid the removal of the original must, the rear of the demijohn is raised up about 20 mm (¾ inch) so that the racking tube can be adjusted to avoid sucking up excess spent, dead yeast cells and fermenting detritus; the object is to transfer the maximum amount of the must in the transferral process and avoiding the introduction of oxygen. It is inevitable that sediment will get drawn up and transferred into the new demijohn; the amount generally is insignificant, and in the next racking the transfer will be negligible and need not overtly be of concern. Place the demijohn on a carpet of absorbent newspaper to pick up possible spillages.

During the transfer process, take a sterilised hydrometer and trial jar and take a sample of the must, recording the SG which should be in the order of 1.05 to 1.10.

Insert a new sterilised airlock (preferably using glycerine in the airlock trap to overcome evaporation) and bung to the newly filled demijohn. There will be a shortfall of the transferred must; topping up can be best achieved by adding to the demijohn warm-boiled water from a sanitised container to within 15 mm (½ inch) of the underside of the bung.

Racking operation [Dave Shannon]

Allow the fermentation to proceed to dryness (1.000); the time taken will depend upon the ambient temperature surrounding the fermentation vessel.

Most importantly, immediately after the racking is completed, clean, sanitise and sterilise the existing fermenting vessel and inspect to ensure no grime is left on the vessel's insides. I have found that undertaking this immediate cleaning procedure is the only solution to keeping fermentation vessels in tip-top shape, which avoids removing stubborn staining at a later date.

Completed Fermentation

Depending upon the yeast, nutrients and other additives used in the production of the finished article, there reaches a point when the vintner needs to decide his options in respect of bottling, bulk storage and maturity issues. There is no real rule of thumb as to when a wine has the completed fermentation process, as a wine can cease working if moved into a cold room or space: conversely, a dormant wine can regenerate itself if moved into a warm environment, resulting in corks being blown or bottles bursting. Nevertheless, should a fermenting wine, situated in ambient conditions of around 20 °C (68 °F), be seen to have no bubbles passing through the airlock in a period of 60 minutes, this wine can be reasonably assumed to be finished.

1. Rack the finished wine into a newly sanitised demijohn vessel. Top up with boiled water as described previously under secondary fermentation.
2. Add to the wine two crushed Campden tablets followed by one level teaspoonful of potassium sorbate (E202] thoroughly stirred into the bulk wine.
3. A wine that is slow to clear can be treated with clarifying agents (see page 119 – Clearing of Meads and Honey Wines). However, a wine that will not clear may well be damaged with a bacterial infection, and as such it will never clear at all; such a batch should be discarded and the vessel, fermentation lock and bung should be thoroughly cleaned, sanitised and sterilised immediately.
4. Rack the wine once more when an appreciable amount of lees is seen at the base of the demijohn. Top up with plain boiled water as described previously.

Controlling Fermentation

Earlier in the text (see page 51 – The Nutrients) mention is made to avoid stressing the yeast cells, as this can so easily happen with the high sugar levels present in the musts of mead and honey wines. To overcome this issue, follow the advice previously given. A number of years ago, I listened to an interesting talk given by Steve Piatz, Eagen, Minnesota, USA, on the problems created by stressing the yeast. He echoed the comments of Ken Schramm in that the best results for a good fermentation is to embark upon adding nutrients to the must in a measured, phased way. Staggered nutrient additions (SNA) should commence following the lag phase (the opening stage). The nutrients are added as discussed earlier in the text (see page 96 – Adding Additional Nutrients – "Staggered Nutrient Additions (SNA)").

USING THE HOT METHOD TO PRODUCE DRY MEAD

As the name implies, external heating is used to pasteurise the contents of the must to a temperature to destroy wild yeasts and any undesirable bacteria that may well be present in the honey and ingredients.

For those making mead or honey wines for the first time, the hot method is relatively a simple operation.

The process for the "Hot Method" is exactly as the "Cold Method" until the Primary Fermentation stage is reached and proceed as follows:

Day 1
Six pints of water are needed. Should the water have been drawn from the domestic water main, do this at least 24 hours previously to disperse any fluoride or chlorine that may be present to allow evaporation. The occasional stir will help to release the chemical fumes.

Sterilisation of the Must

- Make up a starter bottle as described for the "Cold Method".
- Place the prepared water in stainless steel saucepans and gently heat to 55 °C (130 °F). I refer to this as the pasteurisation phase.
- Add half of the honey and stir slowly and deliberately with the sterilised stainless steel mixing spoon until the honey is fully dissolved within the water. Once dissolved, add the remaining honey, skimming off any froth that appears.
- Continue by checking the temperature of the must with a clean, sanitised and sterilised thermometer to ensure its temperature is no more than 55 °C (130 °F).

Proceed as described under the Cold Method

- Ensure everything is fully dissolved by stirring the mass, now referred to as the must. Maintain the must at 55 °C (130 °F) for six to eight minutes maximum, ensuring the temperature is not exceeded.
- Remove from the heat, cover with a clean cloth and allow to cool.
- When the temperature of the must falls to 21 °C (70 °F), pour it into the sterilised fermentation bin or bucket, having removed any further froth or scum.
- Take a sterilised trial jar and hydrometer fill it sufficiently for the hydrometer to float in the contents. Read off the specific gravity which is referred to as the original gravity (OG) which should be around 1.115 but no greater than 1.120. If the SG is too high, dilute with cooled boiled water, or if the SG is too low, add honey; in either situation continually check the SG. Return the contents to the must.
- Add the starter mix bottle contents (see page 92) for how to make up a starter mix bottle) to the must which should be working well, and stir with the sterilised stirring spoon.
- Keep the fermentation bin covered with a clean cloth and place it in a warm place.

Proceed as described under the "Cold Method" – see pages 89-95.

SUMMATION OF USING EITHER THE COLD OR HOT METHOD

After 12 months, the mead should be bright and clear, if the processes of fermentation and cleanliness are readily adhered to, and ready for bottling. It will be ready to drink within another year or, if patience permits, it will improve further if left for up to four years or more. Should there be issues of clearing the wine, see page 135 – Part Three: Mead and Honey Wine Problems – for methods to assist in clearing).

There are arguments for using either method: my recommendation is for the tyro mead vintner to try both processes and use which he feels most comfortable with.

That notwithstanding, in the hot method you must take heed of keeping the temperature of the must at 55 °C (130 °F) for six to eight minutes maximum, ensuring the temperature is not exceeded. Keeping a sanitised thermometer in place is recommended, and frequent stirring to avoid both cold and hot spots in the warming vessel.

If you prefer sweet mead, follow the above method to the letter with the following amendments.

PRODUCING A SWEET MEAD FOR COLD AND HOT METHODS

Proceed to process as with the dry mead by adding one extra teaspoon of tartaric acid and ⅛ teaspoon of malic acid (too much malic acid can make the finished wine acquire a harsh taste), plus two teaspoons of yeast nutrient at the initial first stage of the fermentation (see page 92).

Method

- After the primary fermentation has diminished to an SG below 1.006 (the slowdown in the rate of bubbles passing through the airlock is an indication that the SG is nearing 1.006), add a further 100 g (4 oz) of sterilised honey to the must; the additional honey will allow the fermentation to continue.
- After three weeks test the SG again and, if it is below 1.006, add a further 50 g (2 oz) of honey.
- Repeat this procedure at intervals which might increase between each topping up. This is known as "feeding the must".
- A mead wine for social occasions should not be excessively

strong in alcohol, to this end the Final Gravity is aimed for a SG twixt 1.010 - 1 015. This is achieved by the amount of honey added that should stop at between 1.92kg and 2 kg. (4¼ lb and 4½ lb).

- Should dessert-strength mead be required, continue "feeding" the "must" with sterilised honey at a rate of 25g (1 oz) until the build-up of alcohol reaches a level which overwhelms the yeast's reproductive action, forcing the fermentation to stop; this arises because the yeast can no longer tolerate the new surroundings of increased sugar. This "feeding" may take several months more especially if the mead maker reduces the "feeding" rate to 12g (½ oz)

It is at this point the must retains an appreciable amount of unfermented honey which reveals its level of sweetness. Desirable sweet meads should have an SG between 1.009 and 1.015, and a sack/dessert an SG of 1.021 +.

Naturally, tastes differ and the vintner produces mead to his taste. Heavy sack dessert meads have an SG nearer 1.021+. Such meads are exceedingly strong and potent, and as such not suited as a social or a session drinking wine. These meads are comparable to traditional dessert Sauternes wine.

My preference for sweet table mead is that it should not be too high in alcohol. To achieve this, the fermentation should be stopped at SG 1.010 when a maximum of 1.6 to 1.9 kg (3½ to 4¼ lb) of honey are used in the recipe.

The criteria for bottling are detailed elsewhere (see page 145 – Part Four – Bottling and Cellar-Craft). It is essential to be sure that the mead has ceased working: if it is bottled before the fermentation has stopped, the wine becomes unstable, with bottles bursting or corks being blown. A change in environmental conditions, or if there is a change in temperature where the mead is cellared, is sufficient for a wine to begin restarting a fermentation. Such happenings are very dangerous with possible injury from flying glass, as the detonation happens without warning.

A FEW DO'S AND DON'TS TO CONSIDER WHEN PRODUCING MEADS AND HONEY WINES

- Non-beekeepers need to be aware that honeybees are affected by fatal diseases known as American (AFB) and European Foulbrood (EFB) – their respective names have no geographical significance. Theses dangerous pathogens are found in honey, especially honey traded on world markets. Once containers are emptied of honey, they should be washed out thoroughly (these washings can be used for mead making: see below) and the discarded containers stored away or put for refuse collection. Never leave empty containers to be cleaned up by honeybees, as this creates issues from excitement, bad temper, robbing forays and the spread of these fatal diseases. Honeybees have acute senses of smell: honey left around will soon be found, especially in the active flying season, and in periods of nectar scarcity. Bottled honeys from supermarkets, labelled "honey from more than one country", are honeys that may well harbour bacterial infections injurious to honeybees.
- Do not make short cuts in winemaking: they seldom, if ever, are.
- Make sure you have plenty of time to carry out the initial tasks without being under time constraint pressures.
- Remember the golden rule of cleanliness, always exercise proper cleanliness, sanitisation and sterilisation in your meadery operations: do not throw away in minutes what might have been in years with such folly.
- Use only good-quality honey, and for small batches measure out acids and additives with good, accurate scales to avoid an excess must of either acidity or alkalinity.
- Stock-check that you have all requirements to hand (acids, additives, equipment) before embarking upon the task ahead.
- Good meads and honey wines take time to reach to maturity: good cellar-craft should never be underestimated.

THE USE OF WASHINGS AND COMB-FACE CAPPINGS

The late Douglas ("Doug") Morris of Bramham, West Yorkshire, England, was a well-respected commercial bee farmer from 1934 until the early 1980s. Prior to the Second World War, Doug had been a chemist assistant at the John Smith's Brewery, Tadcaster, West Riding of Yorkshire, England. In the early 1930s, he became a successful semi-commercial beekeeper. In doing so, he used his chemistry knowledge and training to perfect dessert mead table wines much-sought-after by the local aristocracy. The majority of his mead was produced using "washings and cappings" arising from his extensive bee farming activities where he harvested several tons of honey annually. He told me on several occasions that he saved all the "washings water" from the cleaning of the extractors, uncapping trays, buckets and settling tanks (ripeners). After the careful washing out of the equipment, the residual water and its honey content made for an excellent must. The honey from the cappings was allowed to drip into a vessel to become part of the main honey harvest. After draining, the "wet" cappings were ready for washing. Together with the other washings, this water was ready for processing into mead liquor.

The introduction of propolis or beeswax or detritus should be carefully avoided by straining the liquid through strong muslin immediately before the fermentation process begins.

Method

1. Prepare a number of fermenting vessels cleaned, sanitised and sterilised ready for use. The number of vessels is related to the amount of washings available. Filter the washings through a muslin filter to remove every bit of foreign matter, including beeswax, pollen, propolis, bees and debris.

2. Once the washings have been filtered, it is vital that the SG of the leavings (the washings) within the fermentation bin

is measured, using a sterilised hydrometer and trial jar, and duly recorded. The leavings are now the must. This operation will allow the amount (weight) of honey in the must to be calculated. The readings are computed from the specific gravity table (see page 131). This will indicate whether additional honey is needed to raise the SG or new clean water is required to dilute the must's SG. The starting SG needs to be 1.100 (a much higher reading will inhibit the yeast's reproduction).

3. Each fermentation vessel is labelled with its details, especially the original specific gravity (OG). Should (as is most often the case) the SG reading be higher (say, 1.150) than the required SG of 1.100, the must needs to be diluted with additional sterilised clean water. Readings are taken until the SG reaches 1.100.

4. It is often recommended to use a five-gallon cleaned, sanitised and sterilised glass carboy. However, at around 25 kg (56 lb), their weight is considerable when full, making manhandling difficult, no matter the physique of the vintner. There are larger carboys available, but it might be prudent in all situations to decant the liquor into several one-gallon demijohns for ease of use, with tie-on labels giving details of the contents, dates, etc.

5. For a five-gallon vessel: add five totally crushed Campden tablets to the must and the contents swirled around to ensure the tablets are incorporated fully into the must.

6. Place the following in a dry, sterilised beaker for addition to the must:
5 teaspoons (17.75 g) of a proprietary yeast nutrient
25 g citric acid
25 g tartaric acid
25 g malic acid

1 teaspoon (3.55 g) of dried grape tannin
500 mg ascorbic acid (vitamin C)
3 mg thiamine (vitamin B1)
Note: These acids, nutrients and tannin are mixed
thoroughly to ensure that the tannin does not separate
out, which it will do if added to the must on its own; it is
suggested to mix the ingredients together in a beaker, as
described previously. Add the contents of the beaker to the
must, swirling it around to ensure they are fully incorporated.

7. Cover the carboy outlet with a clean towel and place it in a
   warm room, preferably at 21 °C (70 °F). The use of a brewer's
   heating cable around the carboy may be necessary if the
   room's ambient temperature is colder than this.

8. Make up a mixer - starter bottle (see page 92) at least three
   hours in advance of the next operation. After 72 hours,
   the must should be swirled around to expel the sulphur
   dioxide fumes created by the Campden tablets, and shaken
   to introduce oxygen from the atmosphere. The yeast in the
   starter bottle should be well activated before it is added to
   the must. The dead yeast cells present in the starter bottle
   should not be added. The must is swirled around to get
   the yeast well incorporated. The carboy is then sealed with
   an air fermentation lock and bung. Alternatively, once the
   full carboy is working, it can be decanted into one-gallon
   demijohns for ease of lifting and handling.

9. Thereafter, the control and maintenance of the must are
   undertaken as detailed elsewhere in the text.

MEAD AND HONEY WINE PRODUCTION USING LING HEATHER (*CALLUNA VULGARIS*) HONEY

The use of ling heather (*Calluna vulgaris*) honey for making mead is very popular with beekeepers from the heather districts of the British Isles. Ling must not be confused with the port wine-coloured bell heather, whose characteristics are totally different. Owing to its inherent characteristics, the use of ling heather honey can often give mixed results compared with other honeys. By its nature, ling heather honey has high protein and mineral contents compared with other honeys; this quality adds to its uniqueness. This particular intense physical characteristic of high protein content has a profound effect on the finish of the mead; it is a quality not readily acceptable to the majority of non-beekeeping wine makers. Non-beekeeping vintners are not necessarily so keen on the pronounced flavour of ling heather honey so evident when this mead is savoured. The heather honey bouquet is pronounced but pleasing, and the flavour when tasted is generally nice on the palate. Often it has a peaty, smoky taste, an effect synonymous with the locality where the heather flower is grown. Non-beekeeping wine makers are more familiar with meads of a Sauternes nature, very often associated with a sweet dessert type. The non-beekeeper's specialty in mead making veers towards the use of much milder honeys such as acacia, orange blossom, clover, blackberry or rosemary. Many heather honeys differ from one moorland district to another: even those in close proximity are renowned for conveying a differing taste to the finished mead, very much like those malt whiskies that have their own unique taste and flavour. Mead produced from acacia honey probably makes the finest dessert mead, comparable to many a fine Sauternes wine. So do the long-maturing sweet ling heather meads of 10-12 years' vintage, compared with the use of other honeys. Mead dessert wines are of such quality that they, too, are on a par with Sauternes wines. Using ling heather honey for making mead will produce a dry, medium, sweet or a dessert wine

Ling heather honey in the comb, beautifully sealed: note complete absence of pollen
[Brian Nellist]

of full colour, flavour and bouquet and with high alcohol content. To obtain quality heather mead, it is essential that the best-quality heather honey is used, avoiding those honeys that have been heated; these honeys may have acquired a caramelising aftertaste. The beekeeper takes his bees to the upper moorland when the ling is in full bloom, from early August until about 24 August. By the later part of the month, the yield of ling nectar is over and the beekeeper returns the hives home for the honey to be processed.

In periods of very unseasonal high temperatures towards the end of the ling heather flowering period, the bees may well be attracted to late-flowering white clover and rosebay willowherb or other nectar-yielding plants. Such honey is known as a heather blend; nevertheless, it makes excellent mead and honey wines, too. In the large forestry belts, foraging bees will seek out honeydew from the Sitka spruce trees (*Picea sitchensis*) grown in large swathes across vast upper-moorland escarpments. These large forests will readily contaminate true samples of ling heather honey, especially in unseasonal weather. Such tainted honeys should be avoided for

113

mead making, as they contain the impurities of honeydew and propolis, a resinous mixture honeybees collect from tree buds, sap flows or other botanical sources, as these admixtures affect the wine in both flavour and taste. Propolis is used by the bees as a sealant for unwanted open spaces in the hive, and is believed to have aseptic properties. Herbalists recommend it for stomach complaints in humans. Nevertheless, its presence does not bode well for the production of nice meads or honey wines.

Unique Taste and Flavour of Ling Heather Meads and Honey Wines

The majority of wine makers, especially non-beekeeper mead makers, are not by nature admirers of heather honey for mead making, as discussed above. These wine makers are usually experts in producing excellent wines from acacia, rosemary, white clover,

Ling heather (*Calluna vulgaris*): note the purple within the flower, a telltale sign of good prospects for the beekeeper [Brian Nellist]

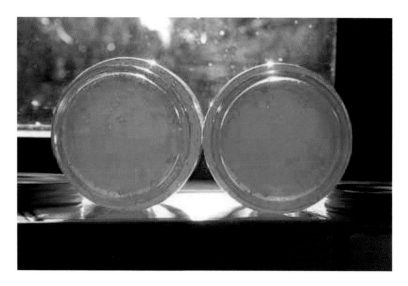

Ling heather honey jars laid on their sides to show its true thixotropic characteristic
[Brian Nellist]

blackberry, oranges, Rosemary and elderflower, and from damson, peach, apricot or other fruits. They prefer meads that are softer to the palate, produced from delicious, light-flavoured and delicate aroma acacia or rosemary honeys.

My experience of the majority of mead and honey wine (honey judges) especially those judges who are very familiar with ling heather are often easily influenced in favour of such meads that use ling heather as the base honey. Regrettably this is because they immediately pick up on its strong bouquet and flavour when tasted and are somewhat prejudiced by putting their own likings before the quality of all the other wines to be judged. They very often discard meads without a heather base because the fine, delicate aroma and the Sauternes taste of other such meads and honey wines are alien to them. Without doubt, heather honeys do impart a distinct, unique flavour to meads. In reality, when it comes down to a social drink, it is what you prefer and, after all, that is what counts.

Ling heather honey as a base for mead comes very much into

its own in sack mead. Most mead makers use a combination of honeys, while others blend floral honeys with heather honey to perfect the mead to their liking, avoiding honeys mentioned as unsuitable (see below). Ling heather honey with its natural high protein levels, plus the water itself, can embody a poorly balanced must unless the mead maker adds the correct acids and nutrients. Generally, the outcome from poorly made up musts is that the fermentation will be slow, possibly resulting in poorly matured mead taking up to eight years before it is drinkable and then being disappointing in flavour and taste. This is especially true of sack meads.

To overcome this impediment, the mead maker introduces nutrients, acids, antioxidants and tannin to the must. These additions will ensure finely produced, stable meads, always providing that good-quality heather honey, free of propolis, is used, with the water free of chlorine/fluoride, and good mead-type yeasts chosen.

HONEYS TO AVOID FOR MEAD AND HONEY WINE MAKING

There are honeys that should not be used for producing mead and honey wines: these include charlock, oilseed rape, ivy and privet. Honey from the yellow, daisy-like flower, ragwort (*Senecio jacobaea*), also makes bitter-tasting mead.

The wine produced from these honeys is far from pleasing, the flavour of these bland honeys revealing itself readily in the finished mead.

Dandelion and borage honey are said by some to make harsh-flavoured meads, yet I have not encountered such problems.

THE PROCESS OF FERMENTATION

The basic principles of fermentation are described in Appendix C. The conversion of the sugars in honey into alcohol is by a process of fermentation through the workings of the yeast in the presence of sugar. The yeasts used are cultured to give high alcohol content and to enhance the character of the wine. The yeast produces the best results when the must (the mixture to be fermented) is allowed to ferment at lower temperatures (15 °C, 60 °F) and is unhurried.

Yeast is a type of fungus which converts the carbohydrates present within the honey sugars into carbon dioxide and alcohols. The yeast requires a number of nitrogenous substances as nutrients which assist it to maintain its health and vitality, very much like we, as humans, require vitamins for our own energy. The correct amounts of added nutrients ensure that the reproducing yeast undergoes a sensational burst in the budding division, thereby ensuring the multiplicity of growth so necessary to ensure all the qualities occur that are needed to make a fine wine.

As a micro-organism, yeast is able to work anaerobically – that is, without the presence of oxygen. A yeast spore uses the honey sugars as its source of energy to continue growing and dividing. Finally, one of the by-products of its own metabolism (alcohol) becomes so highly concentrated that it eventually kills off the yeast, ending the fermentation process. The vintner acts to ensure that this tolerance threshold is not reached too quickly by adding honey to the must in measured degrees. These additions may occur several times, over a period of two or three months or more, all depending on the type of yeast used. Once the tolerance level is reached, the yeast dies.

An advantage with modern yeast strains is that the yeast spore can tolerate much higher levels of alcohol compared with those of yeasts available 30 years or more ago.

The alcohol level does not inhibit the yeast until it reaches 18 per cent or more alcohol by volume (ABV). The mead maker's ultimate goal is to work in harmony with the yeast by creating the perfect conditions in which it can multiply. This is achieved by ensuring that other unwanted organisms in the atmosphere do not gain entry to the must. If these foreign bodies are not excluded, they might well destroy or weaken the yeast colony and ruin a fine wine. Remember the golden rules – cleanliness, sanitisation and sterilisation – are everything.

MALOLACTIC FERMENTATION

Malolactic fermentation (MLF or malolactic conversion) is a process by which tart-tasting malic acid, naturally present in grape must, is converted to softer-tasting lactic acid. While malolactic fermentations can run concurrently with the primary fermentation, they are most usually performed shortly after this is completed. Most red wine production uses the process, as does that for some white grape varieties, such as Chardonnay, where the diacetyl by-product of the reaction can impart a creamy flavour to the end product.

The fermentation reaction is undertaken by the gram-positive bacterium, *Oenococcus oeni*, and various species of *Lactobacillus* and *Pediococcus*: these are lactic acid bacteria (LAB). Carbon dioxide is liberated during the decarboxylation process.

Wine contains two major grape acids, one of which is L- malic acid, associated with the taste of green apples. The LAB convert L- malic acid into L+ lactic acid, which has a much more creamy taste. While this can be a natural process, in commercial winemaking desirable bacteria, such as *Oenococcus oeni*, are introduced to initiate the reaction. This prevents undesirable bacterial strains from producing off-flavours. In order to maintain a more tart or acidic character in white grape varieties such as Riesling and Gewürztraminer, commercial wine makers will actively prevent MLF.

Mead and honey wines where malolactic fermentations have been introduced tend to have a rounder, fuller mouthfeel, with the body and persistence of flavour being enhanced.

The Malolactic Fermentation Equation
COOH.CH2.CHOH.COOH $\rightarrow$ CH3.CHOH.COOH + CO2

malic acid   lactic acid   carbon dioxide

The bacteria present will make the wine undergoing a malolactic fermentation (MLF) cloudy; the diacetyl may produce a smell reminiscent of popcorn. If MLF takes place in the bottle, the contents appear to be fermenting because of the production of carbon dioxide. This is usually considered to be a fault. However, meads and honey wines that have undergone MLF have a fresher taste. MLF is relatively rare in meads and honey wines.

CLEARING OF MEADS AND HONEY WINES

Most wines will clarify on their own account. The mead maker needs to give them enough time, carry out appropriate racking as the sediment (lees) becomes noticeable. Occasionally, a particular mead will not clear. Those made from stone fruits are notorious for not clearing. The problem may be due to pectin or starch haze, or perhaps a metallic contamination from using utensils made from copper, zinc, iron or aluminium.

Such difficulties may have their own cure. However, cloudiness may well be simply caused by very fine suspended particles, or it may be excessive tannin or suspended dead yeast cells. These will clear up over time as the particulates settle out into the lees, but it may be at the cost of adding undesirable off-flavours to the wine. However, if a wine has become contaminated by bacterial infection it will never clear, no matter what treatments for clearing are brought to bear. The salutary lesson is to never underestimate the issues of sanitisation with making wine.

PECTIN ENZYMES

This enzyme is not classified as a fining agent, but their use may greatly improve fining and filtering operations for high-pectin wines by breaking down the pectins known to occur naturally in wines. Their presence is often the cause of cloudiness. Pectic enzyme additions are especially beneficial for press-run wines (from grapes) as well as fruit and country wines, because their musts tend to have much higher pectin content.

Pectic enzyme powder is added at a rate of 1-2 g/hl for white wine, and 2-4 g/hl for red wine, firstly dissolving the compound in cool water. If cloudiness persists after fining, this indicates that the wine may contain excessive amounts of pectin. To test for the presence of pectin, add 50 ml of wine to 200 ml of methanol. If heavy, whitish sediments form, the wine contains excessive pectin and should be treated again with pectic enzymes.

All wine treated with pectic enzymes should be filtered as a means of further clarifying the wine.

FINING AND CLARIFYING AGENTS

Nothing can be more frustrating than a wine that will not clear immediately following the fermentation cycle, or one that continues to discharge sediments (lees) in the bottle. This is usually a telltale sign of meagre winemaking control and, to a degree, poor cellar-craft. Making star-bright, crystal-clear wine is the most important objective in any type of mead and honey wine production. Nevertheless, both cold and heated heather honey can prove difficult to clear due to its high protein content, especially if it is standing in a relatively cool to warm room. Producing wines not up to these criteria is considered to be a serious fault. Ostensibly, clear mead can also throw further sediment in the bottle, especially if a champagne yeast strain has been used. This is a trait often occurring with meads using such yeasts, travelling to a show, the motion seems to reinvigorate the residual sugar to recommence working, thereby throwing a small amount of sediment so often occurring with such yeasts on the base of the bottle. As a mead judge myself and a producer (in quantity, of such wines) plus as an exhibitor, too, it is annoying when a judge throws out such wines, rather than marking them down: such judges in the UK are invariably in my opinion not sound in mead and honey wine production.

Mead wines that are cellared under correct cellar-craft management can undergo malolactic fermentation (see page 118) for reasons not readily understood. Understandably, this is not considered a fault in older mead-type wines which may have been aged for many years and have not clarified except for periodic rackings. Nevertheless, sediments present in early-drinking young wines are a sign of insufficient clarification and rushed mead making. It should be understood that clear (tartrate) crystal deposits either at the bottom of a demijohn, carboy or bottle, or found on the inside end of the cork, are a result of the wine being subjected to cold temperatures. Tartrate crystals should not be confused with other sorts of sediment. I take the view that the presence of tartaric acid, the main wine acid, will cause some precipitation under cold storage conditions. Therefore, it is not related to clarification: it is the effects of storage. The vintner can cold-stabilise the wine prior to final bottling, thereby preventing tartrate deposit.

Many traditionalist wine producers totally avoid the use of additives or filtration to clarify wine in the fear it could be perceived as irregular winemaking. Instead, these wine makers prefer to rely on periodic rackings. For example, they might rack every three months over a period of 18-24 months.

Home wine makers wanting to produce early-drinking wines without the hassle of multiple rackings or having to age wine should always clarify wine using fining agents and/or filtration, such treatments may be detrimental to the finished wine especially filteration. Allowing the wine to clear of its own account is always the best option.

FINING TYPES

Finings, as they are known in the UK, are called clarifiers in the USA. The US term is more helpful in a definition, as these agents are used entirely to remove miasma or haze from a wine that has ceased working. When selecting a fining agent, the vintner needs to consider the main factors of the type of mead, whether white or red, the tannin concentration of the wine, and the desired results relative to colour.

- Early-drinking melomel and pyment produced from fresh juice or grapes should always be clarified prior to bottling using the preferred fining agent. The high protein content in these mead types can cause clarity instability, resulting in a cloudy wine or sediment in the bottle. Concentrated grape juice or other processed juice (such as semi-concentrate or sterilised juice) is perfect for quick mead production and bottling, and therefore these meads should also be clarified.

- Fining agents have varying levels of effectiveness in white and red wines because they contain different concentrations of phenolic compounds. In the context of clarification, tannin concentration is the most significant factor that may cause improper clarification with some fining agents, resulting in a cloudy wine or bottle sedimentation. Grapes, and the process used in red winemaking, impart a higher concentration of phenolic compounds. As a result, red wines have a significantly higher tannin content than white wines. Wines aged in oak barrels will also have a higher tannin content because oak is rich in tannin.

- The primary objective of clarification using fining agents is to produce a clear wine, free of suspended particles that could otherwise affect clarity. There should be a minimal alteration in colour except where this needs to be corrected because of problems such as browning as a result of oxidation. Great care should be taken with some fining agents to avoid over-fining, which would strip colour compounds from the wine.

- Fining agents in solid form should always be dissolved in water first, according to the manufacturer's instructions, unless specified otherwise, before adding them to the wine. Fining agents lose their effectiveness if dissolved or introduced directly into the wine.

Table of Fining Types and Agents

Fining agents and related products	Recommended rate of addition	Quantity for five gallons (Imp)		Wine type
		No. of teaspoons	Weight (grams)	
Positively Charged Fining Agents				
Egg white	5-10 g/hl	¼-½	1-2	Red
Gelatin	10-25 g/hl	½-1½	2-5	White/red
Isinglass	1-3 g/hl	1½-4¼	0.2-0.6	White
Casein	50-100 g/hl	31/3-62/3	10-20	White/red
PVPP	25-75 g/hl	4-11½	5-15	White/red
Sparkolloid®	10-40 g/hl	1½–6	2-8	White/red
Negatively Charged Fining Agents				
Bentonite	25-100 g/hl	1½-6	5-20	White/red
Kieselsol (silicondioxide, also known in the UK as colloidal silica)	25-50 ml/hl	1-2	N/A	White/red

The foggy/misty appearance of a cloudy wine is the result of the suspension of particles of yeast, proteins or polyphenols present in the wine. Polyphenols are found in a wide array of phytochemical-bearing foods, including honey and blackberry. The fining agents bind together the compounds found in suspension and they are removed through precipitation. However, the fining and clarifying agents each work differently as no single fining agent is found to remove every cause of cloudiness. From my experience, I have found that the use of one positively charged agent needs to be followed up later with a negatively charged one.

Positively Charged Fining Agents

Egg White

Egg white (albumen) is regarded as a very effective fining agent. It had long been used for clarifying red wines and it still widely used in modern winemaking. The rich albumen content makes it ideal for softening a wine's astringency by binding and reducing the haze and the tannin content. The use of albumen is most appropriate for fining wines high in tannin, or oak-aged wines. There is a very small risk of over-fining in its use, with colour loss in the wine being minimal when fining and racking are properly controlled.

Gelatin

This fining material is derived from animal tissues. It is a good fining agent for red wines because of its affinity for binding with phenols in precipitating the suspended particles and for reducing the tannin content. It is not recommended for fining white wines, as it will reduce the naturally small amount of tannins present. Experienced wine makers consider that a wine with a low tannin content may not fine adequately. To avoid over-fining white wines, tannin powder can be added before the use of gelatin fining.

Gelatin crystals are an alternative. They are added at a rate of 10-25 g/hl of wine. The maximum rate is used for highly tannic wines or wines having a higher than normal concentration of suspended particles or pectin. The gelatin is stirred thoroughly until dissolved completely. Some gelatin manufacturers recommend soaking the gelatin in cold water, then heating it until it comes to the boil. It is essential to follow the manufacturer's instructions for the gelatin product you purchase. A simple method might be to mix the warm gelatin solution with a little wine – about twice the amount of water used – and then add it to the rest of the wine while stirring. Rack the wine within 2-3 weeks of adding the gelatin.

Isinglass

This is a form of collagen, prepared from the dried swim bladders of fish. It is a popular fining agent among wine makers. Isinglass is less searching than other fining agents; it does not debase the wine's colour to the same degree as other protein-based fining agents such as gelatin or casein. It is most effective in clarifying white wines, particularly those that have been oak-aged. A disadvantage is that it throws a heavier deposit that has a tendency to cling to the wall of the glass fermenting vessel, making racking a little tricky. A second fining with bentonite alleviates this problem and avoids filter pads becoming clogged if the wine is to be filtered.

Isinglass powder is added at a rate of 1-3 g/hl of wine by first dissolving it in water at a temperature between 16 °C and 18 °C (61 °F and 64 °F) while stirring the solution thoroughly. The solution should stand for 15 minutes and then stirred again for two minutes. It is added to the wine while stirring the contents most vigorously. Rack the wine within one to two weeks. Isinglass is also sold as a solution for convenient mixing into wine.

Casein

Casein, a phosphoprotein of milk, flocculates with the wine to absorb and precipitate suspended particles. It is primarily recommended for clarifying white wines, especially for reducing tannin content in those that have been over-oaked. Experienced wine makers use this method for reducing browning resulting from oxidation. Its disadvantages include colour stripping of the wine if used in excess. Stubborn treated meads may well require a second fining with bentonite in order to avoid clogging of the filter pads should the mead or honey wine need filtering.

Casein powder is added at a rate of 50-100 g/hl of wine. Simply dissolve the powder in 100 ml of water for each gram of casein powder used and quickly add the solution to the wine while stirring vigorously. To avoid over-fining, use the lowest rate of addition. However, a higher rate may be needed if the wine is aged in oak barrels. Rack the mead after a couple of days and within one week. For white wines affected by browning caused by oxidation, use up to the maximum rate of addition, depending on the severity of the oxidation problem.

PVPP

Polyvinylpolypyrrolidone is a synthetic polymer that is effective in absorbing and precipitating polyphenols that are responsible for the browning in wines. It also rectifies the excessive bitterness that can occur in red wines. Settling occurs very fast, in as little as one to two hours, depending on the type of PVPP used. Rack the mead immediately after settling and filter it.

Note: There are different PVPP formulations requiring different rates of addition and shorter or longer settling periods. Be sure to follow the manufacturer's instructions for the PVPP product you purchase.

Sparkolloid®

This is a proprietary fining agent based on alginates found in brown algae. It is very effective in settling fine suspended particles in a cloudy-finished fermented wine. It is ideal for red wines, but also suitable for white wines. Sparkolloid's effectiveness is increased by filtering, because the lees is more compacted. Sparkolloid® powder is added at a rate of 10-40 g/hl of wine. First prepare a Sparkolloid® solution by boiling water in a small saucepan. Add the Sparkolloid® powder and stir thoroughly. Boil the solution for 20 minutes, stirring continuously to dissolve all the powder. Add the Sparkolloid® solution to the wine while it is fairly hot, 55 °C (130 °F), stirring continuously. Let the wine settle for at least a week and then filter.

Negatively Charged Fining Agents

Bentonite

Bentonite is a natural absorptive clay that fixes to and precipitates oppositely charged suspended particles in the must. It is used for the clarification of both red and white wines. It is highly recommended for white wine applications because it is excellent for inhibiting haze caused by naturally occurring proteins in the fruit juice. Bentonite's clarifying properties make it a popular choice as a fining agent among wine makers, although the heavy deposit it creates translates into a larger wine loss. One of its principal advantages over other fining agents is that it minimises colour reduction and therefore provides a supplementary safeguard against over-fining of the wine.

Bentonite is added to the must at a rate of 25-100 g/hl of wine. First, prepare a bentonite solution, adding the required amount of powder to a volume of warm water approximately 15 times the weight of the powder, e.g. 20 g in 300 ml. The solution should be shaken vigorously for a few minutes and then allowed to stand for 24 hours, with occasional additional shaking or stirring during this period. It is added to the wine while stirring continuously. The wine should be stored at a temperature between 15 °C and 25 °C (59 °F and 77 °F, respectively) for approximately one week before racking.

Bentonite is most effective when added at the end of fermentation, although it can be added prior to start of fermentation to help the clarification process. When adding bentonite before the start of fermentation, double the rate of the clearing agent used without exceeding the recommended maximum.

Kieselsol

This is colloidal silica that electrostatically binds to and adsorbs positively charged proteins, initiating flocculation and settling. It is an excellent fining agent for both white and red wines. It is particularly effective in wines with a low tannin content. Kieselsol is recommended for wines produced from concentrate, sterilised or fresh juice, or wines that have not been oak-aged in barrels. Experienced wine makers use kieselsol in conjunction with gelatin to increase its effectiveness. Kieselsol is added at a rate of 25-50 ml/hl of wine. Add the kieselsol suspension directly into the wine and stir gently. After 24 hours, add gelatin at the recommended rate and rack the wine within 1-2 weeks.

THE USE OF THE HYDROMETER FOR WINE PRODUCTION

The hydrometer is a piece of precision equipment. It gives a reading of the specific gravity (SG). This reading is indicative of the potential sweetness of the must, enabling the vintner to have control of the fermenting liquor for use as "dry" or "sweet". Nevertheless, the palate (as discussed on page 149) is the real determinant of the relative sweetness in mead and honey wines. The terms used for gravity can be puzzling. "Gravity 0" is 1.000, and a "Gravity 5" is 1.005. The experienced vintner very often relies on the volume/rate of bubbles observed in the fermentation process as his guide to how the rate of fermentation is proceeding. A hydrometer will show a high figure at

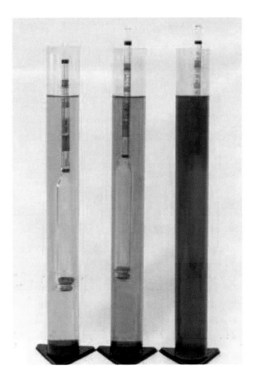

Hydrometer in a trial jar reading receptacle [Michael Young]

the start of the fermentation, and a low one when the fermentation is completed. It gives a useful indication of progress.

To check the liquor is fermenting, the current SG reading will indicate a lower figure than the previous reading. The SG should be ascertained prior to adding (pitching) the yeast at the start of the fermentation. Once the fermentation is underway, a further reading is taken (recommended after two days) by carefully taking a sample from the must to fill a sterilised trial jar and noting the reading. This will be appreciably less if the yeast has been developing fully to its potential. Readings of SG 1.000 or lower, taken over two or three days, indicate that fermentation has probably finished or nearly so. To understand the reality of SG 1.000, a new vintner should fill a trial jar with plain water from the local water supply and ensure its temperature is 20 °C (68 °F). For the perfectionist, the deviation may amount to 3 units of calibration above or below 1.000. To ensure the hydrometer is working correctly, this simple test should be carried out periodically.

The use of the hydrometer and trial jar requires complete sterilisation and sanitisation before and after completion of any trial or test. Do not place the hydrometer or trial jar straight into hot water, as this may cause them to break.

Put a sample of the liquor to be tested into the trial jar (to about two-thirds full), lower the hydrometer carefully into the liquor,

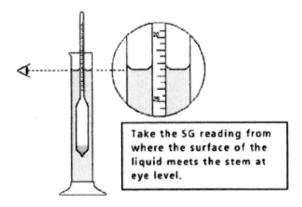

Take the SG reading from where the surface of the liquid meets the stem at eye level.

Measurement and reading of SG by hydrometer [Wikimedia Commons]

and spin or shake the hydrometer to remove any bubbles sticking to its stem. If the liquor is still in the fermenting stage, bubbles on the hydrometer may result in a false reading. In this instance, it is advisable to remove the hydrometer and shake the sample to remove as much gas as possible.

Then the hydrometer is replaced carefully into the trial jar. When it is steady in the liquor, a reading is taken at eye level at the bottom of the main meniscus. After use, rinse, clean and sterilise the hydrometer and trial jar and wipe them dry.

With wine kits, it is convenient to take a reading after honey has been added. With meads and fruit wines it is best to dissolve the honey thoroughly in the water, preferably at about 20 °C (68 °F) as the dissolution will be so much easier and the amount of honey to add can be calculated correctly.

Use the SG 1.005 point to check when the wine is ready for bottling. The hydrometer "reads" the thickness of the liquor, especially if a large amount of fruit is used. The analysis can be used in conjunction with tasting the sampled liquor being tested

.

CALCULATING THE ALCOHOL STRENGTH OF WINES

To calculate the final strength of the honey wine, write down the SG (omitting the decimal point) at the start of the fermentation (i.e. after the honey was added). Subtract this from its final SG and divide the answer by 7.36: that is the percentage of alcohol by volume (abv) of the honey wine.

Starting SG – Final SG ÷ 7.36 = % abv

Multiplying this by 7 and dividing by 4 will determine its strength as proof spirit.

An Example: Sack Dessert Mead
1135 (starting SG) – 1015 (final SG) = 120 ÷ 7.36 = 16.3% abv.
16.30% (abv) x 7 ÷ 4 = 28.5% strength as a proof spirit.

SPECIFIC GRAVITY (SG)

Specific gravity is the ratio of the must at various stages in the fermentation to the density of water at 4 °C. The concept is used in both the brewing and winemaking industries. Specific gravity can be measured with a hydrometer, refractometer, pycnometer, oscillating U-tube or electronic meter. The majority of meadmakers use the hydrometer and trial glass for their deliberations.

The density of the must is largely dependent on its sugar content plus the presence of dissolved salts and solids within the liquor. During the fermentation phase, yeast converts sugars into carbon dioxide and alcohol. The decline in the sugar content and the presence of ethanol (which is appreciably less dense than water) reduce the density of the must. The percentage of alcohol can be calculated from the difference between the Original Gravity (OG) of the must and the current (SG) of the must. By monitoring the decline in SG over time, the vintner obtains information about the health and progress of the fermentation and determines that it is complete when the SG stops falling. If the fermentation is finished, the SG is called the Final Gravity (FG). For example, for mead with a typical strength, OG could be 1.050 and FG could be 1.010.

- The table refers to *sugar* per gallon (4.55 litres). The mead maker should bear in mind that honey consists of approximately 80 per cent fermentable sugar, and an allowance therefore needs to be made for this. In round terms, 1 lb (454 g) of sugar is equivalent to 1.25 lb (568 g) of honey.
- One US gallon (liquid) equals 4 quarts or 3.785 litres.

Specific gravity (SG)	Amount of sugar in 1 gallon (Imp) (ounces)	Amount of sugar in 4.55 litres (grams)	Potential alcohol (%/volume)
1.000	0	0	0.00
1.005	1	26	0.30
1.010	2	55	0.90
1.015	4	125	1.60
1.020	7	195	2.30
1.025	9	265	3.00
1.030	12	320	3.70
1.035	15	410	4.40
1.040	17	480	5.10
1.045	19	535	5.80
1.050	21	590	6.50
1.055	23	645	7.20
1.060	25	705	7.80
1.065	27	760	8.60
1.070	29	815	9.20
1.075	31	870	9.90
1.080	33	930	10.6
1.085	36	1010	11.3
1.090	38	1065	12.00
1.095	40	1125	12.70
1.100	42	1180	13.40
1.105	44	1235	14.10
1.110	46	1290	14.90
1.115	48	1345	15.60
1.120	50	1400	16.30
1.125	52	1455	17.00
1.130	54	1510	17.70
1.135	56	1565	18.40

THE USE OF THE VINOMETER

A vinometer is used when the vintner did not take hydrometer readings at the Original Gravity (OG) and deducts the Final Gravity (FG) (see page 130 for the arithmetical calculation for establishing the alcohol content of a wine).

A vinometer can only produce accurate results in a dry wine (containing little or no residual sugar) once the fermentation is complete. The process works on the principle of capillary action, whereby it measures viscosity that is dependent on the alcohol: water ratio. Its scale is marked as per cent of alcohol.

Vinometer [Michael Young MBE]

The vinometer procedure is as follows:

1. Fill the vinometer with a small amount of dry wine
2. Wait until a few drops of the wine drip out at the other end. If the wine does not start to flow on its own, put your mouth on the funnel side of the vinometer and blow gently
3. Put a finger on the part where the drops form and turn the vinometer upside down
4. Place the vinometer on a flat, secure base, filling reservoir side down. A small plate is ideal as it will catch the wine droplets
5. Release the finger. The level in the capillary will drop to indicate the alcohol content of the sample on the scale (the arrow).

Take two more measurements and determine the average value of the measurements:
average = (measurement 1 + measurement 2 + measurement 3) ÷ 3.

A more precise reading can be obtained by adding 5 ml of wine to 5 ml of water and proceeding as above. The final reading should be multiplied by two to give the alcohol percentage. For example, if the vinometer shows 5 per cent, then the wine will have an alcohol percentage of 10 per cent.

[Note] Make sure there are no air bubbles in the tube. Clean, sterilise and dry the vinometer after use.

PART THREE

MEAD AND HONEY WINE
PRODUCTION PROBLEMS

OPPOSITE

Comparing a good wine (left) with a contaminated one (right) that is failing to clear after two years [Hilary Badger]

TWO GOLDEN RULES

The new vintner should experience very few problems with his mead making, providing the following two golden rules are obeyed. These are:

- Always maintain the highest standards of cleanliness, by sterilising and sanitising all equipment and work surfaces

- Expose the wine to the atmosphere as little as possible; the unnecessary incorporation of air will ruin the finest wine.

Observing these maxims will avoid the majority of problems in mead and honey wine production. Nevertheless, the newcomer may well encounter sporadic problems. The main ones are discussed below.

MEADS AND HONEY WINES THAT "STICK" OR "GET STUCK"

A fermenting mead or honey wine starting off well and stops working after a short time (carbon dioxide bubbles are not visible through the fermentation lock) is said to be "sticking. This is generally caused by the must being overwhelmed with a high sugar content in relation to its water content. The simplest solution is to check the SG. This needs to read 1.100. The must should be diluted by the introduction of clean, cold boiled water, added from a sterilised container, to try getting it working again. This may entail introducing a new yeast starter to regenerate the stuck must by the use of a starter bottle: the starter is made up (see page 92). When the starter is working well (depending upon the yeast used, about two hours), add it by stages to the remaining must in stages by doubling up as the bulk gets working, repeating until the whole of the original must is working. The unassuming remedy in wine production is to start meads and honey wines off with reduced honey content and add the honey by degrees to the fermenting must. A check of the airlock and bung to see both are firmly seated in the fermentation vessel; store yeast in the refrigerator, do not use outdated yeast, too high or low temperature, unclean fermenting vessel or lack of nutrients.

MEAD AND HONEY WINES THAT ARE SLOW TO CLEAR ON THEIR OWN ACCOUNT

Should the wine not have cleared naturally after three rackings at, say, 60 days apart, try putting the vessel in a colder place such as an outhouse or a garage, placing it directly onto the cold floor. Placing it in the refrigerator might be too severe a treatment, but experienced vintners use such a method as a very last resort.

A sudden drop in temperature often starts clarification of the wine, but this may not readily occur if the wine had been overheated during the pasteurisation process, in other words, heating the must beyond the recommended temperature of 55 °C (130 °F).

Mead wine should generally be fermented at 15-21 °C (60-70 °F). The new vintner should note that a 10-degree drop below this will often result in the wine starting to clear naturally. If after 30 days the wine has not cleared, and you have ruled out pectic and starch hazes as a factor, give it more time or try a fining agent (see page 120). This will usually clarify the wine. If it does not, something else is creating the problem. This is most likely to be a bacterial infestation, and you should seriously consider dumping the batch down the drain.

Filtering will clarify many wines, but it can definitely alter its taste and character. I do not usually recommend filtering as I also believe filtering takes out other necessary compounds irrespective of manufacturers stating that it gives a rounded finish to the wine.

There are many fining agents available, some good and some better. All tend to change the taste of the wine somewhat, even if only slightly, and for that reason you should only use fining agents if absolutely necessary. The purpose of fining is to remove suspended particles from a wine that are known to be the cause of current problems or be the basis for future ones.

Many of the unwanted suspended particles in wines possess either a positive (+) or a negative (-) electrical charge while in a low pH, colloidal state. Therefore, it is possible to precipitate these particles by introducing materials which have an opposite electrical charge. Such particles are attracted to, and combine with, the oppositely charged suspended particles. The consequence is relatively large combined particles, usually with a neutral charge (the positive and negative charges having cancelled each other out) that readily precipitates in the wine and even drags other suspended material with them as they fall to the bottom of the fermenter.

MEADS AND HONEY WINES THAT INCUR "OFF-FLAVOURS"

Off-flavours arise because of the lack of the recommended acids added to the primary fermentation. Generally these off-flavours have a medicinal taste. Little can be done to correct such problems once they are detected. If present, a large group of micro-organisms, including lactic acid bacteria, will be responsible for many disorders to a wine. These bacteria are renowned for creating off-flavours which affect sweet wines more than their dry counterparts because of their liking for the residual sugar. However, some species of this bacterium can be said to benefit dry acid wines, as they convert malic acid to the less tart lactic acid, providing the wine with a palatable taste. Nevertheless, the same species may well ruin a sweet wine by the conversion of the residual sugar into other products.

BACTERIAL INFECTIONS

An oily film and ropiness present in a wine are caused by a common species of lactic acid bacteria. The lengthy ropiness is, in fact, a long chain of the bacteria held together by an oily, gelatinous substance that appears to the naked eye as a ropy, oily swirl. The oily swirl immediately becomes visible if the bottle is twirled swiftly. A wine with this obvious characteristic is known to be highly viscous, hence the term "oiliness". That notwithstanding, the flavour of the wine is somewhat impaired while its stark presence and appearance render it undrinkable. The only possible solution is to treat the wine with 100-150 ppm of Campden tablet (sulphite) to kill off the bacteria, then stir it thoroughly to break down the bacteria while introducing and promoting aeration. The bulk is left to settle for six to eight days, then it is racked off into a sterilised container, making sure none of the lees is transferred to the new vessel. Further storage is ill advised and the wine is best consumed at the earliest opportunity.

At the commencement of the fermentation, the vintner should ensure the correct amount and number of acids have been provided with the use of both Campden tablets and potassium sorbate to halt the fermentation and kill off the yeast. Regular racking of the wine plus the addition of a Campden tablet is the surest remedy to overcome such problems.

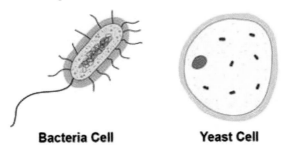

Bacteria Cell   **Yeast Cell**

Bacteria and yeast cell comparisons [Source unknown]

ACETIFICATION OF MEADS AND HONEY WINES

Acetobacter is a genus of acetic acid bacteria. The characteristic of these bacteria is their ability to convert ethanol to acetic acid in the presence of oxygen. *Acetobacter* can oxidise lactate and acetate into carbon dioxide and water. These bacteria have been isolated from industrial vinegar fermentation processes. In essence, they change wine into vinegar and are loosely called opportunistic contaminants of wine and meads. The bacteria thrive in warm conditions in the presence of air, with their growth being inhibited by high concentrations of alcohol and sulphur dioxide. To avoid acetification, wine should not be exposed to the air more than absolutely necessary and scrupulous cleanliness, sterilisation and cleanliness should be maintained at all times.

OXIDISATION IN MEAD AND HONEY WINES

Oxidisation will affect all wine if it is exposed to the air. The liquor will naturally take up oxygen if it is in contact with the atmosphere, thereby browning the wine and leading to a non-sparkling appearance. An oxidised wine looks very much like a bottle of malt vinegar. Simply standing brown malt vinegar alongside a bottle of quality mead will give the clearest indication of what the vintner needs to be aware of. It will clearly demonstrate the dull appearance of the vinegar as against the sharp brightness of the mead.

Adding and maintaining the correct sulphite levels to mead will prevent oxidisation. Oxidisation, as the name implies, refers to the presence of oxygen to a finished fermented wine, although it is not regarded as a real issue for large wine producers; they use barrels in which the wine is matured through tried and proven practice going back centuries. It is really beyond the scope of this narrative to go into great detail of oxidisation methodologies other than to say that the difference between maturing in wood and glass is vague. So the simplest explanation is that wine stored in a wood cask can freely absorb small amounts of air naturally through

Vinegar on the left: note the dullness with bright mead on the right
[Michael Badger]

the pores of the wooden cask without the aid of the vintner. The maturing process includes esterification, the general name for a chemical reaction in which two reactants (typically an alcohol and an acid) form esters as the reaction product. Esters are common in organic chemistry and biological materials, and often have a characteristically pleasant, fruity odour. The presence of esters can add fragrance and enhance flavour.

That notwithstanding, the opposite situation occurs with glass as it is a solid, impenetrable material. Consequently, the oxygen cannot be taken up by the wine in the same way as in an oak cask. Racking the wine at intervals is the only means of adding oxygen to a maturing wine. The danger then arises that oxygen will be added in a series of massive doses that may well exert some sort of disturbing influence upon the maturing process. Because of their composition, wooden casks have the edge over glass ones. Ester formation takes place as the completed wine matures during the ageing process. Under bottle (when the mead is laid down into the bottle) requires storage by expert vintners in commercial meaderies. Here, excellent cellar-craft for maturing the wine comes into its own. Correct storage conditions will also prevent oxidisation. Bottling the wine seals the liquor away from the air, thereby preventing the ingression of oxygen. The tiny amount of air trapped in the bottle will soon become exhausted of its oxygen when the bottle is laid on its side, allowing a vacuum to be created, whereas if the bottle is stored upright, the cork does not become moist and eventually allows in air as the cork dries out. There is no vacuum created when a bottle is stored vertically.

GERANIUM

A term that is attributed to the smell of crushed geranium leaves. It arises mainly through the presence of lactic acid bacteria absorbing sorbic acid added to the wine in the form of potassium sorbate. It is controlled by adding sulphite (crushed Campden tablet) to the wine, followed by 1 level teaspoon of potassium sorbate: never in reverse order.

EXCESS ASTRINGENCY

Astringency is a dry, creasing mouthfeel arising through excess tannin levels added at first stages of fermentation, ingredients with high tannin levels, andageing in barrel. The solution is to blend with other wines known to have lesser tannin levels (Pearson Square, see page 157) or by using a protein-based fining agent like gelatin.

HYDROGEN SULPHIDE

A condition that arises through insufficient yeast nutrition and oxygen at the first stages of fermentation, the practice of staggered nutrient additions (SNA) is recommended as the lack of minimal nitrogen present in the fermentation aids the yeast to produce hydrogen sulphide. Nevertheless, certain yeast strains are known to exacerbate the creation of sulphide aromas; this suggests the use of a different yeast strain for the next lot produced (recording in your log).

The fermented wine can become affected through extended contact with the expired yeast cells (lees) at the base of the fermenter: racking once the fermentation has ceased is an essential action and requirement. In these conditions hydrogen sulphide can be further absorbed into mercaptans and dimethyl sulfide.

MERCAPTANS

A less unstable chemical than hydrogen sulphide having a distinct aroma of cooked cabbage and the odour of natural gas, they arise at post-fermentation through leaving the wine on the lees for excessive periods. Rack at the earliest time after fermentation has ceased.

PHENOLS

The issues of phenolic maladies are generally attributed to the existence of wild yeast contaminants of poor sanitising of equipment and ingredients. The presence of chlorine or amines in the water supply should be removed prior to the first fermentation cycle. Allow the water to stand for 24 hours for the chemical substrates to evaporate, assisted by frequent stirring.

SULPHUR DIOXIDE

The overuse of sulphites can impart bitter features to the wine when it is used to excess. It can stop a fermentation commencing if used in the "Cold Fermentation" process. Their use should be carefully undertaken; nevertheless, they are used for antimicrobial and antioxidant purposes with good effect if used in the 100ppm proportions.

PART FOUR

BOTTLING AND
CELLAR-CRAFT

OPPOSITE

Cellared meads in various stages of maturation [Megan Timms]

TO BOTTLE OR NOT TO BOTTLE?

The art of winemaking is very much on a par with that of the fly fisherman! He needs to be a practitioner with infinite patience so needed because of the length of time involved with meads or honey wines to come to perfection. A wine's great characters truly develop after it has been correctly bottled, added to the natural ageing process that comes to such specialist wines. The facilities of home mead makers may be more basic compared with those used at state-of-the-art commercial wineries; but their skill should never be underestimated, and there is no reason why the results should not be as good – or, for that matter, superior.

Mastering a few basic steps can make bottling a less daunting and more satisfying experience. "When the wine is clear and stable, it may be bottled": this well-known maxim still holds true. While you don't need to be a biochemist to decide when to bottle, there are a few basic considerations needing to be observed and worked to. Principally, if there are any problems with the wine, they need to be sorted before it is in-bottle, and out of reach and out of mind.

Clarity is crucial. While a small amount of sediment will naturally appear in the bottle over time, a murky wine is both unattractive and uninviting. The mead will require decanting and perhaps will have developed off-flavours through lying on the lees. Careful racking, the passage of time and patience are really the prerequisites for laying down a good wine. However, it has to be accepted that mead and honey wines, and most white wines, some blushes and other fruit wines, may obstinately resist clarification without some help by fining, especially heat fining or filtration, or both. Nevertheless, the tyro vintner should remember the following in respect of bottling and "laying down" the finished wine. Three months is the minimum – six is better – nine to twelve + is excellent.

Before proceeding to bottle, it is essential to be satisfied with the wine's condition. Without a doubt, ageing will change and enhance its qualities in terms of taste, body, balance and flavour. Problems put into the bottle remain complications for ever. The vintner cannot dismiss this factual summation. If he does, it is at his own peril!

As you become more talented in winemaking, it becomes both pleasurable and necessary to become familiar with the various types of stability a wine should exhibit. The experienced vintners at commercial meaderies often resort to methods of heat stabilisation; it is a process involving the removal of the protein miasmas that, even if they are invisible during ageing, can reappear when the wine rises above cellar temperature. The veteran vintner with experience of red wines is all too aware that these wines are not heat-stable. To make mead or honey wine heat-stable is to remove the chances of a haze forming when the must is heated or aged: bentonite is often added to the must immediately before or after fermentation. Over time, I have resorted to using a bentonite procedure. I have found that it is cleaner and it gives the liquor more time to settle out. Furthermore, I am of the view that it lessens the shedding and detaching of the essential flavours when added to a wine which has attained dryness.

The recommended solution is to make up a slurry mixture of the bentonite, following the instructions given by the manufacturer. Let the slurry sit overnight so the bentonite can swell. The best way to add the slurry to the wine is to get it swirling and dribble the bentonite mixture into it, ensuring it is mixed well continuously as it is added to the must. This is essential as bentonite works on contact.

Let the wine sit undisturbed (this might be for a few weeks). The bentonite will fall to the bottom of the vessel together with the protein, causing the haze. When cleared, rack the clean wine off carefully and dispose of the sediment.

At the other end of the spectrum, cold stabilisation refers to chilling the wine as a means of precipitating excess tartaric acid (the main grape acid) before bottling. This can be achieved by placing the wine on a cold surface or, more drastically, by refrigeration.

Before bottling, it is essential to establish the wine is fully fermented to dryness unless a sweet wine is required. The vintner may wish to sweeten a specific wine for formal reasons. In either situation the wine has to be stabilised to ensure that any remaining residual sugar does start to re-ferment "in-bottle". Should this be overlooked, it might well lead either to corks popping or, more dangerously, to explosions with flying glass. The newcomer to winemaking needs to have a complete understanding of the principles of fining and filtration for sweet wine: re-fermentation is a common issue.

In general, a hydrometer reading below minus one degree Brix (-1 °Bx) or a Clinitest reading (the urinalysis kits used by diabetics) below 0.2 per cent residual sugar means the wine will not need stabilising. If the wine tests above these readings or is sweetened, the safest stabilisation method is the addition of potassium sorbate at the time of bottling. Potassium sorbate assists as it inhibits re-fermentation. One gram per gallon is usually sufficient preceded immediately by the addition of one crushed Campden tablet when added to the wine.

When using sorbate it is important to make sure that sulphur dioxide levels in the wine are kept in a safe range of 30 to 50 parts per million (ppm). This will help inhibit any malolactic activity that develops a geranium aroma. Potassium sorbate and sulphur dioxide should always be used together if the wine is sweetened or has residual sugar. On the other hand, dry wines do not need the addition of sorbate at all, although a safe sulphur level is a good insurance policy against oxidation or bacterial activity. A rule of thumb is that one-quarter teaspoon of potassium metabisulfite crystals in five gallons of wine yields about 40 ppm of sulphur dioxide. Sodium bisulfite can be used, but this is best reserved for cleaning equipment to avoid adding sodium to the wine.

ADDING OR CORRECTING ACID LEVELS AT THE LAID-IN BOTTLE STAGE

The addition or correction of acids to a laid-in bottle of wine should be undertaken with extreme care. My preference is to check the pH at the early fermentation stage and get it right there and then, rather than tinkering with the finished wine. There are kits available, but caution is needed in their use; it is essential to follow the instructions carefully. If in doubt, don't.

These are the general guidelines for the desired acid levels for various types of wines. Individual tastes may vary, so make adjustments according to your own palate.

- Dry white wine – 0.65%–0.75%.
- Sweet white wine – 0.70%–0.85%.
- Dry red wine – 0.60%–0.70%.
- Sweet red wine – 0.65%–0.80%.

These figures represent total acidity as a percentage by volume, known as the titratable acidity, or TA. Testing the acidity of a wine can be accomplished using an acid testing kit. Titration is a well-established laboratory method of quantifiable chemical analysis used to determine the unknown distillate of an identified analyte or titrand. In this situation, it is establishing the amount of acid in the must or wine. It is commenced by gradually adding a small amount of reagent (often a base, sodium hydroxide [NaOH], whose chemical concentration is known). This addition is continued until there is a change in colour, due to the presence of an indicator (phenolphthalein).

An electronic method uses a specialist pH meter (see page 151). Once testing is completed, by tallying what the acid levels are, the vintner can compare the values to the suggested TA ranges mentioned above.

Methods Available

To increase acidity

Add a proprietary acid blend to increase acidity. The addition of 3.9 g (about three-quarters of a teaspoon) of acid blend raises the acidity of one gallon of must by 0.1 per cent.

To decrease acidity

Add calcium carbonate to lower acidity, but only by 0.4 per cent or less. Do *not* add more than 1.5 teaspoons per gallon.

One teaspoon of calcium carbonate will lower the TA of one gallon of must by approximately 0.1 per cent. Alternatively, a proprietary chemical can be added in place of calcium carbonate. It is essential and critical to follow the manufacturer's instructions to determine the proper dosage.

The Test Procedure

Take a 15 ml sample of must and place it into a sterilised test tube. The test tubes that generally come with the acid test kits are marked with a line specifying the required volume. If not, use a small calibrated plastic syringe to measure the required amount into the test tube. Rinse the syringe thoroughly afterwards.

Place no more than three drops of the phenolphthalein indicator into the test tube, then spin or shake it to ensure the indicator is mixed in with the must.

Using the syringe, draw out 10 ml of reagent (sodium hydroxide), making sure there are no bubbles within the liquid. Extreme care is needed to avoid contact with the skin or eyes as NaOH is highly toxic, burning the skin instantly. Carefully add the sodium hydroxide to the test tube, 0.5 ml at a time. After each addition, twirl or shake the test tube to mix the contents together. The colour of the liquid will change momentarily upon the addition of the reagent.

Testing white wines, the colour change will be to pink; if testing red wine, the colour change will be to grey. Just twirl and swirl until the colour diminishes. To complete the procedure, the colour of the must returns to the original colour. This step is repeated until the colour change becomes permanent.

There are occasions when the colour (either pink or grey) refuses to go away. Stop and calculate the amount of reagent used. At this stage, it is very simple to define the acidity of the must. Each millilitre of reagent used equals 0.1 per cent TA. For example, if you used 6 ml of sodium hydroxide to react with the must, the titratable acidity of your must is 0.6 per cent.

Discard this sample immediately, owing to its toxicity. Do not add it back into the must or wine. Finally, wash and dry the test equipment before storing it away.

MEASURING ACIDITY – USE OF A PH METER

Determining acidity in wine by means of a pH meter is very similar to the titration method described above. Instead of looking for a colour change to indicate that the titration is complete (this can be very difficult to determine depending upon the colour of the wine), simply add the reagent a drop or two at a time until the pH meter reads 8.2, which is the same pH at which phenolphthalein

pH testing unit [Michael Young]

changes colour.

The pH meter method is by far the most accurate and precise way to measure acidity.

pH meters are pernickety things, so handle them with care:

- do not drop the meter or the probe may be damaged
- keep the probe clean and free of debris
- always calibrate your meter with fresh buffering solution before each test
- be sure to stir the sample thoroughly after each addition of the reagent
- store your pH meter in the manner recommended by the manufacturer, taking special care of the probe.

A preferred method for correcting acidity recommended for tyro vintners is to make a blend with other batches of wine, especially those lacking in acid by adding them to those with an excess. Likewise, a wine that is too dry can be sweetened by mixing with one that is too sweet. Blending of wines is commonplace within the commercial world of wine (see page 155 "Blending").

TITRATABLE ACIDITY (TA) – THE OTHER MEASURE OF ACIDITY

The two measures of acidity are titratable acidity (TA) and the potential of hydrogen (pH). Titratable acidity relates to the amount of acid in solution as a percentage or as grams per litre (g/l). This is obtained by multiplying percentage TA by 10, so that a TA of 0.80 per cent becomes 8 g/l. In contrast, pH is related to an acid's strength in solution, measured on a logarithmic scale. On the pH scale, 7 is neutral, values above 7 are alkaline and alkalinity increases as the value increases. Values below 7 are acidic and acidity increases as the value decreases. A pH of 9 is more *alkaline* than a pH of 8, while a pH of 4 is more *acidic* than a pH of 5. This arises through the logarithmic measurements, a pH of 4 being ten times more acidic than a pH of 5.

Although TA and pH are consistent, they are not the same. A solution containing a specific quantity of a relatively weaker acid, such as malic, will have a different (higher) pH than a solution containing the same quantity of a stronger acid such as tartaric.

The pH of a solution is defined as the negative logarithm to the base 10 of the hydrogen ion concentration in gram-atoms per litre. Hydrogen ions (H+) are formed when a dissolved acid partially separates (dissociates) into hydrogen ions and related anions. The concentration of hydrogen ions largely determines the effects acids have on a wine. A stronger acid, such as tartaric, dissociates more than a weaker acid, such as lactic. Thus, the *effective acidity* of a solution depends on the concentration of all acids in the solution, as well as their tendency to dissociate hydrogen ions. *Effective acidity* is measured as pH.

INCREASING AND DECREASING ACIDITY

There are a number of ways of increasing the acidity in the must. Generally, wine recipes will attempt to rectify acid deficiencies by the addition of specific quantities of a precise acid, comprising a blend of tartaric, malic and citric acids (called acid blend), or the juice of some citrus fruit (usually lemon or orange). A word of caution: recipes are established using a series of base ingredients which may differ in natural sugar content or acidity from the same base ingredients you might happen on by chance: the yeast used may have a bearing, too. A recipe that demands a teaspoon of acid blend requires that amount corrected to the acidity in the base constituents the recipe maker had to hand. However, one teaspoon of acid blend *may* or *may not* be sufficient for the base ingredient you have to hand. The reasons for this are various, but basically they are down to differences in varieties, differences in soils, their fertility, and the amount of water available to the host plants, as well as differences in average day and night temperatures, differences in sunlight and intensity, and even differences in the maturity of the base fruit when harvested.

The experienced vintner will measure the acidity of the must, correcting it according to what is required or needed, rather than what a recipe may specify.

The new vintner needs to be aware that there are many formulations of acid blends available commercially. Such acid blends typically contain tartaric, malic and citric acids in a ratio of 40:40:20, 40:30:30, 50:30:20, or 50:25:25. The normal home brew supplier is not usually aware of the specific ratio of the blends available, especially if precision in acidity levels is needed at the onset of the fermentation cycle. The majority of blends are 40:40:20, and the addition of 3.9 g of this ratio blend will increase the acidity in a gallon of must by approximately 0.1 per cent. This same increase can be achieved by adding 3.78 g of tartaric acid to a gallon of must. Fumaric acid, constituted in food-grade powder form, is used as a partial substitute for additions of tartaric acid, as it tends to inhibit malolactic fermentation when used in the range of 1.5 to 5.7 g/gal (thus achieving an increase of 0.05 to 0.15 per cent acidity). Care needs to be exercised when fumaric acid is used in large dosages, as it may so easily affect flavour. Testing its use in a sample of wine is a wise measure before using it throughout.

Citric acid added to a must before fermentation will largely be lost during fermentation. Thus, it is best to add it *after* all signs of fermentation have disappeared. Malic acid can be added at any time but it, too, has a potential disadvantage. Malic acid buffers to a fairly high pH, so it should not be used if the intent is to increase acidity *and/or* lower the pH. In the latter case, tartaric acid is the additive of my preferred choice.

Lowering the acidity in a finished wine is relatively simple through additions of calcium carbonate, a popular compound Acidex®, a so-called double salt of calcium carbonate which, in theory, reduces both tartaric and malic acids equally, or potassium bicarbonate. Cold stabilisation can also be used.

Calcium carbonate reacts preferentially with tartaric rather than malic acid. A dose of 2.5 g/gal of wine lowers the TA to about 0.1 per cent. After its use, the wine should be bulk-aged for at least six months to allow calcium malate, a by-product of the reaction, to precipitate from the wine. The wine should then be cold-stabilised to ensure tartrate crystals do not precipitate out after bottling.

Potassium bicarbonate can be used to de-acidify a wine with a low pH (below 3.5). It should not be used to reduce acidity by more than 0.3 per cent. A dosage of 3.4 g/gal of wine lowers acidity by about 0.1 per cent. After use, the wine should be cold-stabilised as up to 30 per cent of the potential acid reduction occurs during this process. Potassium bitartrate (cream of tartar) is used as a catalyst to promote cold stabilisation. It helps the formation of tartrate crystals. It is used at the rate of 2 to 5 g/gal, followed by vigorous stirring. Its introduction results in an improved and quicker stabilisation.

BLENDING MEADS AND HONEY WINES

As a vintner, it is quite usual to blend your mead and honey wine as a means of finding a wine that you enjoy. A word of caution! If you blend wines you should remember the issues of exhibiting and competition meads, and the essentials of keeping excellent records of your wines. My colleague and mead maker, the late Dennis Rouston, was, as they say in Yorkshire, "a dab hand" at blending meads and honey wines. Dennis was a keen wine maker and a certified wine judge of the National Guild of Beer and Wine Judges (NGBWJ). I learnt a great deal from Dennis on blending these wines. In essence we complemented each other, he with his mead making, and I on helping him with his practical beekeeping.

By definition, blending meads and honey wines is in essence the bringing together of two or more wines in a blended situation to create a new wine.

These are a few codes that are considered when blending meads and honey wines.

- Never, ever, consider blending a top-notch honey wine with an inferior or poor wine. It never achieves the objective. You will be sorely let down with the ruination of a good wine, so don't!

- In your first forays into blending your wines, begin on a small scale. Blend your wine until you accomplish a honey wine that you like. If you start at a larger scale, you might blend a large amount of wine which you do not care for… Forewarned is forearmed.
- Keep detailed notes of your blending activities as a means of repeating the combination of wines that you liked or, for that matter, those you did not.
- Blend wines of the same type, i.e. red with red, and white with white.

There are a number of excellent reasons for a mead maker to consider blending meads and honey wines. They are listed below in no particular order or preference but there may be other reasons, too.

- To enhance the sweetness of a wine.
- To improve the bouquet/aroma of the wine.
- To enrich the colour of the wine.
- To adjust the pH of the mead or honey wine.
- To add or minimise the taste, flavour or bite of a wine.
- To adjust the acidity of wine by either raising or lowering it.
- To raise or lower alcohol levels of a wine.

When undertaking the blending procedures, it is essential that the vintner undertakes the process unhindered. The procedure requires concentration in a well-lit room, free of airborne aromas that might so easily dull the sensory organs of both taste and smell.

BLENDING PROCEDURES

There are a number of techniques that are open to the vintner. These include:

- The Pearson Square
- Fast Tracking and Rough Cuts and Fine-Tuning

The Pearson Square

This is the ultimate blending process as it adopts a simple scientific approach; it is simplicity in itself, involving plain arithmetic utilising the mathematical tool known as the Pearson Square (see Appendix B). This methodology is used in a variety of food-related calculations within the food processing industry, and is also known as the Pearson's Box.

To ensure that the blending has been a success, it is advisable to wait for about two weeks, and re-taste the blended wine. It often happens that wines can lose their appeal to the vintner: this is known as "the taste goes or turns away". This procedure is most important as you wish the laid-down wine to further improve in the ageing process, rather than keeping a wine that, when opened, is found to be wanting.

See Appendix B for a worked example.

Fast Tracking and Rough Cut Methodologies

This is a method that permits you to produce as near as is possible to hone in on the required ratios for future trials. To commence the route you begin with four different glasses of the mixture, each at respective differing proportions of the two being combined. It is essential for absolute accuracy that the glass, shape, size and colour are the same throughout, or prejudice will creep in setting the procedure out of kilter.

Fast Tracking and Rough Ratios

Tag / Label	A % : B %	Parts of A	Parts of B
1	100 : 00	20	0
5	80 : 20	16	4
9	60 : 40	12	8
13	40 : 60	8	12
17	20 : 80	4	16
21	0 : 100	0	20

For simplicity each glass will be in 20 parts; for ease of calculation, a part for this exercise is a tablespoon (5ml).

Note
A represents the first wine – **B** represents the second wine.
The rough-cut blends will change by 1/5 (20%) i.e. 4 parts in 20.
Tag / label an individual glass **A** and another glass **B** before adding the respective wines.

The Process of Tasting and Testing the Bouquet of the Wine A
Stated Example –
Select the wine that has a tad too little of the dominant character:
A Wine has the dominant character with Tag / Label **9** having a tad too much **A**.
Select Tag / Label sample **9** and **5** – Setting these aside to proceed to the fine-tune ratio.

Fine-Tune Blend Ratios

Tag / Label	A % : B %	Parts of A	Parts of B
1	**100 : 00**	**20**	**0**
2	95 : 5	19	1
3	90 : 10	18	2
4	85 : 15	17	3
5	**80 : 20**	**16**	**4**
6	75 : 25	15	5
7	70 : 30	14	6
8	65 : 35	13	7
9	**60 : 40**	**12**	**8**
10	55 : 45	11	9
11	50 : 50	10	10
12	45 : 55	9	11
13	**40 :60**	**8**	**12**
14	35 : 65	7	13
15	30 : 70	6	14

16	25 : 75	5	15
17	**20 :80**	**4**	**16**
18	15 : 85	3	17
19	10 : 90	2	18
20	5 : 95	1	19
21	**0 : 100**	**0**	**20**

Having selected the two coarse end points, the fine-tune procedure for the blend proceeds. The adjustment proceeds at 1/20 (5%) i.e. 1 part in 20 therefore the table above defines all the differing finer blends allowing you to narrow down your objective to three that lie between the two selected in the first rough-cut selection.

To finalise the exercise from the stated example which were **9 and 5, respectively**. Blends for 6, 7 and 8 are selected and each sample is tagged / labelled accordingly. As we proceed we are using five glasses suitably tagged / labelled: Rough-Cuts tagged / Labelled **9** and **5** and three finely blended between these end points and proceed by selecting the single sample that appears to be the best. It may be appropriate to blend a sample into a full bottle and proceed to let it age for, say, three months: sample and evaluate the blend to see if it meets your expectations through seeing if the wine's characteristics have changed through melding during these three months of ageing.

PREPARING TO BOTTLE

The first step is preparing the bottles for use; clean, unchipped, de-labelled and recycled bottles are just fine. De-labelling and cleaning can be accomplished by soaking the bottles in washing soda solution (about one half-cup to a standard sink), brushing with a bottle brush and rinsing. With new cold-stable glues, you need to use one half-cup of ammonia per five gallons of warm water. To avoid glue residues, it is best to de-label and wash in two separate steps. Sterilise bottles with bleach and then do a citric rinse to finish off. There are available proprietary "de-labelling solutions": these readily remove glue residues from the bottle surface with a minimum of effort. Rinse the bottles again in a weak citric acid bath to neutralise any remaining washing soda, rinse again with water, and store upside down until required for use.

CONTAINER TYPES FOR MEADS AND HONEY WINES

A common feature of mead makers in the USA is to lay down mead in both wine bottles and the traditional glass beer bottles, general size 330 ml or 500 ml. The bottles are often recycled, having been thoroughly cleaned and sterilised before use. The closure is a metal crown cork or seal or cap. The cork is best secured to the bottle opening using a twin-lever bottle capper that requires a certain amount of dexterity to clamp and seal the closure securely to the bottle. Saving such bottles in the UK for use will require all the rules of sanitation to come into play, with no skimping.

Wine Bottle Types

At some time a hint of madness entered the world of global commerce in respect of bottle sizes/choices for beers, wines and spirits. European Union (EU) legislation dictated that standard bottles should be 70 cl (spirits), with 75 cl for export to North America. In November 2002, an EU working party resolved to overcome issues of regulated wine and champagne bottle sizes. For many years, the US standard (non-metric) wine and beverage bottle was the "fifth", meaning one-fifth of a US gallon, or 25.6 US fluid ounces (757 ml; 26.6 Imp fl oz). To confuse matters further, some beverages were available in tenth-gallon, half-gallon and one-gallon sizes. From 1979, the US adopted the metric system for wine bottles, with the basic bottle size becoming 75 cl.

It is interesting to note the historical foundation of the 75 cl bottle size; its derivation is believed to have arisen through the strength of air retained by the glass-blower's lungs when expelled in one breath: thus this became the average to the current standard 75 cl bottle size.

There is much interest on the origins of the deep punt (the indentation at the base of wine bottles) in essence. Its origin is lost in the footprints of time. Over the years there have been many concepts put forward as to the background of the punted bottle and its introduction. Some theories are of legend, a deep punt is a sign of quality, although the punt does not have an impact on the wine, other than that some schools of thought regard bottles with deep punts as assisting with the "ageing" of good mead or wine. My researches indicate the punt arose coincidentally as a means of giving the wine bottle a form of structural integrity, and an aid to the glass-blower in its production.

There is a mainstream of wine consumers who believe that a greater, denser bottle denotes quality or status. Vineyards tend to put more expensive wines in what are seen to be superior bottles, in the main with a deep-punted bottom. As I have stated above, it is my contention that the punt came about through the historical process involved in glass-blowing. The mechanism involves the glass-blower attaching the glass to be modelled to a steel shaft encompassing a bulbous rounded end. The glass bottle is held in place whilst the glass-blower produces the bottle. The bulbous end may have an embossing stamp, leaving an imprint within the punt. The punt is known to act (possibly by default) through the slant of the punt, permitting sediment to collect in a constricted area close to the bottle base and wall side, thereby preventing the sediment from blending back into the mead as it's being poured into the glass or decanter. The origin of the "punted bottom" is no doubt an interesting phenomenon.

Commonly Used Wine Bottle Types

There are four bottle shapes.

Bordeaux (also referred to as Claret) The classic Bordeaux/ Claret bottle shape is characterised by straight sides and rounded shoulders. The punt may be deep or shallow, or no punted bottom. There are no specific dimensional limits, but the diameter for a 750 ml Bordeaux/Claret is typically in the range 70 to 80 mm and the height of the bottle is typically 280-340 mm, depending on the bottle width, the height of the shoulders and the length of the neck. This type is the preferred bottle for exhibition of mead-type wines in the United Kingdom.

Burgundy The classic Burgundy bottle shape is characterised by straight sides and sloping shoulders. The punt may be deep or shallow or no punted bottom. There are no specific dimensional limits, but the diameter for a 750 ml Burgundy bottle is typically in the range of 80 to 90 mm and the height of the bottle is typically 270-315 mm,

750ml Bordeaux/Claret with shallow-
punted bottom [Michael Badger]

Burgundy 750 ml bottle with deep-
punted bottom [Michael Badger]

depending on the bottle width, the height of the shoulders and the length of the neck. This bottle is not a characteristic bottle type for the exhibition of mead-type wines in the United Kingdom.

Hock (also referred to as Hoch, Rhine Riesling and Schlegel) The classic Hock bottle shape is characterised by a narrow bottle with straight sides, sloping shoulders and an elongated neck. The punt tends to be shallow. There are no specific dimensional limits, but the diameter for a 750 ml Hock bottle is typically in the range of 75 to 80 mm, and height of the bottle is typically 310-350 mm, depending on the bottle width, the height of the shoulders and the length of the neck. This bottle is not a characteristic bottle type for the exhibition of mead-type wines in the United Kingdom.

Beer bottle Bottles are manufactured in 330 ml, 500 ml and 1 litre sizes and their use is a firm favourite with mead vintners in the USA.

Bottle Colours

All four bottles types can be flint (clear), green or brown, with variations in shade, and occasionally other colours such as blue.

White and rosé wines are bottled in clear glass, whereas coloured wine types are bottled in varying colours, mainly as an aid to avoid colour ageing.

Typical Hock bottle [Michael Badger]   Beer bottle [Michael Badger]

Screw-Cap Bottles
These bottles are usually available in 750 ml and litre size, a common usage for wines to be consumed within a year.

750ml Screw-top version with shallow punt – these bottles are not generally accepted for competition purposes [Michael Badger]

[**Note**]. Participants exhibiting mead and honey wines in the UK (and in other parts of the world) should be aware that show rules and regulations are finite in that they bind both judge and exhibitor: *"Exhibitors exhibit to the schedule rules and regulations, and the judge judges to the schedule rules and regulations"*. The exhibitor should therefore be fully aware that wine for exhibition must be presented to schedule otherwise they may well be disqualified as not to schedule "NTS". A common fault of exhibitors can be to use the *70 cl capacity*, punted bottle primarily used for brandy and other spirits.

TYPES OF BOTTLE CLOSURES

Traditional Cork Closures Wine corks can be made either of a single piece of cork or composed of particles, as in champagne corks. Corks made of granular particles are called agglomerated corks. The cellular structure of cork makes it easily compressible into the neck of the bottle. The cork readily expands to form the required tight seal. The interior diameter of the neck of glass bottles tends to be inconsistent, making this ability to seal through variable contraction and expansion an important attribute. However, unavoidable natural flaws, channels and cracks in the bark make the cork itself highly inconsistent for their use. The wine industry prefers natural cork stoppers, as they allow oxygen to interact with wine for proper ageing, and are best suited for wines purchased with the intent to age. Stoppers which resemble natural cork very closely can be made by isolating the suberin component of the cork from the undesirable lignin. Use of classic cylindrical corks requires a corking tool to compress and insert them.

Screw-Top Closures These are ideal for bottling wine for periods of time and immediate use. The screw tops are quick and easy to use and, with care, are reusable. Screw tops are generally considered to offer a trichloroanisole (TCA), a free seal as opposed to traditional corking that reduces to zero the oxygen transfer rate between the bottle and the atmosphere, a key requirement in ageing. This can lead to a reduction in the quality of the wine over long-time storage.

Champagne Bottles with Muselet-Wired Stoppers A muselet is a wire cage that fits over the cork of a bottle of champagne, sparkling wine or beer to prevent the cork from emerging under the pressure of the self-induced carbonated contents. It derives its name from the French *museler*, to muzzle. The muselet often has a metal cap incorporated into the design carrying the producer's emblem. It is normally covered by metal foil envelope. Muselets are also known as wire hoods or Champagne wires.

Muselet stopper [Michael Badger]

T-corks and Mushroom Stoppers T-corks and mushroom stoppers are usually plastic and used for jug wine. These and screw-top bottles can be closed by hand, but the wine should be used within a year because oxidation is inevitable, owing to the looser seal these closures provide.

Screw Caps A metal closure incorporating a nylon seal on the inside base of cap allows the seal to crumple and bed to form a secure seal protecting the wine from the atmosphere.

Crown Caps Beer bottles with crown caps are used consistently across the USA. These bottled wines are fine provided they do not require transportation, as the vibration is liable to give the contents chance to reinvigorate and re-fermentation arise. This type of closure does not allow wine to age in the same way as traditional corking.

Mechanical crown corker [Michael Badger]

Plastic corks are gaining some acceptance in commercial wineries. Although more expensive than traditional cork, plastic can prevent the very small risk of a contaminated cork. Depending on the quality of traditional corks, some are briefly soaked in water before insertion, more especially if they have been stored for a long time (three months plus) in an open container. However, certain traditional corks are treated with some sort of silicone treatment that debars soaking, as per the manufacturer's instructions.

Various types of closure used in the bottling process [Peter Lewis]

CORKING AND CLOSURE SUMMARY

Traditional corks that require or benefit from soaking may profit from the addition of a standard sulphite tablet solution (two ounces of potassium metabisulfite in a gallon of water). Diluting the standard solution to a ratio of about five to one with water softens the corks and eliminates the risk of any contamination. Do not substitute chlorine for sulphite solution as it might lend itself to cork off-flavours. Soaking for an hour or less should be sufficient using only new corks of grade "extra-first" or at least the equivalent. Extra-first is considered a medium grade. Beware of inferior corks as these can readily ruin the wine. It is well worth the extra cost to use synthetic-quality corks; these will protect the wine and allow it to age under ideal conditions.

Corking screw-cap wine bottles is not recommended. These bottles are in the main an inferior wine bottle in thickness and section; very often the size of the opening for these bottles is not compatible with the size of corks available. Secondly, the shoulders of this type of bottle will often start too early and there is insufficient neck room for the cork. This results in a compressed cork flaring out at the neck bottom while in the bottle. When this occurs, the cork is often drawn down into the bottle by this broadening action.

To ensure a good and correct cork seal for the bottle, use a traditional "straight" cork in contrast to a "tapered" cork. A straight cork is cylindrical and provides the maximum amount of sealing surface. The sealing surface of straight corks is the whole length of the cork, which is paramount to success for sealing. The tapered cork will seal only at the one point along its side where the cork meets the glass.

T-type or Mushroom Corks are straight corks with a plastic top on them for gripping to insert or remove the closure. The tops are prone to snap off during either insertion or removal. Pushed home by hand using moderate force, they fit fairly tightly into a standard cork-finished wine bottle. These types of cork work satisfactorily for temporary exhibition usage or wines to be imbibed within 12 to 18 months.

Straight Corks If you plan storing your wines for longer than a year, you are recommended to use a more conventional straight cork. This type is used for commercially produced bottles of wine due to its reliability. Straight corks are first compressed and driven into the bottle with the aid of a corker. They offer an extremely tight seal because the cork is compressed into a smaller volume.

There are three different grades of corks available: *Superior grade*; *Extra-first grade* and Synthetic. The principal difference between these corks is their density. The denser the mass of the cork, the tighter the seal. Care has to be taken when purchasing straight corks as they are available in more than one diameter. A size #9 is normally recommended for a standard cork-finished wine bottle. This is the size that commercial wineries use. Types of corking machines vary enormously and some are disposed to pinching or mangling the cork before getting it into the bottle correctly. If you have one of these corking machines, it is preferable to use a size #8 straight cork.

For mead and honey wine, Extra-first grade straight or synthetic corks are strongly recommended. These types are preferred due to their higher density than the Superior grade. These corks are recommended for wines that may be stored for more than five years. They are of the same quality used by most wineries and will provide a dependable seal for many years. Synthetic straight corks are produced from man-made materials. They are beige to brown in colour, with a light, swirled design that looks in every way like a natural cork. When these corks are used, you are essentially providing the best seal a cork can possibly provide. These corks are to be recommended for laying down a wine for many years ahead.

BOTTLING DAY AND BEYOND

Wine that is clear and stable is generally ready to bottle. The bottles must be clean, sanitised and sterilised and thoroughly rinsed with clean water. The corks and corker are standing by, and you are prepared. All bottling equipment (fillers and siphon hoses) must be sterilised with bleach and water, then rinsed with citric acid and sulphur, and drained before use. It is essential that equipment is rinsed with lots of water after each chemical sanitising step. Assuming the wine's sulphite level is correct (or not, if you prefer not to use sulphites), the final rinse is with diluted sulphite solution (one teaspoon of potassium metabisulfite crystals and a pinch of citric acid in a small jug of distilled water) to guard against any spoilage organisms that may be lurking in the bottles after they were washed.

Assuming the bottles have been stored upside down (in cases with a sheet of foil on the bottom of each case for a better seal) and that they were thoroughly washed, the alcohol in the wine will be largely responsible for its protection as it goes through the ageing process. It merely needs protection during filling procedures.

When filling each bottle, the aim is to prevent oxidation of the wine. Bottles should be filled, without splashing, to about 15 mm (½ in) below the point where the bottom of the cork will be. Sink the sterilised bottle filler to the bottom of the bottle by letting the wine fill up the bottle with minimum aeration. Some airspace is needed should cellar temperatures rise and the wine expand, and a minute amount of air is useful in ageing.

Once the bottle is filled, it is best to cork it promptly. The bottles should be given a final water rinse on the outside to remove any droplets of wine. Label immediately. After filling is complete, leave the bottles standing, cork up, for three to five days. This allows the internal pressure to equalise down to normal, to prevent the wine pushing and leaking when the bottle is placed on its side. This procedure allows the cork to breathe off any residual sulphite. The bottles are stored on their sides or upside down in the coolness of a traffic-free situation. Almost all wines benefit from three to six months in-bottle, some for much longer.

It should be remembered that the wine ages in two ways: firstly aerobically, while it is fermenting, being pressed, racked and prepared for bottling; and secondly, anaerobically after bottling, when the countless subtle chemical changes occur away from the air (other than that dissolved in the wine at the bottling stage). It is this ageing that produces a true bouquet and the intricacies of flavour.

GOOD AND BAD CORKING

It is essential when hand-corking wines using a handheld device that the corking implement is used correctly. Ensure the bottle's base is held and placed firmly on a solid foundation, thereby ensuring the cork is forced home properly and securely into the neck of the bottle. Correct corking can only be guaranteed if the right purchase pressure has been applied. A badly corked bottle, as illustrated above, should be checked periodically; or a better solution is to uncork it, ensuring the removed cork does not shed cork shavings into the wine itself, then re-cork. If shavings do fall into the wine, it should be re-filtered and rebottled, adding a single Campden tablet prior to re-corking.

Good and bad corking of bottles: the bottle to the right is correctly corked, whereas the other is incorrectly corked [Michael Badger]

BOTTLING GEAR AND APPARATUS

The kit that can be used for filling the bottle is:

- UPVC siphon tubing 1500 mm long x 6 mm in diameter with a tap at the discharge end. Siphoning is ideal for small amounts, but can be messy, with spillages and wastage of precious wine through overfilling.
- Bottle washing brush/es. Vigo Ltd manufactures a bottle siphon filler manufactured in AISI 304 stainless steel. This is ideal for bottling wine. Bottles are filled gently via long filling tubes to reduce foaming.

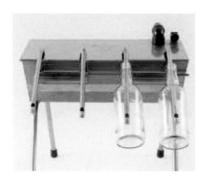

Vigo Ltd bottle siphon filler [Vigo Ltd]

Typical double-handled corker
for small batches [Michael Badger]

OUTWARD FINISHES TO THE BOTTLED WINE

There are three types of decorative neck capsules for wine bottles: these add the *je ne sais quoi* finishing touches to a well-produced wine.

Neck Capsules are sleeves that sit over the neck of the wine bottle, as used extensively by the large commercial wine producers. These sleeves not only add decoration to the wine bottle, but also have two other more practical functions. They help to eliminate the growth of mould and bacteria on the outwardly exposed surface of the cork while laid in storage, and they help to keep the cork in place, should it decide to push out of the bottle.

Heat Shrink Capsules are made of a thin PVPP (Polyvinyl-polypyrrolidone) plastic that shrinks when exposed to heat. They can be applied to a wine bottle very easily by placing them over the neck and then dipping this into hot water for a few seconds. Heat shrink capsules add a very professional look that sets the wine off to perfection. They come in many different colours, from gold to burgundy.

Left Typical heat-shrink capsules [Michael Badger]
Right Sealing corks with molten beeswax using a bain-marie unit [Peter Lewis]

Gold Foil Capsules are similar to heat shrink capsules in function, but they are made from foil instead of plastic. You apply them to the neck of the wine bottle by simply crimping them down by hand. The inside of the capsule is lightly coated with an adhesive that will stick to the neck of the bottle when it is moistened. Gold foil capsules are a very attractive decoration that fits well with a dinner party or celebration.

Long Time Storage of Corked Bottles

It is good practice to seal the cork ends of in-bottle wine by sealing the ends with hot beeswax. This ensures the enclosed wine is unaffected by conditions of corkage and admission of oxygen to the contents.

WINE LABELLING

Wine bottle labels are another way to bring panache and a professional look to the wine in-bottle. Several factors can be taken into consideration. First, the colour of the neck capsule on the bottle should also be on the label you select. It does not necessarily have to be the main colour of the label: a few spots of it here and

Mead labels [Samuel Timms]

there are fine. The colour of the wine bottle being used should also be considered. A green wine bottle will be more welcoming to certain labels than a blue wine bottle, and vice versa. If you are using a clear bottle, then obviously you will need to consider the colour of the wine when choosing a label.

AGEING OF WINE

Mention has been made elsewhere that meads and honey wines, when laid down after time, may be affected by ageing this arises through natural chemical processes / reactions arising within the wine through the prescence of within the acidsacidity levels combined with the levels of esterification in that the acidity and levels of esterification in the acids. Change may also occur with the joining of alcohols in a blending process from other meads whose own levels of acids form esters as a means to enhance a

Robert Mondavi, 7801 St Helena Highway, Oakville, CA 94562, USA
[Michael Badger]

wine's qualities and characteristics. Red-based wines are said to fare better than white wines in the ageing process, no doubt due to their naturally higher tannin levels and phenols known to be present. Yet high-acid white wines are resilient to ageing over a red wine. Whilst visiting wineries in Napa Valley, California, my hosts exclaimed that in their experience white wines aged in French oak barrels pick up desirable phenols enhancing the wine's ageing potential over time in good cellar-craft conditions.

The esterification enhancement very often makes melomels fruitier as the phenolic compounds begin to amass within the bulk mead which settles out, often changing the colour of the wine and reducing the tannin levels, too. The honeys used are absent of both phenols, tannins and a noticeable lacking of acids, too: this is why ageing of meads needs to take account of these anomalies by the vintner being ahead of the situation, using his expertise to right such shortcomings. The meads of pyment and melomel have the advantage over straight meads, due to the presence of phenols and tannins within the fruit, but lacking totally in plain meads. As mentioned elsewhere, cellar-craft is most important, as vibration and temperature variation are an anathema to maturing mead, as is excess bright daylight – this, too, will accelerate oxidisation. Oxidisation to wines is much reduced in barrels and corked bottles, provided the criteria of temperature and vibration are heeded.

SUMMARY OF STORING AND SERVING MEADS AND HONEY WINES

The storage and cellar-craft of wines is most important. The finished wine should be stored in an area free from undue vibration. If available, a cellar is ideal as it is generally cool and will have the ideal temperature that is between 10 °C and 13 °C (50 °F and 55 °F, respectively). Nevertheless, it has to be accepted that the perfect situation is not always available to the amateur vintner. The use of an external garage is usually adequate for storage purposes. Never be tempted to store wines in a roof loft space or under greenhouse staging because of the excessive temperatures that arise in summer months.

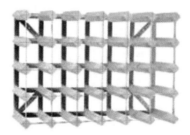

Simple wine rack for securing to a wall to
ensure stability [Michael Badger]

Custom-made wine racks
[Tanglewood Accessories Ltd, with permission]

Custom-made fitted-out wine cellar
[Tanglewood Accessories Ltd, with permission]

Experienced vintners have their own methods for storing their wine. The late Andy Andrews retained his wine in bulk, using standard demijohns suitably labelled, ready to bottle as required. Others store in-bottle laid on their sides so as to keep the cork moist. I use both methods for storage, recognising that, laid down in this manner, the wine is likely to throw a deposit that will settle on the bottle's side, making decanting somewhat problematic if a cloudy wine is to be avoided. The advantage of the demijohn is that the deposit (lees) falls to the base of the container, allowing the wine to be siphoned into the bottles without disturbing the deposit; possibly the final bottle may be a little cloudy. It is essential that once you have taken wine from the demijohn, the remaining airspace is ideal for unwanted oxidisation to take a hold: it is best avoided by bottling up the remaining wine.

Either the bottle or the demijohn should be filled to within 15 mm (½ in) of the bottom of the bung or cork, providing the bare minimum of airspace to avoid oxidisation issues.

The stored wine must be clearly identified with a label identifying the characteristics: type (dry/sweet, etc.), date, honey and ingredients, together with any notes particular to the batch produced, the most important being that, on a year-on-year basis, honey is variable and this can affect the finished wine.

When blending batches of mead, a crushed Campden tablet should be added to each batch to ensure the stability of the wine, so that re-fermentation is not encouraged to restart due to changes in environmental and physical conditions of the blending process. Mead and honey wines mature and improve with age; generally, dry mead needs two years, sweet mead requires at least five years, and heavy sack mead, eight years or longer.

To serve the mead is an art in itself. Should the wine have been stored in-bottle laid on its side, it needs to be carefully stood in an upright position for a minimum of two days before decanting it into a wine glass or a decanter itself. The deposit "lees" will collect in the punted area of the bottle, making it less likely to be disturbed when the wine is decanted.

All meads and honey wines are best served chilled. They can be stored in a refrigerator for several hours and then stood in a traditional ice bucket containing ice cubes.

The wine served for consumption is best from a plain-glass, tulip-shaped goblet. The tradition is that when the wine is drunk, this shape plays an important feature in that it helps to maintain the bouquet (or "nose") of the wine.

It is generally agreed that dry meads and honey wines with Melomel are more acceptable to accompany food, with the sweeter varieties taken as "social wines" for drinking on their own. Sack meads, being dessert wines, are very much in a league of their own; this arises because of their high alcohol content. These meads are very much akin to the Sauternes wines that end a fine banquet; such wines are anything but a session drinking beverage at barbeques and the like.

BANQUETS AND DINNERS

The Worshipful Company of Wax Chandlers uses mead and honey wines for its loving cup ceremony, an ancient and traditional ceremony exercised by a number of the livery companies of the City of London at their banquets and dinners.

THE LOVING CUP

The custom of the loving cup is believed to have originated in the 9th century when Alfred, King of the West Saxons from 871, had suzerainty over the whole of England, but did not directly control the Danish Kingdom of York, so that the country was still divided. Many attempts were made to get Saxons and Danes to live peacefully together, but treachery was common, especially during the act of drinking. So Oslac the cup bearer, who was also a grandfather of Alfred, arranged for the leaders of the two sides

A Loving Cup of the Worshipful Company of Wax Chandlers [Erica Osborn]

179

Guests partaking in the loving cup ceremony at the Worshipful Company of Wax Chandlers' Livery and Escorts dinner in May 2012 [Georgina Brown, Clerk to the Wax Chandlers' Company]

to pledge their goodwill in public to maintain the King's peace. To make sure that the dagger hands of their unruly followers were visible and occupied, every drinking cup was fitted with a cover which had to be held by the man facing the drinker. However, his back was still unprotected and, in about 978, Edward the Martyr is said to have been stabbed from behind while drinking. As a result, it became the custom for a second man to stand back to back with the drinker, thus giving the additional protection required.

In the London loving cup ceremony, as used by the Wax Chandlers, the Master, as host, and the principal guest drink first, the cover being held aloft by the principal guest and the Master's back being guarded by his other dinner neighbour. To the playing of music, the cover is replaced and the principal guest turns to his next neighbour, who is now standing, while the Master guards the guest's back. The other two both bow and the new neighbour removes the cover. The principal guest now drinks and his neighbour replaces the cover and turns to the next guest. The ceremony is repeated by everyone in turn, and so the cup passes around the table. While anyone is drinking, his neighbour who had previously drunk the cup stands back to back with him in order to prevent an attack from behind.

Your neighbour with the cup in his hand will turn round to face you. You will rise from your chair and you will bow to each other. You will raise the lid of the cup aloft in your right hand and he will drink and wipe the rim of the cup with the table napkin attached to the handle. You will replace the lid and take the cup. You will bow to one another again. You will then turn to your neighbour on your other side. He will rise and you will bow to one another. He will raise the lid. You will drink and wipe the rim. He will replace the lid and take the cup from you. You will bow to one another again. He will then turn to his other neighbour. At the same time you will turn to face your original neighbour, thus protecting the back of your second neighbour while he is drinking. When he has finished drinking and wiped the rim of the cup, you will sit down. Three – and only three – persons should be standing at the same time.

For information on the Loving Cup process, thanks are due to John Dummelow, Master Wax Chandler, 1960–62.

A MEAL FOR A FUTURE KING

Casserole of Pheasant: "Prince of Wales"
– Michael Young MBE

Ingredients

A brace of pheasants
purchased as dressed.
To ensure flavour, it is
suggested they are allowed
at least a further 10 days
past the statutory sell-by
date to ensure the bird meat
is sufficiently "high".
2 Chantenay-type carrots cut
into pieces, baton-style

2 parsnips, preferably
winter-frosted
8 small onions or shallots,
peeled and left whole
160 g (6 oz) heather honey or
dark flavoured honey
1 orange, segments free of pith
100 g (3.4 oz) unsalted butter
1 garlic clove, crushed

Ingredients for the sauce

100 g (3.4 oz) unsalted butter
The leftovers from the cooked
pheasants
4 rashers hickory-smoked
back-bacon
200 g (7 oz) fresh wild
mushrooms

114 g (4 oz) sweet chestnuts
4 sprigs thyme
200 ml (7 fl oz) blackberry
melomel or plain dry mead
1,500 ml (53 fl oz) chicken
stock
114 g (4 oz) plain flour

Method

Wash the inside and outside of the birds under cold running water.
Dry with a paper towel. Remove the breasts and legs. Chop up the
remains of the carcasses, ready for the sauce. Wrap the breasts and
legs in a piece of hickory-smoked bacon. Put on a separate tray to
the side. Brush the meat liberally with honey.

The Sauce

Heat a medium-sized, thick-bottomed saucepan on the stove. Add
the butter. Once the butter has melted, add the chopped carcasses
and bacon. Cook until brown, stirring occasionally, ensuring the
pan is very hot at all times to get a good brown colour and lots of

Casserole of Pheasant Prince of Wales [Michael Young]

flavour from the bones, etc. Add the onions, carrots and parsnip trimmings, mushrooms and sprigs of thyme. Cook out for a few minutes, always moving the ingredients with a wooden spatula to avoid burning. Lastly, add half of the blackberry melomel or dry mead. (If the mead used is as good as Ken Schramm's, that is a real treat.)

With care, keeping your face away from the pan, tilt it and let the flame catch the alcohol and flame the melomel. The pan should be still hot. With this dish it is good to use all natural ingredients; your blackberry melomel should preferably be dry and strong.

Having reduced the mead by half, sprinkle the plain flour over the mixture, stir for a few minutes to get the contents into a mushy state, add the chicken stock, and bring to the boil. Turn down to simmer for 20 minutes.

Next operation
Place a knob of butter (100 g) into a thick-bottomed frying pan. When nice and hot, place the pheasant breasts and legs into the

pan until golden brown, turning the meat over. Place all the meat in a good flameproof earthenware casserole dish. Set aside for the remaining food items. Note: glassware is known to hurt the cooking process.

Having removed the meat from the frying pan, add a further knob of butter and fry off the garlic, carrots, parsnips, shallots and wild mushrooms until lightly browned.

Place these ingredients on top of the pheasants within the casserole dish. Sprinkle the chopped chestnuts and tiny thyme leaves over the meat pieces, season with sea salt and a hint of cracked black pepper. Finally, add the sauce which should be a beautifully deep brown colour. Strain this through a coarse sieve (to catch small bones and lead shot). Pour over the pheasant meat and cover well.

Place a dessertspoon of flour into a small cup. Add a touch of water to make a thick paste. With your finger, spread this mixture around the edge of the casserole dish and onto the lid of the dish prior to putting this in the oven. By doing so, the lid will be sealed, capturing the essence of the pheasant.

Place the casserole on the middle shelf of the oven and bake at 160 °C (320 °F) or, in a fan oven, at 140 °C (285 °F). for 1¼ -1½ hrs (depending on the size of the bird) Serve with seasonal vegetables and braised red cabbage.

You can add a bit of spice by serving this dish in a novel way to appeal to your guests. View the photograph and dress the casserole, which is set in the centre of the salver with all the trimmings and garnish. Place the birds' feet in boiling water for one minute. Remove, cool and strip the first layer of skin from the bone, then lightly brush them with oil. Place to one side. Prepare a loaf of bread by cutting it in half, so it is able to stand up. Straight bake it in a hot oven until it becomes hard. When cold, insert the tail feathers into the top of the loaf. Place the feet at the front of the loaf and place it at the back of the salver. Boiled vegetables can be placed around the outside of the dish or served separately, if required.

PART FIVE

THE REQUIREMENTS FOR PRODUCING MEADS AND HONEY WINES

OPPOSITE

A heavy duty press for apples and fruit [Megan Timms]

SOME IMPORTANT CONSIDERATIONS

Producing mead and honey wine is about practice, combined with patience and theory, and more practice than theory until you have perfected a type of drink that is to your liking. This is achieved through excellent selection of ingredients, including the quality and type of honeys, strain of yeast, water and accepted additives that are available. The highest standard of cleanliness, sanitisation and sterilisation is essential, combined with the use of first-class equipment, faultless in every respect, and it is essential that detailed records are kept of each batch produced. This will allow the analysis of the characters and points of the beverage to be assessed, and these can then be considered when making another batch. Tie-on labels on each demijohn/carboy are essential to identify the date, content and history of the wine. The reliance on memory or notes written on paper placed through the demijohn/carboy handle is not satisfactory, as they can so easily fade or be lost. Use black ink or reproductive biro ink.

YEASTS AND
THE FERMENTATION PROCESS

There are two types of fermentation: anaerobic (in the absence of oxygen) and aerobic (when oxygen is present).

The Fermentation Equation

Anaerobic

$$C6H12O6 \rightarrow 2C2H5OH + 2CO2$$

Fermentation converts sugar (glucose) into alcohol and carbon dioxide

Aerobic

$$C6H12O6 + 6O2 \rightarrow 6CO2 + 6H2O + 2900 \text{ kJ/mol}$$

glucose + oxygen = carbon dioxide + water + energy

Anaerobic fermentation turns the must into carbon dioxide and alcohol. The must is a combination of honey, water, yeast, acids and nutrients. Given the correct temperature and pH level, the yeast begins to ferment. The fermentation process is a somewhat complex chain of reactions whereby the yeast cells metabolise (break down) the single larger molecule (sugar) into two simpler molecules, ethanol and carbon dioxide.

The fermentation process can be so easily be spoiled by a combination of factors which create problems of "off-flavours" in the finished wine. These off-flavours arise when the yeast population becomes stressed, mainly because of poor amounts of nutrients added at pitch (adding) stage, using aged yeast past its recommended use-by date, and an incorrect pH level in the must, with the wrong temperature for the fermentation to begin (either too cold or too hot, coupled with poor aeration issues). Conversely, a correct fermentation, justly called a clean fermentation, is what the mead maker strives for.

FERMENTATION PATHWAYS

To simplify matters, the process of fermentation begins immediately the yeast is introduced to the specially prepared must. The process follows a biological process through four pathways:

1. the lag period
2. the aerobic or respiratory phase
3. the fermentation phase
4. the flocculation or yeast-settling phase.

1. The Lag Period
This is referred to as the "lag phase" in the USA
Once the yeast is added to the must, it needs time to acclimatise to the new aqueous solution. Some yeast strains are more active than others, starting the fermentation cycle within the hour. Others can take up to 48 hours or more. The new surroundings (the must) will require a routine acceptable sugar amount: this avoids a blatant excess sugar level tolerance to the yeast. Intolerably high sugar content will stop the yeast from reproducing. The pH needs to be correct for yeast replication. Reproduction of the yeast spores requires the necessary acids, compounds and nutrients to be in solution at the right amounts. As the term implies, the lag period is the time the yeast needs to adjust to its new environment. Different yeasts used in mead and honey wine production have varying periods before they appear to begin multiplying into the reproduction phase. This is essentially a period when the yeast cell walls thicken and the cytoplasm begins hoarding nutrients in readiness to produce the enormous number of multiplying offspring that will arise once the reproduction phase is enacted.

2. The Aerobic or Respiratory Phase
The terms "aerobic" and "respiratory" relate to the yeast's requirements for oxygen in this particular phase of the fermentation process. For the reproducing yeast to reach the required concentrations, its cells must replicate over and over again. Individual yeast organisms will

do this until they totally deplete their reserves. The yeast cell creates a bulge, termed a "bud", within the cell wall. Its nuclear chromosomal counterpart reproduces, suffuses into the bulge and finally slices off the "bulged bud" creating a new autonomous yeast cell. This asexual budding process requires the generation of large amounts of new cell wall tissue. This, in turn, requires a large number of nutrients with the vintner duty-bound to ensure the yeast is well provisioned for this reproduction. The production of this new cellular membrane utilises oxygen, nitrogen and the other nutrients rapidly. Different strains of yeast very often require different levels of dissolved oxygen and nutrient levels in the new must. These compounds are essential for ensuring a satisfactory fermentation.

3. The Fermentation Phase

During the transition from aerobic (with oxygen) to anaerobic (without oxygen) fermentation, there is a phase when the growing yeast exhausts the supplies of molecular oxygen used for the creation of new cell wall tissue. During this phase, the population of yeast cells shifts its focus from reproduction to fermentation, and the yeast population can accelerate to its maximum level which can exceed 1.5×10^8 cells/ml.

Before the real conversion of the dissolved sugars to alcohol commences, the yeast cells utilise transport compounds, known as permeases, to move the sugars across their cell walls. The fermentation process begins in a series metabolic phases reducing the glucose to trioses (simple sugars). This is followed by glycolysis where the trioses are reduced to pyruvic acid, leaving two molecules of adenosine triphosphate (ATP), a nucleoside triphosphate used in cells as a coenzyme, often called the "molecular unit of currency" of intracellular energy transfer. ATP transports chemical energy within cells for metabolism. The amount of ethanol and carbon dioxide formed often varies between the strains of yeasts used. The fermentation stage may begin within one to four hours or up to 12 to 48 hours once the yeast is "pitched" (added) into the must. Once begun, fermentation generally reaches its peak in five to nine days. However, if the vintner is seeking to produce sweet/dessert

A demijohn of mead covered in black plastic sheet to keep out
the light to assist the yeast in its reproduction [Michael Badger]

mead, he will add amounts of honey to the must. These are added
on the premise of little and often, judged by the rapidity of the
expelled carbon dioxide seen through the airlock. The additions
will eventually cease once the yeast has become worked out in the
fermentation. When fermentation has peaked, the population of
yeast cells begins to drop and follows the natural bell-shaped graph.
*(The bell curve is the most common type of distribution for a variable.
The term comes from the bell-shaped line resulting from the graph's
data.)* The yeast will work according to the prevailing conditions,
resulting in a medium to higher alcohol content, affected ultimately
by lower nutrient levels or the pH level. Understandably, a very
healthy yeast culture will continue within the fermentation phase
until the yeast has fully consumed all the available sugar in the
must. In essence, it has reached its alcohol tolerance level and is
exhausted. By this time the yeast cells are on the wane, and the
yeast is entering the final stage of the fermentation process.

4. Flocculation
The final stage of fermentation is when the sugar solution becomes
consumed. It has begun to tail off as the yeast cells dye. The cells
are now exhibiting changes in their cell wall structure and forming
into clumps called "flocs". With most modern yeast strains, the
clumps fall to the bottom of the fermentation vessel. The degree
to which this happens is indicated by the clarity of the clearing

mead, and is dependent upon the strain of yeast used. A strain of yeast that settles quickly to form a firm yeast bed at the base of the fermentation vessel is said to "flocculate well". Naturally, it is the genetic make-up of the yeast strain that determines this feature.

OTHER FACTORS THAT INFLUENCE FERMENTATION

There are other critical issues the mead maker needs to consider when preparing the must. The yeast's activity greatly influences the flavour of the finished mead. The vintner has many opportunities to prepare the must to its optimum composition in order to achieve a successful outcome. These include:

- nutrient levels and the quality of the nutrient used
- pH levels
- aeration
- temperature.

Above all, the quality of the honey and the chosen yeast used, freshness, origin and type all play their part.

Nutrient Levels
The most critical ingredient for a robust fermentation is the total amount of nitrogen available to the reproducing yeast. The most important is the available nitrogen, known as free amino nitrogen (FAN). There is a limited amount of FAN in honey, with the lowest levels being found in the lightest honeys. The must requires a minimum of 130 mg/l of FAN, with a recommended level of 300-500 mg/l. Additional nutrients are therefore required to ensure a satisfactory fermentation. Specially prepared nitrogen-based nutrients from a local home brew store can be used. The commonest is diammonium phosphate (DAP; $(NH4)2HPO4$) which now replaces the once-popular ammonium sulphate, commonly referred to in dated textbooks on the subject, so beware. The new mead maker should be aware of packaged "yeast

energisers" which are more or less the same product. DAP adds 258 ppm of fermentable nitrogen when added to a must at the rate of 1 g/l. The use of such compounds can nurture an aggressive fermentation or restart a stalled (stuck) fermentation, resulting from higher concentrations of sugars present in the must, possibly when it was made up and the SG was not checked, so the vintner was not aware of the highly sugary solution within the must. The only way (and it is no secret) is to start off with the correct amounts of ingredients and instigate a dynamic fermentation from the outset, rather than getting into difficulties with one that is slow and sluggish. When using purchased yeast nutrients or energisers, it is essential to read the dosage instructions carefully and adhere to them.

Ken Schramm recommends that nutrients should be added to the must under the regime of staggered nutrient additions (SNA) by instalments, dividing the desired amount into five equal portions. Ken suggests two-fifths should be added after the yeast has been pitched to the must after about 12 hours, with one-fifth added on each of the three remaining days as near as possible on a 24-hour cycle.

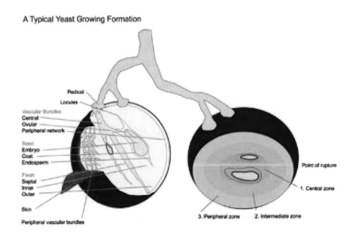

Section through a yeast bundle [Damien Timms©]

In the production of melomel or other mead variants involving fruit, it is essential that a balanced nutrient is used. As discussed previously, it is critical for the production of the permeases: these are membrane transport proteins which deliver the necessary nutrients to the growing yeast cell for its reproduction. These fruit-type meads may have additional nutrient sources within the fruit itself for feeding the reproducing yeast cells other than the honey itself.

(b) pH Levels

During the lag and aerobic phases of the fermentation process, the growing yeast needs the specific resources to enable it to reproduce. In this mechanism, it takes in all that is required to nourish and feed it from the many nutrients available, together with mineral compounds known to be present in the yeast itself, and the amino acids naturally present within the honey. All these nutrients, compounds and acids act as a kind of shield ensuring the must's pH is kept within the necessary bounds enabling the yeast cells to readily assimilate a possibly high sugar content in the must. As the assimilation continues, the pH consistently falls. This can and does inhibit the fermentation, more especially if the pH falls to below 3.00, i.e. the solution becomes more acidic should this happen, the rate of fermentation also falls, resulting in the fermentation proceeding at a slower degree possibly over many months. This slowdown may be of natural concern to the vintner. When the yeast becomes exhausted, it also becomes both strained and stressed, leading to the possibility of other undesirable compounds being produced during the later stages of the fermentation. It is these substances and substrates that may affect both aroma and taste in the finished wine. The experts recommend a pH of 3.7 to 4.3 as the optimum for mead and honey wines. The lowest end of the pH range is quite adequate to ensure the yeast can metabolise sufficiently to keep unwanted bacteria and other undesirable compounds at bay. The new wine maker is advised not to add other acids during the fermentation period. By doing so, they may unwittingly make matters worse. The pH in the wine can be adjusted once it is finished. It should be noted that lemons, limes, elderberries and berries used in melomel and honey fruit wines will add extra acids to the must. This needs to be taken into account when making additions to the must.

(c) Aeration

Before fermentation begins, it is essential that sufficient oxygen is introduced into the must well in advance of adding (pitching) the yeast. Oxygen can be introduced by pouring the must from one sterilised container to another. The wine maker should be aware that yeast strains differ in the time they take to work and reproduce. I have observed some wine makers leaving the fermentation vessel open to the atmosphere as a means of drawing in oxygen. This should never be done; it is pure folly by exacerbating oxidisation to the wine, more especially when vinegar flies are active in the summer months.

(d) Temperature

This plays a vital part in successful fermentation. The ideal condition for the yeast to multiply is a stable temperature between 18° C (65° F) and 21° C (70° F). The yeast is inhibited at temperatures either below 13° C (56 °F) or in excess of 27 °C (80 °F). The preferred environment is where the fermentation proceeds in an orderly fashion: neither too slow, nor too fast. Modern yeasts no longer require fermenting vessels to be placed in warm cupboards, as recommended in the past.

A more contemporary method of averaging out fermentation is to use an electric heating belt, heating mat or an insertion-type heater. Whatever kit is used, they are best controlled by the use of a thermostatic device.

The manufacturers state that these devices maintain a favourable temperature during the fermentation. The majority of the heating belt fits around the outside of a 25-litre (5½ UK gal) fermenting vessel or bin, or it is wrapped in a figure of eight when two demijohns are used in harness. These devices provide gentle warmth to the must in a convenient and economical way.

The heating belt must be placed around the fermenter and adjusted by trial and error according to the ambient temperature. The manufacturer's instructions are quite specific as to how the heating belt should be attached to the fermenter. There are immersion-type heaters for use with 1 gal. demijohn or 5 gal. carboy, also heating mats for vessels for the must to be kept at a set temperature; the manufacturer's instructions are simple to implement.

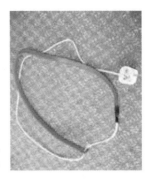

Belt-type heater cable for wrapping around demijohn or carboy [Michael Badger]

YEAST SELECTION

The yeasts widely used by vintners have been developed from the species of a yeast commonly referred to as *Saccharomyces cerevisiae*. This strain of yeast is widely used; it is derived from hundreds of different strains with over 100 used purely in the beer and wine industries. Wine makers are known to use other closely related strains, *S. bayous*, and *S. bayanus uvarum*. The experienced vintner goes to extraordinary lengths to obtain and use a yeast strain known to hold the characteristics he knows will produce the flavour and aroma he requires in the finished wine. These experienced vintners are all too aware that yeasts behave differently in varying musts, made and enhanced through the different honeys, nutrients and temperatures used during the fermentation process.

Yeasts are available in three distinct forms:

1. *dried yeast* sold in sachets or foil packets
2. *liquid cultures* distributed in either vials or foil pouches
3. *culturing kits* for the experienced microbiologist

Yeast suppliers generally market two categories: wine yeasts and beer yeasts. Specific wine yeasts are labelled as dry or sweet.

YEASTS IN COMMON USAGE WORLDWIDE FOR RED WINES AND WHITE WINES

Red wines

Name	Origin	Narrative
Assmann-shausen	Germany, Rhine region, in the state of Hesse	Medium- to full-bodied red wines. Alcohol to 15 per cent
Bourgovin	France, Burgundy region	Full-bodied red wines. Used for darker fruits. Alcohol 14 to 16 per cent
Côtes du Rhône	France, Rhône region	Flocs well. Excellent for dry meads. Alcohol 12 to 14 per cent
Épernay	France, District of Marne, Épernay. Marne region	Champagne yeast. Alcohol 16 to 18 per cent
Flor	Spain, Andalucía	Sherry-type yeast. Develops a film (flor) on the surface of the wine. Creates the green almond, Granny Smith and nougat characteristics found in sherry. Alcohol 16 per cent
Montrachet	France, Côte de Beaune subregion of Burgundy	A very good fermenter. Good alcohol tolerance that is useful in producing dry, full-bodied red and white wines. Alcohol 15 per cent
Narbonne	France, Languedoc-Roussillon-Midi-Pyrénées region	Cabernet wine yeast. Alcohol 15 per cent
Pasteur Red	France, Institut Pasteur, Paris	Dry. A strong fermenter. Produces full-bodied red wines. Particularly well suited for grapes from the Zinfandel and Cabernet families as well as berry and cherry wine, Gamay, Merlot, Pinot and Syrah. Alcohol 15 per cent

White wines

Name	Origin	Narrative
Côte des Blancs	France, South, Marne region	One of the most traditional aromatic strains for white wines. An excellent choice for fruity wines. Alcohol 15 per cent
Épernay	France, Épernay, Marne region	Neutral, classic yeast, used to produce sparkling wine, cider, dry meads, and dry wines
Montpellier	France, capital of the Languedoc-Roussillon-Midi-Pyrénées region	A vigorous and competitive fermenter. Very well suited to fruit wines, as well as wines made from grapes. Alcohol 16 to 18 per cent
Pasteur Champagne	France, Champagne area of Épernay	All-purpose and vigorous, a moderately foaming and extremely good fermenter. Very high alcohol tolerance. Recommended for treating stuck fermentations. Alcohol 18 per cent
Prise de mousse	France, Champagne area of Épernay	A low-foaming, vigorous and fast fermenter. Good for both reds and whites. Ideal for cyser and sparkling wines. Alcohol 18 per cent
Rüdisheimer	Germany, Rüdesheim am Rhein in the Rhine Gorge	Riesling for very sweet meads and wines. Alcohol 9 to 12 per cent
Sauternes	France, Bordeaux, Gironde valley	Sweet dessert wine flavour. Alcohol 12 to 16 per cent
Steinberg	Germany	High fruit/ester production. Moderate fermentation characteristics. Cold-tolerant. Alcohol 12 to 14 per cent
Tokay d'Alsace	Germany, Alsace-Lorraine	Obsolete name for Pinot gris grapes, Alsace. Medium sweet. Can be flaccid with certain honeys. Alcohol 9 to 12 per cent
Narbonne	France, Languedoc-Roussillon-Midi-Pyrénées region	Semi-dry white wine yeast that will enhance fruit flavours and add fruity esters. Can be used with whites, rosés, nouveaus and concentrates. Alcohol 14 per cent.

Commonly Available Yeasts for Meads and Country Wines

GERVIN	
GV 1 – Green Label	(*S. cerevisiae*, Narbonne Strain) Universal; General-purpose wine yeast – redcurrant and rose hip melomels.
GV 2 – Red Label	(*S. cerevisiae*, French Strain) Full-bodied red and white wine yeast – Melomels – blackberry, blackcurrants, bilberries, elderflower and sloes.
GV 3 – Yellow Label	(*S. cerevisiae*, Institut Pasteur Strain) Sparkling Wine yeast – champagne / sparkling mead, cyser, elderflower.
GV 4 – Purple Label	(*S. cerevisiae* French strain) High-alcohol wine yeast.
GV 5 – Grey Label	(*S. cerevisiae*, French Strain GVN) White Wine Yeast; apricot, peach and strawberry Melomels and Honey Country Wines.
GV 6 – Orange Label	Light Dessert Yeast; For true Sauternes-type meads.
GV 7 – Brown Label	Yeast for restarting stuck fermentations with too much residual sugar within the must.
GV 8 – Burgundy Label	(*S. cerevisiae* Narbonne selection strain) Red table wine yeast; Bordeaux / Claret-style wines.
GV 9 – Black Label	(*S. cerevisiae*, Narbonne selection strain) White Wine yeast; German-style wine for Melomels and Honey Country Meads.
GV 10 – Gold Label	*S. cerevisiae* (bayanus) Light Sparkling Wine yeast; Superior Sparkling and Rosé Wine.
GV 11 – Dark Red Label	Red fruit Country Honey Meads and Wines yeast; ideal for fruit wines with high levels of malic acid.
GV 13 – Dark Green Label	Cyser and Cider yeast.

FERMENTIS	
B C – S 103	Recommended for "stuck" fermentations and production of high-alcohol meads.
C K – S102	Ideal for citrus-based Melomels and Cyser meads.
S – 101	Melomels with high-red fruit colours.
LALLEMAND (LALVIN)	
K1 – V 1116 *Saccharomyces cerevisiae*	Ideal for giving added esters to a finished mead. Recommended for white grape varieties such as Sauvignon blanc, Chenin blanc and Seyval.
E C – 1118 *Saccharomyces bayanus*	Champagne and sparkling meads. Recommended for all types of wines, including sparkling, dry white, late-harvest wines and cider.
71 B – 1122 *Saccharomyces cerevisiae*	Melomels, Pyments and Cyser meads. Recommended for blush and residual sugar whites / late-harvest wines, nouveau and young red wines.
D 47 Strain [L'institut coopératif du vin]	Red Melomels or Red country wine meads. Recommended for dry white wines such as Chardonnay and rosé / blush wines and residual sugar wines. An excellent choice for producing mead. It is essential to supplement with yeast nutrients, especially usable nitrogen. Malolactic fermentation proceeds well with ICV D47.
RC 212 *Saccharomyces cerevisiae*	Red and rosé-type meads and country wine meads. Recommended for red-coloured varieties of wines.
BM4X4	Universal yeast for red and white Melomels and Country Wines.
QA 23	White wine yeast; Chardonnay, Sauvignon blanc and Sémillon wines.
Lalvin 43	This yeast was selected for its exceptional ability to restart stuck fermentations. Alcohol tolerance is at least 18%.

RED STAR	
Première Cuvée	*S. cerevisiae* (bayanus) Davis 796 strain; High alcohol, for wine that requires no residual sugar desired.
Montrachet	*S. cerevisiae*; A strong fermenter with good ethanol tolerance, will readily ferment grape musts and fruit juices to dryness. Montrachet is noted for low volatile acidity, good flavour complexity, and intense colour.
Côte des Blancs	*S. cerevisiae*; Derived from yeasts perfected by the Geisenheim Institute, Germany. It is recommended for reds, whites, sparkling cuvées and non-grape fruit wines.
Red Star Pasteur Red®	*S. cerevisiae*; Derived from yeasts perfected by the Institut Pasteur in Paris. It is a strong, even fermenter that produces full-bodied reds. This yeast encourages the development of varietal fruit flavours, balanced by complex aromas.
Pasteur Champagne	*S. cerevisiae* (bayanus); Derived from a pure culture slant of the Institut Pasteur in Paris. This strain has been widely used in the US since 1968. It is a strong fermenter with good ethanol tolerance, and will readily ferment grape musts and fruit juices to dryness. Useful for restarting stuck fermentations.
Épernay	Champagne yeast. Épernay is used in bottle fermenting because it ferments slowly and is tolerant to cold temperatures with moderate foaming.
WHITE LABS	
WLP – 775	Cyser meads
WLP 720	Sweet meads
WLP 720	Sweet and dessert-type meads
WYEAST	
4632	Dry Meads and country wines
4184	Sweet meads and country wines
4021	Pasteur Champagne

NON-TRADITIONAL YEASTS

The commonly used yeasts by vintners are being challenged by *brettanomyces* alias *Botanical Mayces*, a non-spore-forming genus of yeast in the family Saccharomycetaceae, and is often colloquially referred to as "Brett". The yeast is only available in liquid culture form that requires making up into a starter bottle for adding to the must. Brett fermentations are renowned for working out to dryness, a quality not always appreciated by vintners.

PREPARING THE YEAST FOR FERMENTATION

Note: The mead vintner should exercise every aspect of cleaning, sterilisation and sanitisation throughout.

Producers of yeasts for the vintner label them as "ready for use". These yeasts are best added to the must (pitched) by using a tried and proven method. They are available as dry yeasts, best prepared using proper rehydration methods, and liquid yeasts where a starter is the preferred method to add them to the must, especially for the new vintner.

Rehydration Methodology.

Add sterilised water to the dry (dehydrated) yeast culture in readiness to add it to the must. The simplest method is to take 60 ml (2 fl oz) of water at the temperature recommended by the manufacturer for each 5 g (0.16 oz) of yeast to be rehydrated. Place the sterilised water into a sterilised container. Sprinkle the yeast carefully on the surface. After 15 minutes, carefully stir the yeast slowly and deliberately into the water at a temperature of 21 °C (70 °F), avoiding any yeast adhering to the container's walls. When it is working well, add it to the must. Shake well to incorporate extra oxygen to give added impetus to coax the yeast to start the first reproductive phase of budding. Certain yeasts are not freeze-dried and the vintner needs to make up a "starter bottle" to get them working before adding them to the must (see below, page 204).

Starter Methodology for Liquid Yeasts

The vintner should exercise the same care in regard to cleanliness, sanitisation and cleanliness. The principal object is to have the greatest number of yeast cells being produced before adding (pitching) the yeast to the must. This is best achieved by making up a starter-mix bottle (see page 93). A healthy must may have 10 x 106 (1 million) cells/ml.

Another Yeast Starter Method Commonly adopted in the USA

The procedure for making 1 gallon (Imp). It is highly recommend using a scale to weigh these products for the accurate dosage.

1. Take 120 ml (4¼ fl oz) of boiled water or treated water with sulphite compound; heat the water gently to blood-heat 37 °C (98.4 °F), but not to exceed 40 °C (104 °F). Check temperature with a sanitised thermometer.

2. Add Go-Ferm to the water at a rate of 1.25 g per 1 g of yeast. Due to its natural properties, it is difficult to incorporate into the water: I use a sanitised eggcup half-filled with the water and press the nutrient into the side of this smaller vessel, gradually blending into this liquid and equal amounts of water and nutrient until fully dissolved, and then add to the remaining water to ensure it is fully and thoroughly mixed.

3. Prepare Fermaid K at approximately 1 g per gallon: 1 g DAP per gallon by placing in a sanitised discarded chemicals container, and secure lid and shake to incorporate. Set aside for incorporating into the must at the appropriate time (approximately three days after the primary fermentation is underway).

Mixing Container for Nutrients [Charlotte Lewis]

4. Add the contents of the packet of chosen yeast to the water that has the blended Go-Ferm and stir in slowly but deliberately. Seal the container with cling film and set a timer to 15 minutes.

5. Add the yeast mixture, set aside to the must.

[Note] Yeasts of different strains multiply at different rates, in differing musts and in environmental conditions of hot or cold.

Record all timings and actions in your logbook.

OXYGENATING THE "MUST"

Successful fermentation requires the must to have adequate oxygen which will ensure that the yeast can, and will, reproduce quickly, getting off to a vigorous start. To accomplish this, the must should be stirred or shaken vigorously to integrate air and oxygen. In essence, you cannot over-incorporate air at this stage of the fermentation. Some vintners use hand or electrical blenders or other devices to agitate the must for up to five minutes. The original specific gravity (OG) is recorded and noted at this stage.

SULPHITES AND CAMPDEN TABLETS

Potassium metabisulfite (K2S2O5), more often known as sulphite, is the commonest compound used for both cleaning and sanitising equipment and sterilising musts. It is the most active constituent of Campden tablets.

There is much discussion about the use of such compounds in all spheres of wine production because of their formulation and chemical properties. They are essential for sterilising and cleaning, and it is a matter of choice whether to use them in sterilising fruit and honey in a formulated must or to resort to traditional methods of pasteurisation. There are concerns by some vintners to use non-chemical usage; however, the cleansing, sanitisation and sterilisation are a real issue and should be taken very seriously.

STOPPING THE FERMENTATION

When the desired SG has been achieved, the fermentation needs to be stopped. This is best achieved by racking the must into a new fermentation vessel, avoiding incorporation of any additional oxygen during the transfer. One crushed Campden tablet is added per gallon of must and the vessel shaken well to ensure thorough distribution. One level teaspoon of potassium sorbate is stirred into the must. The vessel is topped up to 15 mm below the airlock with cold boiled water for a dry wine, or cold boiled water sweetened with sterilised honey for a sweet wine.

RACKING (DECANTING) THE WINE FROM THE FERMENTER.

Racking is the process of decanting the wine from one fermentation vessel into another. The primary objective is to get the completed fermented wine away from the spent yeast as the precursor to separating it from other particles in suspension by regularly racking, as this assists in clearing the mead.

To avoid disturbing the sediment (lees), some vintners use a racking cane. This is a stout, hollow plastic tube secured to the siphon tube to ensure it does not disturb the sediment unduly, while at the same time allowing the siphon to operate without the end of the tube leaving the must.

A simple aid to clearing a racked wine is to remove the vessel to a cold room, a cellar, garage or outhouse, and place the container directly onto a solid concrete floor.

Left Racking of mead – the sanitised syphoning tube is made to reach the bottom of the demijohn to avoid the introduction of oxygen into the must [Michael Badger]

Right Racking of mead: the syphon tube should be placed into the bulk to avoid incorporation of oxygen when racking – shown here purely for effect of how not to rack mead [Michael Badger]

Melomel Vinegar
of Raspberry/cherry
Mother of Vinegar
Water. Medium Sweet

Cyser Vinegar
Medium Sweet
Cyser mead
mother of vinegar
water.

PART SIX

RECIPES FOR MEADS, HONEY WINES AND MEAD-BASED VINEGAR

OPPOSITE
Melomel Vinegar (*left*) and Cyser Vinegar (*right*) [Rupert Palmer]

GENERAL CONSIDERATIONS

In all recipes, the vintner has to take heed of cleanliness, disinfecting, sanitation and sterilisation of all work surfaces, places of work and equipment used.

Fill the fermentation lock with glycerine to ensure the airlock never evaporates.

It is good practice to envelop the fermenting vessel with a black plastic cover to exclude the light as, in normal situations, the yeast develops in anaerobic conditions and total darkness.

For recipes using pectolase and Rohamet P (a special, multi-active enzyme that releases aromatic components bound to sugars present in the must, enhancing colour and flavour), refer to the manufacturer's detailed instructions for their use.

The Specific Gravity (SG) of honey is 1.425: therefore you will need 0.56 kg (1.25 lb) of honey for the equivalent in sugar of 0.454 kg (1 lb).

Natural grape juice or grape concentrate should be procured from commercial wine-grown grapes. Dessert grapes or grape juice from health shops are devoid of the essential efficient acids found in commercial wine grapes, and should not be used.

The remedy for producing good sweet wines is to start the fermentation off with a lower addition of honey, adding small quantities of sterilised honey incrementally as the fermentation slows down to about 1.08: at best, the maximum for a social wine should be 4¼ to 4½ lb honey.

A dry wine can easily be made sweet by adding a proprietary sweetening agent.

Grape juice concentrate from wine kits is an ideal medium.

To avoid duplication and clarity in wording, the following is noted:

• The term "make-up starter bottle" is described on page 92
• Water is deemed to have been evaporated for chlorine / fluoride, water from borehole or well water should be sterilised by boiling this water or by use of osmotic filter.

sterilised to by boiling for borehole or well water
- Rainwater is deemed have included a 1/16th of Epsom salts (magnesium sulphate) added at the gallon rate
- Remove all stalks from fruits as stalk remains will impoverish the wine
- To "stop fermentation" refers to adding 1 Campden tablet and one level teaspoon of potassium sorbate per gallon
- To "bottle" means lay down in-bottle generally when the wine is star-bright, usually free of lees and at least 12 months old.
- The specific gravity (SG) of honey is 1.425. Therefore you will need 0.56 kg (1.25 lb) of honey for the equivalent in sugar of 0.454 kg (1 lb).

Dry and Sweet Mead

The recipes described earlier in the text on pages 88 to 107 inclusive have not been repeated here. However, the vintner may wish to use either a general purpose-type or specific yeast type. The quality of the honey used, combined with the appropriate permitted acids and nutrients, together with excellent cellar-craft, determines the quality of the finished product. The new vintner will become more proficient, the more meads and honey wines he produces: his knowledge base will improve with more practice, and this is the only way forward to producing good wine.

SPARKLING MEADS AND HONEY WINES

Producing such volatile wines requires extreme caution because of the pressures that naturally build up within the bottles. Those with experience of producing beers are all too aware of the typical pressures, which run to about two atmospheres – that is, twice the pressure exerted in the airspace of the bottle than at normal pressure at room temperature. Standard wine bottles should never be used for such wines: they are of a much-reduced section; being thinner, they will literally explode without warning, with flying glass causing serious injury or damage.

The pressure generated in sparkling mead wines and champagne is increased to four atmospheres by the introduction of carbon dioxide, so the bottles used for such wine need to be of considerable strength and robustness. They are both corked and wired to avoid the stopper being forced out while under these

Far left Champagne bottle
[Michael Badger]
Left Muselet-type corking
arrangement for highly
carbonated wines
[Michael Badger]

Left White plastic champagne
cork [Michael Badger]
Below Wiring in place: plastic
champagne cork [source unknown,
believed to be the Amateur Wine
Maker publications]

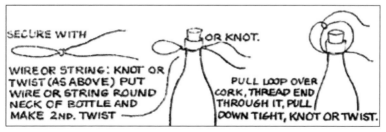

SECURE WITH OR KNOT.

WIRE OR STRING: KNOT OR TWIST (AS ABOVE) PUT WIRE OR STRING ROUND NECK OF BOTTLE AND MAKE 2ND. TWIST

PULL LOOP OVER CORK, THREAD END THROUGH IT, PULL DOWN TIGHT, KNOT OR TWIST.

extreme pressures. The use of the typical champagne bottle is the preferred option, due to its robustness.

These types of wine require a process of carbonation by the addition of a small amount of honey or sugar "priming" which is added prior to bottling. Fundamentally, the small amount of yeast that remains in the wine will consume any sweetener added, producing a small amount of carbon dioxide and alcohol to produce a nice sparkling wine exhibiting the characteristic foaming and burst of wine when opened by the unwary.

[**CAUTION**] This procedure requires 10 to 30 days to produce a reconciled sparkling wine. The mead or honey to be used may be aged, whereby the residual yeast present may be exhausted. In this case, it may be prudent to replenish this by adding a small portion of fresh yeast to ensure that carbonation takes place. This is where good record keeping allows you to use the same strain of yeast as in the original fermentation. A different strain of yeast may have a higher alcohol tolerance, and this could run the risk of generating a higher pressure, resulting in bottles exploding or corks blowing. It is best to serve the sparkling mead (chilled) by decanting it carefully off the sediment into another jug, avoiding the inclusion of the lees as it moves to be poured. The new vintner is advised not to experiment with producing higher-rated carbonation levels using priming sugar or honey as this causes problems with creation of additional sediment with the serious danger of the bottle bursting or the cork blowing. When opened, the internal pressure will naturally cause venting of the contents, spurting out uncontrollably, and the turbulence will mix any lees and deposit into the served mead.

In 2015, I was invited to the champagne cellars of Munn & Co in Rheims, France, to see the practice of "méthode champenoise" for champagne production, allowing me to see first-hand the two-handed operation of this very intricate method of sugar priming.

Ingredients are as for dry mead, with the exception that a champagne yeast should be used with a light honey, rather than ling heather honey.

Method

1. Proceed as for the dry mead recipe, leaving sufficient space to receive additional honey and keeping a watchful eye on the progress of the fermentation. Check the original SG and record it.
2. When the must has achieved a dryness reading below 1.005, add 227 g (½ lb) of honey to the demijohn, mixing well. Replace the airlock.
3. Place the demijohn in a warm place and after a few days, when fermentation is seen to be active, rack the mead into proper champagne bottles, leaving an airspace of 25 mm (1 in).
4. Cork with champagne-type plastic stoppers, wiring the corks into position (see the diagram). This procedure is most important.
5. Store the bottles on their sides at a steady temperature of about 15° C for at least six months before opening.

PYMENTS

Pyment is produced with natural grape juice or grape concentrate or from a wine kit, plus honey, permitted additives and water.

White Pyment (One)

Ingredients (using natural grapes)

4 litres (7 pints Imp; 9 kg) commercial grapes for pressing
1 kg (2.2 lb) medium honey
½ teaspoon tartaric acid
¼ teaspoon malic acid
¼ teaspoon grape tannin or 4 tablespoons of strong, cold tea

1 teaspoon citric acid
1 teaspoon yeast nutrient
1 tablet thiamine (vitamin B1)
1 tablet ascorbic acid (vitamin C)
1 sachet Chablis-type yeast
Campden tablets
Potassium sorbate

Method

1. Extract the juice from the grapes either by crushing or by pressing, or from the can holding the concentrate.
2. Add the honey (slightly warmed to aid dissolving) and stir until mixed into the grape juice.
3. Place the must into a demijohn, adding a crushed Campden tablet. Stir well and place the demijohn in a warm place for 24 hours. Stir several times during this period.
4. Make up a starter bottle using the sachet of Chablis yeast. When the yeast is working, add the starter bottle contents to the demijohn and stir well. Add a fermentation lock and place in a warm room, preferably at no more than 15-18 °C (60-65 °F).
5. As the yeast flourishes in natural grape juice, if the room is too warm, there is a strong possibility that the fermentation will become violent, causing the must to froth and overflow. In this case, the demijohn should be removed to a cool place.
6. When the fermentation is complete, rack the must into a

clean demijohn, add a crushed Campden tablet and store in a cool place.

7. Rack again when an appreciable amount of deposit or sediment is seen at the base of the demijohn.
8. Pyment should be allowed to mature for at least two years.
9. Bottle.

White Pyment (Two)

Ingredients (using grape concentrate)
White grape concentrate is used extensively by wine makers and mead makers alike. Obtain the concentrate from your local winemaking supplier. The winemaking supplier will be most helpful in advising you which grape concentrate to use and will give you full instructions. Follow the instructions meticulously; bearing in mind the instructions for the concentrate will be referring to cane or beet sugar, and not honey – for every 454 g (1 lb) sugar its equivalent in honey is 566 g (1.25 lb). Follow the method above for its production.

MELOMELS

Melomel is a fruit-based mead and honey wine derived from any fruit other than grapes or apples.

There are many fruits, whether fresh, dried or as juices (concentrated juices from commercially grown wine grapes), that can be used for making a mead or honey wine. Either can be sweet or dry. Some fruits are better than others, and some are ideal for particular meads, while others are not. Some create difficulties because of their high tannin and pectin levels. Most difficulties with fruit meads concern clearing but, with proper cellar-craft, these obstacles can be overcome easily.

Blackberry Melomel

Made from blackberry purée.

Days 1 and 2
Use the production method described previously for dry mead on page 89.

Ingredients
5.50 litres (1.2 gal Imp) cold water
13.36 litres (3 gal Imp) cold water
2.73 kg (6 lb) light honey or clover honey
1 teaspoon citric acid
1 teaspoon pectic enzyme
1 teaspoon malic acid
1 teaspoon tartaric acid
3 teaspoons yeast nutrient
1 tablet thiamine (vitamin B1)
1 tablet ascorbic acid (vitamin C)
1 sachet Côte des blanc wine yeast
5 Campden tablets
2 teaspoons potassium sorbate

Method
Sterilise and sanitise a food-grade plastic bucket inside and out, then add 5.50 litres (1.2 gal Imp) of cold water and cover with a clean cloth. Add the honey and stir using a sterilised stainless steel

mixing spoon to dissolve the honey. Add two crushed Campden tablets and stir in thoroughly until fully dissolved. Cover with a clean cloth. Place the must in a warm place and stir it periodically with the sterilised spoon.

Day 2

Prepare a starter bottle: froth indicates that it is working and is ready for adding to the must.

Give the must a vigorous stir with the sterilised spoon to remove all traces of the sterilising Campden tablet. Leave for a minute and stir once more to add further oxygen. Add the citric, malic and tartaric acids, the yeast nutrient, crushed vitamin B1 and vitamin C tablets and, finally, the pectic enzyme. Stir thoroughly to ensure all the ingredients have been thoroughly integrated. Stir vigorously to add oxygen. Make up the must with the remaining water. Take a reading of the must's SG and record it. It should be around 1.100. If it is higher, you will need to dilute the must by adding cold boiled water until the SG reads around 1.100. Conversely, a lower reading requires honey to be added. Use the starter bottle to add the contents to the must, stirring slowly but deliberately. Cover the must and place it in a warm room to allow the yeast to start working. The time before the must can be seen to be working depends on the type of yeast used, the honey used, the correct additions of acids and nutrients, and the ambient temperature where the fermenting vessel is located. The yeast will generally be seen to be working from about 24 hours onwards.

Day 4 onwards

Transfer the must to a 25-litre (5.5 gal Imp) carboy and top up with cold boiled water to 25 mm (1 in) of the top. Fit an airlock and allow fermentation to proceed for three weeks. Check the SG and record it. If a dry melomel is required, there is no need to check the SG, just allow the must to complete to dryness.

Should you require a sweet melomel, the SG needs to be 1.010 to 1.015. If the SG of the must falls in this range, it is time to stop the fermentation.

Different colours of starbright bulk mead – labelled and ready for bottling
[Michael Badger]

Lift the full carboy carefully to a raised work surface. Avoid disturbing the sediment at the bottom. Leave for a day to allow the sediment to stabilise.

Rack the contents into a new carboy carefully, again avoiding disturbing the sediment. When the transfer is complete, add two crushed Campden tablets and two level teaspoons of potassium sorbate. Fit an airlock containing glycerine. Place the carboy in a cool space and encapsulate it in black polythene.

After 56 days, check the must. Take a note of the SG. If this has dropped to near 1.010 because of previous rackings, all is well. Should it be nearing the lower limit, take two dessertspoons of honey and dilute them in the added water (while still hot, as it dissolves better) before topping up.

Rack once more, adding one crushed Campden tablet after racking. Top up to 15 mm of the fermentation bung with cold boiled water.

After 12 months, bottle. This mead will be ready to drink by its second year.

Peach Melomel (Sweet)

Ingredients

1.80 kg (4 lb) ripe peaches	Pectolase
1.36 kg (3 lb) light or medium honey	Rohamet P
	1 tablet thiamine (vitamin B1)
½ can white grape concentrate	1 tablet ascorbic acid
¼ teaspoon grape tannin	(vitamin C)
1 teaspoon yeast nutrient	Sachet Sauternes yeast
1 teaspoon citric acid	Water to make to the gallon
1 teaspoon tartaric acid	Campden tablets
¼ teaspoon malic acid	Potassium sorbate

Method

1. Carefully remove the stones and quarter the peaches.
2. Place them into a large fermentation bucket and cover with five pints of cold water.
3. Add 454 g (1 lb) of the honey plus the grape concentrate, citric acid, grape tannin, yeast nutrient, crushed vitamin B1 and C tablets, pectolase and Rohamet P (as per the manufacturer's instructions). Stir well to mix the ingredients and add one crushed Campden tablet. Cover with a clean cloth.
4. After 48 hours, prepare a starter bottle using the Sauternes yeast. When it is working, add the contents to the must and stir in well.
5. Allow the must to ferment on the pulp for five days, stirring twice daily.
6. Strain the contents through a jelly bag and put the must into a demijohn. Top up with cold boiled water to within 20 mm (¾ in) of the fitted airlock and bung. Place in a warm position.
7. Check the specific gravity. If it is below 1.010, add 115 g (4 oz) of honey by stirring it into a small amount of the must before adding to the bulk.

8. Check the SG when the bubbles from the fermentation lock slow down to a trickle. If the reading is below 1.010, add a further 115 g (4 oz) of honey, as above.
9. Continue to add honey, as above, until fermentation stops. The SG should be in the range 1.010-1.020.
10. When fermentation has stopped at the required SG, rack into a clean demijohn. Add one crushed Campden tablet and top up with cold boiled water to within 15 mm (½ in) of the fermentation bung.
11. Rack again when a significant amount of sediment is visible at the base of the demijohn.

After 12 months, bottle: this sweet melomel is an ideal social wine which is best left to mature for at least two years.

Redcurrant Melomel

Ingredients

1.3 kg (3 lb) redcurrants	1 tablet ascorbic acid
1.36 kg (3 lb) light or medium	(vitamin C)
honey	1 sachet Bordeaux yeast
½ can white grape concentrate	Water to make to the gallon
1 teaspoon yeast nutrient	Settled mains cold water to
1 teaspoon tartaric acid	disperse chlorine
Pectolase	Campden tablets
Rohamet P	Potassium sorbate
1 tablet thiamine (vitamin B1)	

Method

Day 1

The fruit needs to be ripe and of good quality. Remove stalks from the fruit as stalk remains will impoverish the wine.

Place the fruit into a fermentation bin, add six pints of water, and mash the fruit. Add one crushed Campden tablet and the pectolase. Cover the bin and put in a warm place. Stir occasionally.

Day 2
1. Make up the starter bottle with the yeast.
2. Add the grape concentrate, yeast nutrient, crushed vitamin tablets, 900 g (2 lb) of honey and stir well to dissolve the honey.
3. Add the yeast starter and ferment upon the pulp for five days, stirring twice per day.

Day 7
4. Strain the contents through a jelly bag, collecting the must into a one-gallon demijohn, stirring well. Add the remaining honey and stir well.
5. Top up the liquid with tepid boiled water. Add an airlock.
6. Ferment to dryness. If a sweet wine is preferred, add extra honey as described previously.

Blackcurrant Melomel (Sweet)

Ingredients

1.36 kg (3 lb) blackcurrants
1.36 kg (3 lb) light or medium honey
0.45 kg (1 lb) very ripe bananas
½ can red grape concentrate
1 teaspoon citric acid
1 teaspoon tartaric acid
1 teaspoon yeast nutrient
Pectolase

Rohamet P
1 tablet thiamine (vitamin B1)
1 tablet ascorbic acid (vitamin C)
¼ teaspoon grape tannin
1 sachet Bordeaux yeast
Water to make to the gallon
Campden tablets
Potassium sorbate

Method

Day 1
1. The fruit needs to be ripe and of good quality.
2. Place the fruit into a fermentation bin, adding five pints of water. Add the chopped banana pieces and mashed fruit. Add one crushed Campden tablet, the pectolase and

Rohamet P. Cover the bin and place in a warm place. Stir occasionally for two days.

Day 3
3. Prepare the starter bottle with the yeast.
4. Mix the yeast nutrient, grape tannin, crushed vitamin tablets and citric acid as dry matter to ensure the grape tannin is incorporated. Add this mixture, 454 g (1 lb) of honey and the grape concentrate to the must, stirring well.
5. Add the contents of the starter bottle.
6. Cover the fermentation vessel with a clean cloth and ferment on the pulp for three days.

Day 7
7. Strain the contents through a jelly bag and add the liquid to a demijohn.
8. Add 454 g (1 lb) of honey and stir well. Top up with tepid boiled water, fit an airlock and place in a warm place.
9. Adjust the specific gravity until it reaches 1.005 by adding 110 g (4 oz) of honey at a time to the must by adding small, drip-feed amounts over a number of days.
10. Repeat this procedure until all this remaining honey is used or fermentation ceases.
11. When fermentation has stopped, rack into another demijohn, add one crushed Campden tablet and one level teaspoon of potassium sorbate. Top up with boiled cold water and store in a cool place.
12. Rack again when lees is seen at the base of the demijohn. Envelope the demijohn with black plastic.

Bottle: sweet blackcurrant melomel needs three to four years to mature.

Raspberry Melomel

It is essential that only *dry*, good-quality raspberries are used for this recipe.

Ingredients

1.36 kg (3 lb) raspberries
1.36 kg (3 lb) light or medium
   honey
0.45 kg (1 lb) very ripe
   bananas
½ can white grape concentrate
1 teaspoon citric acid
1 teaspoon tartaric acid
1 teaspoon yeast nutrient
Pectolase

Rohamet P
1 tablet thiamine (vitamin B1)
1 tablet ascorbic acid (
   vitamin C)
¼ teaspoon grape tannin
1 sachet Sauternes yeast
Water to make to the gallon
Campden tablets
Potassium sorbate

Method
Follow the method given for blackcurrant melomel and allow for maturity of 30 months to three years.

Damson Melomel (Dry)

It is essential to use only *dry*, good-quality damsons for this recipe.

Ingredients

1.81 kg (4 lb) damsons
1.81 kg (4 lb) light or medium
   honey
½ can red grape concentrate
2 teaspoons citric acid
1 teaspoon tartaric acid
1 teaspoon yeast nutrient
Pectolase
Rohamet P

1 tablet thiamine (vitamin B1)
1 tablet ascorbic acid
   (vitamin C)
¼ teaspoon grape tannin
1 sachet Burgundy or
   Bordeaux yeast
Water to make to the gallon
Campden tablets
Potassium sorbate

Method

Day 1

1. The fruit needs to be ripe, firm and of good quality. Remove the stalks. Place the fruit into a fermentation bin and add six pints of boiling water.
2. When cool, mash the fruit and remove the stones. Mix one crushed Campden tablet, the pectolase, Rohamet P, yeast nutrient, grape tannin, crushed vitamin tablets and citric acid. Add the mixture to the fermentation bin, cover it and place it in a warm place. Stir twice daily.

Day 2

3. Make up a starter bottle. Add the grape concentrate and stir well. Add 0.9 kg (2 lb) of honey and cover with a clean cloth. Leave for seven days in a warm place, stirring daily to break down the fruit.

Day 10

4. Strain the contents through a jelly bag and add the liquid to a demijohn. Add the remaining honey, top up the demijohn with clean boiled water, insert a fermentation lock and ferment to dryness.
5. Rack the liquid into a clean demijohn, adding a crushed Campden tablet and a level teaspoon of potassium sorbate.

To make a sweet damson wine you need an extra 0.45 kg (1 lb) of honey. Follow the procedure up to step (4) above and then:

1. Check the SG. When it has fallen to 1.010, add 110 g (4 oz) of honey. Repeat this process until all the honey is incorporated.
2. Check the SG after the addition of the final amount of honey and when it drops to 1.010, stop the fermentation by racking into another sterilised demijohn, topping up the level to 15 mm (½ in) of the fermentation lock. Add two crushed

    Campden tablets and one level teaspoon of potassium sorbate.
3. Rack the wine as sediment appears, adding a crushed Campden tablet at each racking and topping up with plain cold boiled water.

Bottle: sweet damson melomel mead needs to be kept at least 30 months and up to three years in a cool place with the demijohn covered in black plastic to help retain the colour.

Gooseberry Melomel (Dry)

For this recipe, it is essential to use only the green variety of gooseberry, and when they are nearing ripeness.

Ingredients

1.36 kg (3 lb) gooseberries	1 ascorbic acid tablet
1.36 kg (3 lb) light or medium honey	(vitamin C), crushed
½ can white grape concentrate	¼ teaspoon grape tannin
1 teaspoon tartaric acid	1 sachet Chablis yeast
1 teaspoon yeast nutrient	Water to make to the gallon
Pectolase	Campden tablets
Rohamet P	Potassium sorbate
1 thiamine tablet (vitamin B1), crushed	

Method

Day 1
1. The fruit needs to be of good quality, firm and almost ripe. Remove by topping and tailing stalks from the fruit. Place the fruit into a fermentation bin, adding six pints of boiling water.
2. When cool, crush the fruit and add the pectolase, Rohamet P and one crushed Campden tablet. Stir well.

Day 2

3. Make up a starter bottle with the yeast. Mix the grape concentrate, yeast nutrient, grape tannin and crushed vitamin tablets, and add to the must. Add 0.9 kg (2 lb) of the honey to the must and stir well to dissolve. Add the yeast starter and stir it into the must. Ferment on the pulp for five days, stirring twice daily.

Day 7

4. Strain the contents through a jelly bag into a clean demijohn. Add the final amount of honey, topping up the jar with tepid boiled water. Add a fermentation lock and ferment to dryness.

Bottle: allow three years to reach maturity.

Gooseberry Melomel (Sweet)

The ingredients are the same as for the dry gooseberry melomel, with one additional teaspoon of tartaric acid. Add 0.45 kg (1 lb) honey extra to the fermenting must. This is added in increments as described in other recipes. A Chablis yeast is suggested.

Bottle: allow at least three years to mature.

Fresh Apricot Melomel

The ingredients and method are exactly as described for peach melomel, substituting apricots for peaches, and amending the recipes for sweet or dry wine.

Apricot Melomel Using Dried Fruit

Ingredients

0.45 kg (1 lb) good-quality
  dried apricots
0.45 kg (1 lb) very ripe
  bananas
1.36 kg (3 lb) light or medium
  honey
½ can white grape concentrate
2 teaspoons citric acid
1 teaspoon tartaric acid
1 teaspoon yeast nutrient

Pectolase
Rohamet P
1 tablet thiamine (vitamin B1)
1 tablet ascorbic acid
  (vitamin C)
¼ teaspoon grape tannin
1 sachet general-purpose yeast
Water to make to the gallon
Campden tablets
Potassium sorbate

Method

Day 1

1. Cut the apricots into small pieces and soak them in 2.3 litres (4 pints Imp) of water overnight.

Day 2

2. Simmer the apricots for five minutes in the water, allow to cool. Transfer to a fermentation bin, add the bananas by mashing into small pieces. Mix pectolase, Rohamet P, grape concentrate, yeast nutrient, citric acid, grape tannin and the crushed vitamin tablets, and add to the must. Stir well, keeping warm, and cover with a clean cloth.

Day 3

3. Activate a starter bottle. Add its contents and 0.9 kg (2 lb) of honey to the must and stir well. Ferment on the pulp for seven days, stirring daily to break up the apricots.

Day 10

Strain the contents of the fermentation bin through a jelly bag into a demijohn. Add the remaining honey and ferment to dryness, all as described for other recipes.

To make a sweet apricot melomel, you need another 0.45 kg (1 lb) of honey. Follow the method above up to stage (4), then:

1. Check the SG. When it has fallen to 1.010, add 110 g (4 oz) of honey in stages, repeating the process until all the honey is incorporated.
2. Check the SG after the addition of the final amount of honey: when the SG drops to 1.010, rack into another sterilised demijohn, topping up the level to 15 mm (½ in) of the fermentation lock. Add two crushed Campden tablets and one level teaspoon of potassium sorbate.
3. Further rack the wine as sediment appears, adding a crushed Campden tablet at each racking and topping up with plain cold boiled water.

Bottle: sweet apricot melomel mead needs to be kept at least 30 months and up to three years in a cool place.

CYSER

Cyser is mead made from apples, or pure apple juice, and honey. The honey is used to sweeten the apple juice to the desired specific gravity, which should be finished to about 1.000. Very often it is difficult to determine the amount of honey required because of the variability in the initial specific gravity of available apple juices. Cyser mead is generally finished as medium-to-dry, with an alcohol content of 13-14 per cent. Mead makers who have their own apples will use the fruit for the must. Three recipes are given.

Cyser (One)

Ingredients

2.25 litres (4 pints Imp) pure apple juice (not concentrate)
1.1 kg (2½ lb) light or medium honey
½ can white grape concentrate
½ teaspoon citric acid
Pectolase
¼ teaspoon grape tannin
1 teaspoon citric acid

1 teaspoon yeast nutrient
1 tablet thiamine (vitamin B1)
1 tablet ascorbic acid (vitamin C)
1 sachet Chablis-type yeast
Water to make up to 1 gallon (Imp)
Campden tablets
Potassium sorbate

Method
1. Pasteurise all the apple juice and add water to about ¾ gallon.
2. Prepare a starter bottle using the Chablis yeast.
3. Heat the contents to a maximum of 55 °C (130 °F) and hold them at this temperature for a maximum of five minutes.
4. Mix all the ingredients into the must and stir until all are fully dissolved. Allow to cool and transfer to a sterilised fermentation bin.
5. When the must reaches 21 °C (70 °F), add the contents of the starter bottle to the must.

6. Stir the must for 30 seconds and place the fermentation vessel in a warm room.

7. Once the primary fermentation is over (it is usually very vigorous), strain and pour the contents into a demijohn. Top up with tepid boiled water to within 15 mm (½ in) of the fermentation lock.

8. Ferment to dryness and, when complete, rack into another sterilised demijohn. Add one Campden tablet and one teaspoon of potassium sorbate: top up to 10 mm (3 in) of the fermentation lock. Place the demijohn in a warm place.

9. Rack into another sterilised demijohn when an appreciable amount of sediment (lees) is present, usually after three months. Top up with tepid boiled water. Add one Campden tablet. Remove the demijohn to a cool place. Further rackings may be necessary.

Bottle: The cyser should be suitable for drinking within 15 months.

Cyser (Two)

Ingredients

4.5 kg (10 lb) mixture of dessert and cooking apples
1.36 kg (3 lb) light or medium honey
½ can white grape concentrate
¼ teaspoon citric acid
Pectolase
Rohamet P
1 teaspoon yeast nutrient

1 tablet thiamine (vitamin B1)
1 tablet ascorbic acid (vitamin C)
1 sachet Chablis yeast
Water to make up to one gallon (Imp)
Campden tablet
Potassium sorbate

Method

The apples used should be ripe and clean. The advantage of using fresh apples instead of apple juice is the natural presence of tannin in the skins and seeds. Use a fruit press or juice extractor to obtain 3.4 litres (6 pints UK or 0.900 gal US). Set aside the remaining apples for the next stage.

1. Pasteurise the apple juice and 900g (2 lb) of honey.
2. Heat the contents to a maximum of 55 °C (130 °F) and hold at this temperature for a maximum of five minutes.
3. Allow to cool and transfer to a fermentation vessel.
4. Stir the must for 30 seconds. Place it in a fermentation bin in a warm room.
5. Add four pints of cold water to the fermentation bin together with the citric acid, one crushed Campden tablet, pectolase and Rohamet P.
6. Wash and clean the remaining apples, removing any bad or bruised parts. Immediately cut the apples into small, bite-sized segments and place them into the fermentation bin to avoid discolouration. Cover and place in a warm room for 24 hours.
7. The next day, prepare a starter bottle using the Chablis yeast. Stir the grape concentrate, the remaining honey, yeast nutrient, crushed vitamin tablets and citric acid into the must.
8. Add the starter bottle to the must. Stir well and cover the fermentation bin. Place it in a warm room and ferment on the pulp for at least seven days, stirring daily to break up the apples.
9. Strain the pulp through a jelly bag and transfer the liquor to a demijohn. Add a fermentation lock and ferment to dryness.
10. Store in a cool place to aid clearing. Rack as the cyser clears and allow it to mature for two years. At each racking, top up with cold boiled water.

Cyser (Three)

My colleague and mead enthusiast, Erica Osborn, produced a recipe for quick mead production and, best of all, it is perfectly drinkable within four to six months.

Ingredients

1½ litres water
1 litre apple juice (not concentrate)
1 litre elderflower juice (not concentrate)
¼ teaspoon (maximum) Epsom salts
4 teaspoons tannin or strong, cold tea (not scented)
½ teaspoon bentonite
1 rounded teaspoon yeast nutrient
3 teaspoons tartaric acid

1 teaspoon citric acid
¼ teaspoon Marmite
2 tablets thiamine (vitamin B1)
2 tablets ascorbic acid (vitamin C)
3½ lb best-quality honey (not heather or oilseed rape)
1 packet of general-purpose yeast for cider (Gervin GV13 Dark Green Label)
Campden tablets
Potassium sorbate

Method

1. Place the water, apple juice and elderflower juice into stainless steel pans and heat to an absolute maximum of 55 °C (130 °F) for three minutes.
2. When the must is warming up, add the honey and stir constantly with a sterilised stirring spoon until dissolved. Pasteurise at this temperature for a maximum of three minutes, skimming off the froth as much as possible. Cool to 21 °C (70 °F), then place in a demijohn. Add the remaining chemicals except the yeast and bentonite. Dissolve by shaking at least twice for 30 seconds each time.
3. When cooled, take a sample into a sterilised trial jar to establish the must's opening gravity (OG) with a hydrometer and record it.
4. Add bentonite and stir vigorously for 30 seconds.
5. When it has settled and froth is minimal, sprinkle yeast on the surface of the must. Add a fermentation lock and bung

and then leave well alone. Put the demijohn in a warm room and allow the must to work out.

6. Once the primary fermentation is complete, add cold boiled water to about 15 mm (½ in) from the underside of the fermentation bung.

7. When bubbles from the air trap slow down, check the SG to the desired 1.010. Stop fermentation by racking off into another sterilised demijohn. Add two Campden tablets.

8. Top up the demijohn with cold boiled water to within 15 mm (½ in) of the airlock. Place it in a cold place to clear: setting it down on a concrete surface is ideal. Rack again when sediment (lees) appears and the mead is clearing: rack as described previously, adding a Campden tablet.

After four months, bottle and store on its side. Identify the contents. It is generally drinkable after six months. Serve chilled after refrigerating for 24 hours.

HIPPOCRAS

Hippocras is pyment mead to which spices and herbs have been added. It is believed to originate with the famous Greek physician, Hippocrates (circa 460-357 BC).

Method
1. Prepare pyment mead as described earlier.
2. When fermentation is complete, rack into a clean demijohn.
3. Make up a small muslin bag to hold the spices and herbs. Secure the bag so that none of the contents can escape into the pyment.
4. Suspend the bag in the pyment on a piece of strong thread and seal the demijohn.
5. Sample the pyment at the third day onwards.
6. Remove the muslin bag once a satisfactory flavour has been achieved.

Only very small amounts of spices and herbs are required to flavour the hippocras. They are to be used sparingly when immersed into the must.

METHEGLIN

Metheglin is mead that is made with spices only and can be regarded as hippocras without herbs. It is produced as either dry or sweet. This pyment is ideal if made with orange blossom honey. An easy recipe to follow is vanilla metheglin. Only one type of spice is needed: two Mexican or Bourbon vanilla beans.

Method
1. Prepare pyment mead as described earlier.
2. When fermentation is complete, rack into a clean, sterilised demijohn and top up to 15 mm (½ in) of the fermentation lock.
3. Cut the vanilla pods lengthways to expose the seeds. Add to the mead.
4. Leave the vanilla pods in the liquor for about three months to allow the mellow vanilla flavour to infuse the mead. Taste the mead each month to ensure that the spice does not become overpowering and impair the pyment.
5. When ready, remove the vanilla pods carefully.
6. Bottle.

COUNTRY MEAD AND HONEY WINES

Mead producers are adept at making variations of mead and honey wines. The recipes are often a concoction of flowers or fruits with additives made up by the vintner. In essence, any of the majority of flowers and fruits can be put to good use for such liquors. It is a question of trying, analysing the finished product and, through detailed records, it is relatively easy to trace both good and bad points of such wines.

Elderflower Honey Wine

The white or whitish-yellow flowers of the elderflower are pleasantly fragrant and impart a Muscat-like flavour to the mead. Elderflower honey wine is an acquired taste and not appreciated by everyone. It is a very nice barbeque drink on warm summer evenings. It is essential not to use too many flower heads, otherwise the finished wine will be almost undrinkable. Do not exceed the amount specified for the one-gallon recipe below.

Ingredients

1.25 pint fresh elderflowers
1.36 kg (3 lb) light or medium honey
355 ml (12 oz) white grape concentrate
1 teaspoon citric acid
1 teaspoon tartaric acid
¼ teaspoon malic acid
Pectolase
Rohamet P

1 teaspoon yeast nutrient
1 tablet thiamine (vitamin B1)
1 tablet ascorbic acid (vitamin C)
1 sachet Chablis
1 crushed Campden tablet
Potassium sorbate
Water in addition to make up to one gallon (Imp)

Method

Day 1
Separate the flowers from the stalks and wash them to remove insects and dust. Put the flowers and grape juice concentrate

into the primary fermentation vessel and pour boiling water over them, stirring well. When the temperature of the must falls to 55 °C (130 °F), add the honey, acids, pectolase, Rohamet P and vitamins, and stir well to dissolve them. When the temperature falls to 21 °C (70 °F), add one crushed Campden tablet and stir it into the must. Cover the vessel with a clean cloth. Stir several times over 24 hours.

Day 2

Make up a starter bottle. Add yeast nutrient to the must. Prepare a starter bottle, add it to the must and leave it to ferment on the flowers for six days.

Day 8

Strain the must through a jelly bag and collect the strained must in a demijohn. Top up to within 20 mm (¾ in) of the top. Add a fermentation lock and allow fermentation to proceed to SG 1.005.

At SG 1.005, stop the fermentation by racking into a fresh sterilised demijohn, adding two crushed Campden tablets and a level teaspoon of potassium sorbate. Top up with cold boiled water to 15 mm (½ in) of the fermentation lock bung. Store in a cold place to help the must to clear. Rack again when there is an appreciable amount of sediment visible. Top up with cold boiled water and sweeten to retain an SG of 1.005.

Repeat the racking if further sediment appears. The wine will be ready to drink at about nine months.

Elderberry Mead

Ingredients

1.6 kg (3.5 lb) fresh
  elderberries
1.36 kg (3 lb) light or medium
  honey
355 ml (12 oz) red grape
  concentrate
1 teaspoon citric acid
1 teaspoon tartaric acid
1 teaspoon malic acid
2 small oranges
Pectolase

Rohamet P
1 teaspoon yeast nutrient
1 tablet thiamine (vitamin B1)
1 tablet ascorbic acid
  (vitamin C)
1 sachet Gervin GV1 Green
  Label wine yeast
1 crushed Campden tablet
Potassium sorbate
Water in addition to make up
  to one gallon (Imp)

Method

Day 1

Separate the berries from the stalks and wash them to remove insects and dust. Put the berries and grape juice concentrate in the primary fermentation vessel and pour boiling water over them. Stir well. When the temperature of the must falls to 55 °C (130 °F), add the honey together with the acids, pectolase, Rohamet P and vitamins. Stir well to dissolve. When the temperature falls to 21 °C (70 °F), add one crushed Campden tablet and stir into the must. Cover the vessel with a clean cloth. Stir several times over 24 hours.

Day 2

Make up a starter bottle. Add yeast nutrient to the must. When the starter bottle fermentation is working well, add it to the must and leave to ferment on the berries for six days.

Day 8

1. Strain the must through a jelly bag and collect the liquor in a demijohn. Top up to within 20 mm (¾ in) of the top. Add a fermentation lock and allow fermentation to proceed until the SG is 1.005.

2. At SG 1.005, stop the fermentation by racking into a fresh sterilised demijohn. Add two crushed Campden tablets and a level teaspoon of potassium sorbate. Top up with cold boiled water to 15 mm (½ in) of the fermentation lock bung. Store in a cold place to help the must to clear.
3. Rack again when an appreciable amount of sediment is visible. Top up with cold boiled water and sweeten to retain the SG at 1.005.
4. Repeat the racking if further sediment appears.

Bottle: The wine will be ready to drink at about nine months.

Elderberry Rosé Honey Wine

Retain the pulp from the must used in the elderberry mead.

Ingredients

1.6 kg (3.5 lb) retained pulp
1.36 kg (3 lb) light honey
0.45 kg (1 lb) fully ripe
   bananas
1 handful quality California
   raisins
355 ml (12 oz) white grape
   concentrate
1 teaspoon citric acid
1 teaspoon tartaric acid
1 teaspoon malic acid
2 small oranges

Pectolase
Rohamet P
1 teaspoon yeast nutrient
1 tablet thiamine (vitamin B1)
1 tablet ascorbic acid
   (vitamin C)
1 sachet Burgundy wine yeast
1 crushed Campden tablet
Potassium sorbate
Water in addition to make up
   to one gallon (Imp)

Method

Day 1

1. Place the retained elderberry pulp in a fermentation bin. Add the honey, acids, pectolase, Rohamet P and vitamins, and stir well to dissolve. Carefully slice the bananas into slivers and cut the raisins in half. Add both to the must.

2. Add one crushed Campden tablet and stir it into the must. Cover the vessel with a clean cloth. Stir several times over 24 hours.

Day 2

3. Make up a starter bottle. Add yeast nutrient to the must. When the starter bottle fermentation is working well, add it to the must and leave it to ferment on the pulp for seven days.

Day 11

4. Strain the must through a jelly bag and collect the liquor in a sterilised demijohn. Top it up to within 20 mm (¾ in) of the top. Add a fermentation lock and allow it to ferment to dryness with an SG of 1.000.

At four weeks and beyond

5. If the mead is still working towards the desired SG, leave it for another 21 days and then check its progress. Continue this procedure until the SG measures 1.000. Once the fermentation has worked to dryness, rack it into a fresh sterilised demijohn and add two crushed Campden tablets and a level teaspoon of potassium sorbate. Top up with cold boiled water to 15 mm (½ in) of the fermentation lock bung. Store in a cold place to help the must to clear.
6. Store in a cool place and rack when an appreciable amount of sediment is seen at the base of the demijohn.

Bottle: This mead is drinkable in 18 months. It is not one that improves with ageing.

The Author's Shakespearean Sack Mead

My great-uncles were great producers and imbibers of cider, country wines, beer and meads. This was one of their favourite wines: they produced it in quantity.

Ingredients

1.9 kg (4.25 lb) medium honey (not light or ling heather)

1 small sprig of purple sage herb

1 small sprig of rosemary herb

1 small piece of fennel root

1 small sprig of rue

1 teaspoon of citric acid

¼ teaspoon of tartaric acid

½ teaspoon ascorbic acid (vitamin C)

½ teaspoon of yeast nutrient

1 gallon (Imp) of water

1 sachet White Labs WLP700 Flor yeast (sherry type)

Method

The must can be produced by either the hot or the cold method.

Make up a starter bottle.

Boil the 3.5 ls (6 pints imp) water for three minutes, adding the sage, rosemary, rue and fennel when the water begins to boil. Discard the herb and vegetable additions, save the water by pouring into a sanitised demijohn; allow to cool to 21 °C (70 °F).

Add the acids and nutrient, ensure all fully dissolved and incorporated into the water.

Add 1.6 kg (3½ lb) of the honey to the must, mixing well and achieving an Opening Gravity (OG) of 1.100: add the starter bottle contents, shake the must vigorously to incorporate extra oxygen. Fit fermentation lock. Place in a warm room.

Observe the fermentation. When it slows, check the SG; once it is in the range 1.05-1.09, add a further increment of 115 g (¼ lb) of the remaining honey mixed with cold boiled water to the must. Repeat this procedure once again as the fermentation falls; repeat the process until all the honey is used up.

When the fermentation is complete, rack into a sterilised demijohn, add two crushed Campden tablets plus a level teaspoon of proprietary yeast stabiliser. Rack the wine as the wine clears and there is an appreciable amount of lees visible; this can be exercised several times, topping up to 15 mm (½ inch) of the fermentation bung. After 12 months, bottle.

This mead wine will need three to four years to achieve a good flavour: being a heavy sack mead, it will age and improve up to and over ten years. This will be strong mead that is far from being a session drinking wine, so beware.

Sack Mead with Hops

Ingredients

1.8 kg (4 lb) medium honey or ling heather or a heather blend

7 g (¼ oz) good-quality hops

226 g (8 oz) chopped and pared good-quality sultanas

½ teaspoon of citric acid

¼ teaspoon of tartaric acid

½ teaspoon ascorbic acid (vitamin C)

1 teaspoon of yeast nutrient

1 gallon (1mp) of water

1 sachet White Labs WLP700 Flor yeast (sherry type)

Method

Boil up the hops as described in Hops and Their Use for Meads and Honey Wines (page 67). Add further cold boiled water to replenish the water evaporated when boiling the hops.

The must can be produced by either the hot or the cold method.

Make up a starter bottle.

Add 3.5 litres (6 pints Imp) water into a pan, adding 1.35 kg (3 lb) of the honey and warm to assist the honey to be incorporated into the water, add the sultanas, acids and yeast nutrient, and allow to cool to 21 °C (70 °F); add the starter bottle contents, shake the must vigorously to incorporate extra oxygen. Add to a sterilised demijohn. Fit fermentation lock. Place in a warm room.

After 5 days remove the sultanas from the must.

Repeat the remaining procedure as in "Author's Shakespearean Sack Mead Recipe".

[**Note**] This mead is a melomel type, due to the use of sultanas and hops: be aware that it should not be entered into straight mead classes of the large specialist honey shows.

The hops flavour will be identifiable notifiable when the mead is fresh, but over time will abate to nothing once the mead has reached maturity. The addition of hops acts as a preservative, giving a much-deserved partial acerbity to the mead as described in Hops and Their Use for Meads and Honey Wines (page 67).

Parsnip Mead

Ingredients

1.8 kg (4 lb) medium honey or ling heather or a heather blend

1.8 kg (4 lb) small young parsnips – avoid older parsnips as they are woody

1 heaped teaspoon of grape tannin or three tablespoons of cold, unscented tea

½ teaspoon of citric acid

¼ teaspoon of tartaric acid

½ teaspoon ascorbic acid (vitamin C)

1 teaspoon of yeast nutrient

1 gallon (1mp) of water

1 sachet White Labs WLP700 Flor yeast (sherry type)

Method

The must can be produced by either the hot or the cold method. Make up a starter bottle.

Scrub and wash the parsnips, cutting them into four pieces as for the table. Bring to boil in one gallon of water: parboil until they can be pierced by a knife and no longer, otherwise the wine will be difficult to clear. Strain the liquid into another sterilised vessel. (The discarded parsnips can be used for a main dinner course by baking in the oven until golden brown, firstly seasoning with coarse sea salt, ground pepper and butter.)

Make up the strained liquor to one gallon with cold boiled water and add to a sterilised demijohn. Warm two pints of the liquid, adding 1.35 kg (3 lb) of the honey and warm to assist the honey to be incorporated into the water, add the acids and yeast nutrient, and allow to cool to 21 °C (70 °F); add the starter bottle contents, shake the must vigorously to incorporate extra oxygen. Fit fermentation lock. Place in a warm room.

Repeat the remaining procedure as in "Author's Shakespearean Sack Mead Recipe".

This mead is known to improve dramatically if stored in a French oak cask for about eighteen months; then bottle.

Strawberry Melomel (Sweet)

Ingredients
2.75 kg (6 lb) top-grade ripe strawberries
1.8 kg (4 lb) medium honey
½ teaspoon of citric acid
¼ teaspoon of tartaric acid
½ teaspoon ascorbic acid (vitamin C)
1 teaspoon of yeast nutrient

1 gallon (Imp) of water
115 g (4 oz) red grape concentrate
GV 2 – Red Label – *Saccharomyces cerevisiae*-type yeast for blush-type wines

Method
Make up a starter bottle.

Remove unripe, damaged strawberries, remove stalks: place in a sterilised fermentation vessel and crush into a pulp; add 2.85 litres (5 pints) of cold water; add one crushed Campden tablet to the must. Stir several times over the next 24 hours.

Add 1.35 kg (3 lb) of the honey and warm to assist the honey to be incorporated into the water, add the grape concentrate, acids and yeast nutrient, and allow to cool to 21 °C (70 °F); add the starter bottle contents, shake the must vigorously to incorporate extra oxygen.

Allow two days of active fermentation on the strawberry pulp, stir twice daily. Press the must and the pulp through a jelly bag into a sterilised demijohn, top up to the gallon with cold boiled water. Fit fermentation lock. Place in a warm room.

Repeat the remaining procedure as in "Author's Shakespearean Sack Mead Recipe".

Cowslip Mead

Note that Cowslip is a protected plant in Great Britain.

Ingredients

Fill a one-gallon container with cowslip flowers
1.6 kg (3½ lb) light honey
14¼ g (½ oz) citric acid
1 heaped teaspoon of grape tannin or three tablespoons of cold, unscented tea

¼ teaspoon of tartaric acid
½ teaspoon ascorbic acid (vitamin C)
1 teaspoon of yeast nutrient
1 gallon (Imp) of water
Vierka Tokay yeast

Method

The must can be produced by either the hot or the cold method.

Carefully remove yellow florets from the calyx.

Make up a starter bottle.

Warm 1.7 litres (3 pints) of water, add to a sterilised vessel, adding the honey, warm to assist the honey to be incorporated into the water, add a further three pints of water, add the acids, tannin and yeast nutrient, allow to cool to 21 °C (70 °F); add the starter bottle contents, shake the must vigorously to incorporate extra oxygen. Decant into a demijohn. Fit fermentation lock. Place in a warm room.

Once the fermentation is thoroughly active, add the cowslip florets, and after three days press out the florets in the must; strain and decant into a sterilised demijohn; fit airlock and allow fermentation to fall to 1.005; add remaining honey by dissolving within a sample of the fermenting liquor; add to the must; allow fermentation to work until fermentation is completed.

Rack once appreciable sediment is seen and further rack until clear, topping up with cold boiled water after each racking procedure.

Bottle when clear; store in a cool, vibration-free space.

Rose Petal Mead

Ingredients

2 quarts of fresh red rose petals (loosely packed) approximately 66 g (2¼ oz). White and yellow petals make an inferior mead.

1.6 kg (3½ lb) light honey

14¼ g (½ oz) citric acid

1 heaped teaspoon of grape tannin or three tablespoons of cold, unscented tea

¼ teaspoon of tartaric acid

½ teaspoon ascorbic acid (vitamin C)

1 teaspoon of yeast nutrient

115 g (4 oz) red grape concentrate

1 gallon (Imp) of water

Burgundy-style yeast: Lalvin RC212 or Gervin No. 2 – Red Label yeast

Method

The must can be produced by either the hot or the cold method.

Make up a starter bottle.

Place the petals into a sterilised fermentation bin; pour one gallon of boiling water over the petals. Cover and leave the petals to infuse for twenty-four hours. Press out the petals and remove from the liquor by straining into a sterilised vessel. Warm 1.7 litres (3 pints) of water, add to the sterilised vessel, adding the honey, warm to assist the honey to be incorporated into the water, add a further three pints of water, add the acids, tannin and yeast nutrient, allow to cool to 21 °C (70 °F); add the starter bottle contents, shake the must vigorously to incorporate extra oxygen. Decant to a demijohn. Fit fermentation lock. Place in a warm room, allow the fermentation to fall to 1.005, add remaining honey by dissolving within a sample of the fermenting liquor; add to the must, allow fermentation to work until fermentation is completed.

Rack once appreciable sediment is seen and further rack until clear, topping up with cold boiled water after each racking procedure.

Bottle when clear, consume when fresh: it has a short shelf life, it deteriorates after two years.

HONEY VINEGAR

There is no real mystery about making honey vinegar other than that any mead can readily be turned into vinegar, whether by choice or design. The simplest method is to take a bottle of either dry or sweet mead and remove the stopper. Place the bottle, exposed to the atmosphere, in a warm conservatory or greenhouse to allow vinegar flies access. After eight to ten weeks, the mead should have been "turned". Strain the contents into a clean bottle and seal it from the atmosphere.

My mother regularly made mead vinegar. She had a constant supply of mother of vinegar, produced by mixing a small amount of cheap cooking sherry with vinegar. It was added to alcohol to ferment it to vinegar. Vinegar is produced by acetic acid bacteria which cause ethanol to ferment. Mother of vinegar is composed of cellulose and acetic acid bacteria. It is added to the ethanol to speed up vinegar production. The finished vinegar is siphoned off into a clean bottles, corked and labelled accordingly to avoid mishaps in use.

The use of a different stopper (coloured top) is recommended as a ready identification and a prompt that the bottle contains vinegar and not wine.

Honey vinegar: note the use of burgundy-type bottle
as an aide-mémoire that the contents are not mead or
honey wine [Michael Badger]

HINTS AND TIPS – AIDE-MÉMOIRE

The adage "not seeing the wood for the trees" oft comes to mind when knowing where to start or commence operations of producing meads and honey wines. Listed below are a number of pointers which might prove useful:

- Draw up a list of your needs and requirements to overcome forgetting essentials from water treatment, ingredients, acids, etc.
- Be alive to airborne wild yeasts, cleanliness, sanitation, disinfecting and cleanliness at all times, more especially in the summer months.
- Be careful in the use of bleaches and chemicals at all times.
- Immediately after racking or decanting wines from vessels ensure that they are cleaned immediately, removing all stains and grime, sanitising and washing and ensure all droplets in containers are removed by storing upside down.
- The importance of keeping detailed records of each and subsequent fermentations: dates, times, temperatures, quantities, ingredients used or added, of acids, yeasts to honeys, opening OG, final SG, finings, stabilisers, bottling, etc.
- Introduce a mechanism of reference for each batch undertaken by using tie-on labels indicating instant criteria with a unique number that is back to back with the detailed records.
- At the beginning of fermentation incorporate plenty of oxygen to assist the budding yeast cells to multiply. Conversely when racking, take care to avoid introducing air and oxygen into the finished must.
- A "stuck fermentation" is when the fermentation that stops well before all the available sugar in the wine has been converted to alcohol and carbon dioxide, and can be attributed to a number of causes: check the airlock and

bung to see both are firmly seated in the fermentation vessel; excess sugar to liquid, commencing with a high SG; use of outdated yeast; too high or low temperature; unclean fermenting vessel; lack of nutrients.

- Pitch the yeast in accord with instructions of the yeast supplier.
- Starting SG should range from 1.09 to 1.1 or lower.
- Rack a completed wine once an appreciable amount of sediment is seen in the fermentation bottle.
- Bottle only fully stabilised wines in sterilised containers.
- Store in cool, vibration-free conditions.

Part Six – Recipes for Meads, Honey Wines and Mead-based Vinegar

PART SEVEN

ADVANCED
MEAD-MAKING TECHNIQUES
AND PRACTICES

OPPOSITE
Dual keg set-up [Wikepedia Commons]

ESSENCES FOR MEADS AND HONEY WINES

A term commonly used in the USA is tinctures, or additions. Using such items needs to be undertaken carefully: adding any commodity to finished mead needs to be both exact and precise, otherwise you will alter the characteristics of the wine to an extent that it cannot be rectified or remedied. Additions are in effect focused solutions of regarded characters essential to increase the well-being of the fermented-out wine. Such additions may be water, mead, substrates of mead, simple additions of alcohol (usually vodka) mixed carefully to a syrup solution of boiled-up honey or sugar cane. These additions are mentioned in depth elsewhere in the text as diverse as fruits to flowers to wood to spices. All manner of concoctions can be included. For competition purposes the question of straight meads should not be forgotten.

The late Andy Andrews used sanitised "Grolsch" glass swing-top bottles, using a thimble of vodka to sanitise the insides of the cleaned vessel before adding the ingredients to it, and, if mead-based, the vessel was filled to within 6 mm (¼ inch) of the stopper to obviate oxidation issues. When adding any substances, care needs to be taken that you do not restart fermentation due to the remaining fermentable sugars within the mead.

For most ingredients to be used, it is recommended to remember that the components added to the make-up vessel will be nominally extracted within days more than weeks for the required characters to be obtained. The obtained substrate, if it is water-based, will need to be stored in a refrigerator to enhance its shelf life, whilst those of distilled spirits need not.

KEGGING SYSTEMS FOR MEAD AND HONEY WINES

The significant advantage of using a kegging system is the certainty that the use of CO_2 will provide a protective barrier eliminating oxygen absorption; thereby the wine is permitted to improve without the issues of oxidisation. On the downside, kegging is so often perceived to be a preserve method for the enthusiastic mead maker rather than the run of the mill vintner. However, if you use mead in quantity it is well worth the time and effort to get it set up. As Ken Schramm says, "it is a blessing well worth the effort and expense".

The Equipment Required

- Cornelius-style soda keg – capacity of either 22.75 litre (5 gal. Imp.) or 12 litre (2.65 gal. Imp)
- CO_2 storage bottle fully charged with CO_2
- CO_2 regulator
- Hoses, connectors, valves for connecting the regulator to the keg, plus dispensing tap or faucet
- Keg maintenance kit comprising extra numbers of replacement rubber "0" rings plus accessory kit if you use the Blichmann Beer Gun system for connection to the kegging equipment

Supplementary Equipment for Kegging Systems

- A hydrometer and test jar for testing residual fermentation of the fermented beverage
- Simple weighing scales (kitchen-type ideal) for use if the liquor needs sweetening
- Wine thief or pipette
- Potassium sorbate to stop re-fermentation that can reoccur when adding sweetening agents to an existing liquor

Top left Kegging Gear Pressure Gauges plus hose
Top right Partially Filled Keg
Bottom left Kegging Gear Pressure Gauges Connected to Co2 Gas Cylinder
Bottom right Leaking Seal to Kegging Unit
[Dan Daugherty, Cidersage, Colorado, USA]

- Sanitiser spray bottle for use around components and checking for leaks
- Auto-syphon kit for transferring contents from fermenter to the storage keg

Kegging Procedure

- Cleaning, sterilisation, sanitation and cleaning
- Assessing the honey sugar content and adjusting if required (Note: 0.57 kg or 1.25 lb honey equivalent compared to cane sugar at 1 lb per gallon)

- Decanting mead from storage vessel to keg vessel
- Set-up of regulator, hoses, connections between keg and CO2 bottle
- Carbonation

Sanitisation, Sterilisation and Cleaning

Much has been discussed elsewhere in the text on the importance of this procedure: it is most important that it is undertaken seriously throughout the set-up operation and beyond.

Assessing the Sugar Content and Adjusting if Required

Little needs to be mentioned other than that now is the time to satisfy yourself that the liquor is of the correct sweetness or, if too sweet, undertake remedial action at this juncture.

Decanting Mead from Storage Vessel to Keg Vessel

In this operation it is essential that the bare minimum of lees is introduced into the keg. The use of a sanitised purpose-made syphon vessel is used for the transfer. The keg should be filled to about 85% capacity to allow "head space" between the liquor and the outlet: this is the area that permits the absorption of gas to the liquor.

Set-up of Regulator, Hoses, Connections Between Keg and CO2 bottle

Once the decanting is complete, secure the keg filling lid correctly, checking that the "0" is not pinched or constrained, otherwise leakage will occur. The regulation equipment instructions need to be read before assembly.

- Connect the delivery hose to the valve on the regulator.
- Attach the main regulator to the CO2 bottle using the provided fibre washers, tighten hand-tight and finish using a monkey wrench. Do not overtighten otherwise you will break the fibre washer, and then leakage will occur.

Kegging Gear all set up [Dan Daugherty, Cidersage, Colorado, USA]

- Connect the pressure hose to the keg, ensuring that all valves are locked-closed. Due to fragility of the metal components you should avoid overtightening connections.

Carbonation Procedure

With the keg lid sealed securely, hoses properly connected (double-check before charging):

- Carefully open the CO_2 bottle regulation valve about half a turn. The bottle pressure gauge is the indicator of the contents of CO_2 in the bottle. A fully charged bottle is about 55 bar (800psi)
- Adjust the delivery gauge to the desired pressure of between 0.7bar (10.15psi) and 1.03 bar (15psi). For still mead the operating pressure can be reduced to 0.55bar (8psi). Increasing the volume of CO_2 for highly sparkling meads will create foam
- Pull up the release valve on the keg for 2 to 3 seconds to release the common air trapped in the head space; slowly replace it with CO_2 to preserve the contents within the keg vessel
- Check all joints with the sanitiser spray for leaks. Either any leaks will be audible for major ones, or air bubbles will disclose minor leaks.

Serving Kegged Mead and Honey Wines

Once the soda keg vessel is fully charged you can serve the liquor directly from the keg or into sterilised bottles using the Blichmann Beer Gun to give carbonated mead straight into the bottle. Enthusiasts of kegging systems usually have additional refrigeration cabinets to store their products – ideal in summer months when it is barbeque time.

Serving Wine from a Corked Wine Bottle

A recent innovation is the Coravin ™ Model Two Wine System, a method of pouring wine from the bottle without removing the cork. The operation is by a purpose-made Wine Needle that ensures an air-tight seal with the use of pure argon gas to protect the wine from oxidation. The device is simplicity in itself.

Coravin ™ Model Two Wine System [with permission]

DISTILLED MEADS

There is a growing trend to add distilled spirit to meads. Port is a dessert wine fortified with the addition of distilled grape spirit (aguardente, a spirit similar to brandy). Portuguese vintners are adept at fortifying port wines through halting fermentation before all the sugar is converted to alcohol. For the mead maker, adding neutral spirits is a real art requiring consummate skill best achieved by experimenting with small volumes of fermenting liquor by firstly measuring out the alcohol spirit to a point reached as to when to stop the fermentation. It is a growing practice carried out by skilled vintners: perhaps it is best left to those who like imbibing such liquors to their mead.

PART EIGHT

FLORAL SPECIES, NECTAR AND HONEY

OPPOSITE
Ling Heather (*Calluna vulgaris*) in full bloom [Brian Nellist]

GENERALLY

The many factors involving the production of honey – from the harvesting of nectar by the foraging worker honeybee, the plants, flowers and trees – are worth considering by the vintner. The constituents of nectar, its transformation to honey, the different sugars, acids, proteins and minerals, plus the physical properties of viscosity, flavour and aroma are of interest, too. Blended honeys and the issues of adulteration need consideration in their procurement due to possibilities of fraudulent use by an unsuspecting mead maker. Nevertheless, the honeybee will forage and seek out other sugary substances and harvest them accordingly, thereby ruining all the good work and effort for the beekeeper.

(The term "bees" refers to all species of foraging bees.)

THE WESTERN HONEYBEE (*APIS MELLIFERA*)

Western honeybee working heather (*Calluna vulgaris*)
[Brian Nellist]

This is the honeybee species we, as mead vintners, are grateful to for providing the finished product, honey, that we use in our mead and honey wines.

A typical honeybee colony consists of the following:

- a laying queen who is fertile and has a lifespan of up to five years
- worker honeybees (foragers) are sterile females. They number from several thousands (over the winter period) to up to 80,000 at the height of the breeding cycle. Their lifespan during the active season is four to five weeks, extending to several months if they are born late in the autumn
- drones are male bees who number several hundred plus in a colony. They are reared from late spring until late July, and discarded once the major honey flows cease.

THE MECHANISMS INVOLVING THE FORAGING HONEYBEE AND NECTAR-YIELDING PLANTS

In layman's terms, a bee visiting a source of nectar will be seen to drift near to the flower head by sensing the odour of the nectar through organs within its antennae. It is attracted by the strength of the nectar, i.e. its sugar concentration, as nectar with a sugar content less than 15 per cent in solution is rarely collected.

Interestingly, the number of flowers visited during one foraging foray to maximise a consignment of nectar varies in relation to the amount of nectar available in any one flower. During the heady days of bee research at ICAR Rothamsted, Harpenden, Hertfordshire, researchers established that the number of visits made by bees to flowers was fairly elastic, varying from 30 to 1,600. The length of a foraging flight might well be just a few minutes or up to three to four hours, depending upon the distance travelled and the ease of access to the forage.

The bee's honey sac (crop), in which the foraging bee carries the nectar, can accommodate up to 100 mg, but the average load is around 40 mg. This means that to collect 454 g (1 lb) requires 2,000 to 24,000 journeys, equating to something like three orbits around the world.

Honey is developed from nectar, a sugary solution harvested by honeybees from the nectaries of flowers. The bee's foraging activity requires her to use some of the collected nectar to fuel the metabolic activity of her flight muscles through the hydrolysis of sucrose to glucose and fructose. The surplus nectar is retained in the bee's honey sac for transportation back to the nest: enzymes are added from specific glands in the bee's head during the return flight to the hive nest, beginning the inversion of the sugars within the nectar. At this point, the nectar has a water content of approximately 80 per cent. At the nest, it is converted to honey for long-term storage and the water content is reduced to 18-20 per cent.

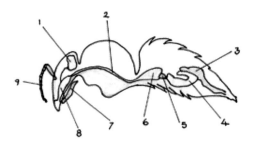

Sketch of bees' honey crop and digestive system [David Lumb]

1. Salivary Glands	4. Ventriculus	7. Proboscis
2. Oesophagus	5. Proventriculus Valve	8. Pharynx
3. Small Intestine	6. Honey Crop	9. Antennae

The shape, aroma and odour of flowers attract the bee to visit the flower head. While it is sucking up nectar, its hairy body becomes dusted with pollen which is then transported from one flower to another to effect pollination. The nectar reward attracts the bee and her visit will ensure that the plant's pollen is transferred to other plants, effecting cross-pollination. Some plants, like Himalayan balsam (*Impatiens glandulifera*), have developed elaborate mechanisms that ensure visiting pollinators are adequately dusted with pollen during their visit.

Beekeepers can tell when their bees are visiting this particular species as they are reminiscent of "Dusty Miller", by getting smothered in dull cream pollen.

THE SIMPLE BIOLOGY OF PLANTS

Flowers are the defining botanical characteristic of angiosperm plants. These form a large group that comprises plants with flowers which produce seeds enclosed within a carpel. They include herbaceous plants, shrubs, grasses and most trees. The flowers are the mechanism for reproduction and spread. These plants dominate our world, illustrating the success of their reproduction strategy. Evolution was at its most creative when

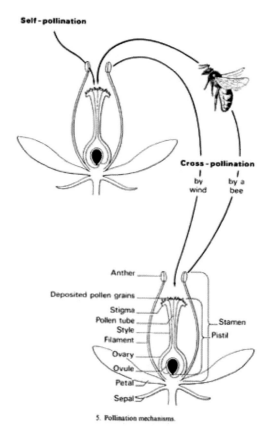

Self-pollination

Cross-pollination

by wind

by a bee

Anther

Deposited pollen grains

Stigma

Pollen tube

Style

Filament

Ovary

Ovule

Petal

Sepal

Stamen

Pistil

5. Pollination mechanisms.

Pollination mechanisms [IBRA with permission]

the first flowers appeared. Clearly the colourful or scented flower evolved in harmony with the evolution of insects. There is general agreement between both botanists and entomologists that flowers and pollinating insects evolved together in a process called 'co-evolution'. It could be argued that the two developed ways and means of helping each other survive and therefore succeeded through a symbiotic relationship embracing mutual co-operation and coordination. One provided the transportation and the other provided food. Another theory is that flowers appeared and insects visited them. Flowers improved, insects improved and an

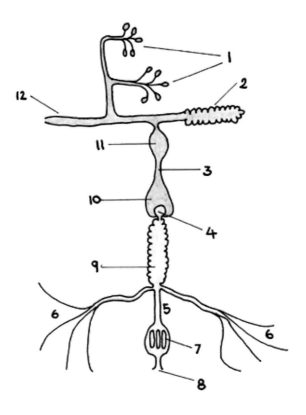

Drawing of honeybee's digestive tract [David Lumb]

1. Salivary glands	4. Proventriculus	tubules	10. Crop
2. Hypopharyngeal	valve and filter	7. Rectum	11. Pharynx
glands	5. Small intestine	8. Anus	12. Proboscis
3. Oesophagus	6. Malpighian	9. Ventriculus	

evolutionary spiral took off. Over many millennia, flowers have developed and produced a great number of inducements to get the various animal species on land and in the air to distribute their pollen and seeds. Flowers need pollinators as much as pollinators need flowers. Although some plants are self-pollinated, others need cross-pollination. The bees themselves are thought to have evolved from wasp-like insects, circa 150 million years ago.

WHAT IS HONEY? – HOW IT IS PRODUCED BY THE WORKER HONEYBEE

The processing of the nectar begins with the addition of enzymes from the salivary and hypopharyngeal glands in the head and thorax. Two pairs of salivary glands, the post-cerebral and thoracic, provide the enzymes for digestion and possibly sucrase (invertase). The hypopharyngeal glands produce sucrase and glucose oxidase which are responsible for starting the inversion of the sucrose in the nectar during its transportation back to the hive. This admixture then passes through the pharynx, the first part of the digestive tract occupying the front central part of the head, into the honey sac.

The bees in the hive nest reduce the water content from 80 per cent to around 20 per cent; the resulting elaborated honey is stored in cells in the honeycomb. It may be as long as 20 minutes until the product reaches storage quality. Nectar left at a high moisture content will attract natural yeasts, causing the sugars to ferment. Hive bees circulate air around the hive which evaporates water from the honey, reducing its moisture content to about 18%. This raises the sugar concentration, thereby preventing fermentation. The bees then cap the comb cells with beeswax to seal them. Beekeepers remove this capping in order to extract the honey using wax cappings for mead making.

SALIVARY GLANDS WITHIN HONEYBEES HEAD

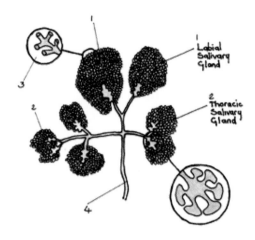

Drawing of salivary and thoracic glands [David Lumb]

1. Labial Salivary Gland   3. Thoracic Salivary Gland

2. Reservoir   4. Common Salivary Duct to Honey Sac

When sealed combs of honey are removed from the beehive by the beekeeper, the honey is extracted into storage containers for future use. Honey is hydroscopic: when stored correctly, bulk-stored honey has a relatively long shelf life and will not ferment if properly sealed from the atmosphere. Honey that is stored over a long period can be affected by both fermentation and an increase in the level of hydroxymethylfurfural (HMF) (see Appendices E and F). Bulk honey must be stored in the correct ambient conditions.

THE CONSTITUENTS OF HONEY

The basic constituents of honey are:

- water
- acids
- proteins
- amino acids
- minerals and other substances

The Nectar

Nectar is made up of a series of compounds, the most important being the disaccharide, sucrose. In addition, there are simple sugars that include fructose and glucose. The exact ratio of sugars varies between floral species, the variation arising because of different soils and environments in which the trees, shrubs and plants grow. Honeys can vary enormously as the soil and environment vary from locality to locality, very often within relatively close proximity, more especially in an urban setting compared with those rural areas of monoculture in the wider farming landscape. The quality of the honeys can also vary between the years through climatic and environmental factors. The mead maker needs to be aware of the nectar's susceptibility to contamination by wild yeasts: these are always present as airborne particles and destined to find a host in which to regenerate. Honeys gathered earlier in the season may be less affected by airborne yeasts, as the concentration of these is known to peak towards the end of summer.

Much of the flavour and aroma of honeys is attributed to colloidal substances. A colloid is a mixture where insoluble microscopic particles are suspended throughout another substance and do not settle out. The suspended particles can result in turbidity, and the resulting cloudiness or haziness is the death knell of a good show mead or honey wine. Honey normally comprises fructose, proteins, other colloidal substances and water. Light honeys may only contain 0.1 per cent of colloidal substances, but cloudy, opaque honeys have around 1 per cent. Colloids are regarded as the compounds that produce honey's distinctive properties. So, just as including the skins, stems and seeds of grapes results in the variations in taste, bouquet, flavour and colour that add to a wine's character, so these colloidal substances contribute to the variations in honey because of the different amounts in plant nectars. Indeed, meads may be enjoyable not because of what is taken out in the early production stages, but because of what is left in the must. Water, with additional dissolved compounds, forms the liquid part of the colloidal substances.

Water, sugar, acids, proteins and minerals are highlighted in the *Guide to the Composition of Honeys by Floral Source* on page 306.

Water

Honey is naturally hygroscopic so the water content varies between honey types. Viscous honeys are generally richer in flavour and aroma, believed to be enhanced by their greater density. Honey with an 18 per cent moisture content by weight has an SG of 1.417, so honey weighs roughly 11 lb 12 oz (5.33 kg) per gallon (UK) (4.55 litres).

Honey contains many complex sugars. The main one is sucrose that is split into its constituent monosaccharides, glucose and fructose. Honeys also contain many other sugars in small amounts. These include the disaccharides maltose, isomaltose, maltulose, turanose and possibly kojibiose. The oligosaccharides present are known to include panose and theanderose.

The Acids

The acids found in honey make up approximately 0.58 per cent by weight. For successful mead making, the mead maker is obliged to know the pH and total acid content of the honey being used and what it is in the must. *The Guide to the Composition of Honeys by Floral Source* (page 305) shows that the pH of honey is variable and can range from 3.84 (white clover) to 6.1 (prune).

The principal acid is gluconic acid produced by enzymatic

action on glucose. Other acids include citric, malic, formic, lactic, pyroglutamic, succinic, acetic, butyric and a number of other amino acids.

Honey by its constitution contains low amounts of these acids, so the mead maker needs to add specific acids to ensure that the finished mead will have the right flavour. Above all, the presence of these acids helps to enhance the keeping qualities of the honey, so essential for a fine wine. Citric and malic acids, present in apples and citrus fruits, are renowned for being tart, but not unduly unpleasant. All these particular acids provide the necessary balance together with taste, aroma and the ultimate keeping quality to the wine.

Other acids present in honey include butyric: its presence leaves an impression of a cheese flavour on the palate. Acetic acid gives an indication of a vinegar taste; liquids with concentrations in excess of 20 per cent are known as vinegar.

There are other non-aromatic organic acids present in the honey which no doubt contribute to its flavour, although they represent less than 0.5 per cent of honey's constituents. However, their presence makes an important contribution to its organoleptic, physical and chemical properties. Approximately 30 non-aromatic organic acids have been identified in honeys, but relatively little attention has been paid to these components in either research or value terms.

The main amino acids found in random in trials of Spanish honeys revealed five different types with a single botanical origin. They include proline, phenylalanine, tyrosine and lysine, followed by arginine, glutamic acid, histidine and valine. They will be present in other honeys, probably in varying proportions. Lavender honeys have been shown to have the highest concentrations of tyrosine, which is one of the primary amino acids in all types of honey.

The Proteins

The proteins present within honey include the enzymes added by the bees during the transformation from raw nectar to the finished honey. The mead maker may also need to add a supplement to the must in the form of nutrients required by the yeast for its division and reproduction.

The Minerals

Honeys can contain an exceptionally wide range of minerals, especially when comparing dark honeys with light ones. Dark honeys commonly have higher mineral contents and higher pH readings, often causing a pronounced strong flavour. Averages for potassium content can be more than eight times higher in a dark honey than in a lighter honey. Sulphur is present in dark honeys, giving them a much higher aroma threshold than lighter honeys. Sodium, a flavour-enhancer, is also present at up to 400 ppm in the darkest of honeys, a level four times higher than that in lighter-coloured honeys.

The mead maker may also need to add a supplement to the must in the form of mineral nutrients required by the yeast in its fermentation stage to enhance division and reproduction.

Minerals found in honeys include potassium, chlorine, manganese, sulphur, sodium and magnesium, and many others in the minutest amounts.

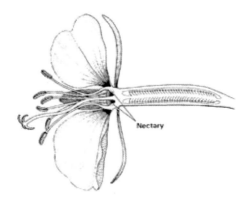

Section through the flower of Rosebay Willowherb or Fireweed
[Copyright the International Bee Research Association (IBRA) –
reproduced with permission]

The Nutritional Value of Honey per 100 g (3.5 oz)

Energy	1,272 kJ (304 kcal)
Carbohydrates	82.4 g
Sugars	82.12 g
Dietary fibre	0.2 g
Fat	0.0 g
Protein	0.3 g
Vitamins	
Riboflavin (B2)	0.038 mg
Niacin (B3)	0.121 mg
Pantothenic acid (B5)	0.068 mg
Pyridoxal-5-phosphate; vitamin (B6)	0.024 mg
Folate B9	2 µg
Vitamin C: ascorbic acid	0.5 mg
Minerals	
Calcium	6 mg
Iron	0.42 mg
Magnesium	2 mg
Phosphorus	4 mg
Potassium	52 mg
Sodium	4 mg
Zinc	0.22 mg
Other Constituents	
Water	17.10 g

Source: USDA National Nutrient Database

[**Note**] The hydroxymethylfurfural (HMF) level is not constant, being increased by temperature and over time. Honey should be stored at the correct temperature in airtight containers to minimise this increase.

FLAVOUR AND AROMA WITHIN HONEYS

Honeys are, in essence, very highly supersaturated sugars, with most honeys crystallising freely. Glucose is much less soluble in water than the other sugars, such as fructose, present in a given sample. It is glucose which routinely crystallises in the majority of honeys so the granulation will be partially controlled by the amount of supersaturated glucose present. Should the proportion of glucose be high, as it is in oilseed rape honey, granulation will be extremely rapid, whereas in a sample of honey from *Robinia* there will be practically none, owing to the high proportion of fructose.

The varying and somewhat complex sweetness offered by the sugars present in honey controls its flavour. Understandably, the exact assortment of these sugars varies considerably depending on the floral source from which the nectar was obtained.

A honey that is in its first stages of crystallisation [Gerald Collins]

Naturally, these variances have a bearing on the honey's flavour, body and taste, producing both favourable (and unfavourable) by-products in the finished wine. Honeys chosen for mead making must therefore be of a high order from the onset. It is accepted that particular honeys impart their own flavours to the finished mead, both good and bad.

Using heather honeys to produce mead (see page 288) often imparts a distinct flavour to the finished wine. It is generally strong, often with a smoky aftertaste, arising from the compounds in the nectar as a result of the subsoil where the heather was grown, which varies from one upland moor to another. Mead from oilseed rape has an unpalatable, cabbage-like flavour the mead maker should avoid at all costs. Types of mead made from honey from the same floral source can differ because of the variances in both mineral and acid contents of that particular honey. All these variances make mead making such fun and so interesting.

THE PHYSICAL AND CHEMICAL PROPERTIES OF HONEY

The physical properties of honey differ, conditional on its water content, its floral source, temperature and, above all, the proportion of the specific sugars it contains. Fresh honey is a supersaturated liquid, containing more sugar than the water present can typically dissolve at ambient temperatures. At room temperature, over time, the glucose in honey will precipitate as solid granules from a solution with fructose and other ingredients.

Phase Changeovers

The melting point of crystallised honey is between 40 °C and 50 °C (104 °F and 122 °F), dependent upon its composition. Below these temperatures, it can be in a metastable state, meaning that it will not crystallise until a "seed honey" is added. Very often, it is saturated with enough sugars to crystallise spontaneously. The rate of crystallisation is affected by many factors, the primary one being the ratio of the main sugars: fructose and glucose. Honeys that are supersaturated with a very high percentage of glucose, such as *Brassica*-sourced honey, will crystallise almost immediately after harvesting, while those with a low glucose percentage, such as sweet chestnut or tupelo honey, do not crystallise. Some types of honey may produce very large but few crystals, while others will produce many small crystals.

Crystallisation is also exaggerated by water content: a high percentage of water will inhibit crystallisation. A high dextrin content will also trigger crystallisation. Temperature also affects the rate of crystallisation, with the fastest rate of growth occurring between 13 °C and 17 °C (55 °F and 63 °F). Crystal nuclei (seeds) tend to form more readily if the honey is disturbed, by stirring, shaking or agitating, rather than left at rest. However, the nucleation of microscopic seed crystals is greatest between 5 °C and 8 °C (41 °F and 46 °F). Therefore, larger but fewer crystals tend to form at higher temperatures, while smaller but more numerous crystals usually form at lower temperatures. Below 5 °C, the honey will not crystallise and, thus the original texture and flavour can be preserved more or less indefinitely.

Viscosity

The viscosity of honey is affected by changes in both temperature and water content. At very low temperatures, honey will not freeze to a solid. Instead, as the temperatures become lower, its viscosity increases, making it thick and sluggish. The higher the water content, the easier honey flows. Above honey's melting point, the water content has little effect on viscosity. Setting aside water content, the composition of honey has little effect on viscosity, with the exception of a few types of honey. At 25 °C (77 °F), honey with 14 per cent water content generally has a viscosity of up to 400 poise, while a honey containing 20 per cent water has a viscosity around 20 poise. Increase in viscosity due to temperature occurs very slowly at first. A honey type containing 16 per cent water will have a viscosity of around 2 poise at 70 °C (158 °F), while at 30 °C (86 °F), the viscosity is around 70 poise. As cooling progresses, honey becomes more viscous at an increasing rate, reaching 600 poise around 14 °C (57 °F). However, while honey is very viscous, it has a rather low surface tension. Only a few types of honey, such as ling heather or manuka, have unusual viscous properties, both displaying thixotropic properties. These honeys enter a gel-like state when motionless, but liquefy when stirred.

Electrical and Optical Properties

Because honey contains electrolytes in the form of acids, minerals and other substances, it exhibits varying degrees of electrical conductivity. Measurements of the electrical conductivity are used to determine the quality of honey in terms of ash content.

The effect honey has on light is useful for determining the type and quality. Variations in the water content alter the refractive index. Water content can easily be measured with a refractometer.

Photograph of refractometer [Michael Badger]

Typically, the refractive index for honey ranges from 1.504 at 13 per cent water content to 1.474 at 25 per cent. Honey also has an effect on polarised light, in that it will rotate the plane of polarisation.

The polarimeter light box with a jar of floral honey being illuminated [Michael Badger]

The fructose gives a negative rotation, while the glucose produces a positive one. The overall rotation can be used to measure the ratio of the mixture of these two sugars. Honey may vary in colour between pale yellow and dark brown, but other bright colours may be found occasionally, depending on the nectar source.

Hygroscopy and Fermentation

Honey has the ability to absorb moisture directly from the air; it is hygroscopic. The amount of water absorbed depends on the relative humidity of the air. Because honey contains natural yeasts, this hygroscopic nature means it has to be stored in sealed containers to prevent fermentation, which usually begins if the water content rises much above 25 per cent (see Appendix D). Honeys tend to absorb more water in this manner than the individual sugars would on their own, which may be due to other ingredients it contains.

Fermentation of honey will usually occur after crystallisation because, without the glucose, the liquid portion of the honey primarily consists of a concentrated mixture of fructose, acids and water, providing the yeast with enough of an increase in the water content for growth. Honey that is to be stored at room temperature for long periods of time is often pasteurised to kill any yeast by heating it above 70 °C (158 °F).

Thermal Characteristics of Honey

Honey, like all sugar compounds, will caramelise if heated appropriately, becoming darker in colour, and finally it will burn. Fructose caramelises at lower temperatures than glucose. The temperature at which caramelisation commences varies, depending on the honey's composition, but is typically between 70 °C and 110 °C (158 °F and 230 °F). The acids in honey act as reagents, reducing the caramelisation temperature even further. The small amounts of amino acids play a vital role in the darkening of honey. They form darkened compounds called melanoidins generated in the late stages of the Maillard reaction between amino acids and reducing sugars that gives browned food its desirable flavour. The Maillard reaction will occur slowly at room temperature, taking from a few to several months to show visible darkening. However, it will speed up dramatically with increasing temperatures. The reaction can also be slowed down significantly by storing the honey at colder temperatures.

Honey has very poor thermal conductivity, taking a long time to reach thermal equilibrium. Melting crystallised honey can easily result in localised caramelisation if the heat source is too hot or if it is not evenly distributed. It will take substantially longer to liquefy when just above the melting point than it will at raised temperatures. Heating up 20 kg of crystallised honey at 40 °C (104 °F) can take up to 24 hours, while 50 kg may take twice as long. These times can be halved by heating at 50 °C (122 °F). It needs to be recognised that important minor substances in honey can be affected significantly by heating, thereby changing the flavour, aroma and other properties. Heating is therefore usually carried out at the lowest temperature possible for the shortest amount of time.

BAKER'S HONEY

The mead maker needs to be aware that bulk supplies of commercial honey, known as baker's honey, are available. This honey is not suitable for mead and honey wine production as it is inferior to beekeepers' honey. Its marketing and sale have special provision in the UK. Where baker's honey and filtered honey are sold in bulk containers, the full product name must appear on both the container and on any accompanying trade documents. Baker's honey must be accompanied by the words "intended for cooking only".

Some processors use other appropriate and accurate descriptions or claims. However, some of these, e.g. organic or those relating to health or nutritional properties, are subject to specific additional rules and requirements.

It is not unknown for producers to add other ingredients to bulk honey. Honey may be mixed with other foodstuffs. However, such products are no longer "specified honey products". In the UK, these foodstuffs are subject to the general food composition and labelling requirements in the Food Labelling Regulations 1996. Any honey used as an ingredient of such a product has to be a specified honey product. Nevertheless, the name used should clearly describe the product to ensure that it cannot be confused with a product with a reserved description. A durability indication is the date up to and including that which the honey can reasonably be expected to retain its specific compositional qualities, if stored properly. (If storage is critical, storage information should be given to the purchaser.)

BLENDED HONEYS

Honeys of mixed origin are often available in bulk or at supermarkets or health shops. In the UK they may well be labelled with all the countries concerned, or this may be replaced with one of the following, as appropriate:

- blend of EU honeys
- blend of non-EU honeys
- blend of EU and non-EU honeys.

ADULTERATION OF HONEY

Those purchasing honey for mead and honey wines need to be aware that adulterated honey is sold in large volumes. Honey adulteration appeared on the world market in the 1970s when high-fructose corn syrup was introduced by industry. The sugars (60.7-77.8 per cent) are the major components of honey and the most dominant are the monosaccharides, fructose and glucose (accounting for 85-95 per cent).

Consumption of honey and honey products has grown considerably over the past few decades. However, at the present time, the traceability of this food is limited to the quality of each processor's documentation. In case of doubt or fraud, there is no standardised analysis available that can discriminate or determine the botanical (floral or vegetable) and geographical (regional or territorial) origin of the honey. Counterfeiting and product adulteration are now commonly practised in the global food marketplace. Honey from the same floral source can also vary because of seasonal climatic variations or different geographic origins. Aside from the definition of honey in the *Codex Alimentarius* (1992), there are additional definitions in the regulations of many countries and the European Union (EU). Various physical types (pressed, centrifuged and drained) and forms (comb, chunk, crystallised or granulated, creamed and heat-processed) of honey are on the market. In 2001, the European Commission (EC) adopted Council Directive 2001/110/EC concerning honey. This Directive lays down common rules relating to honey. Allowable names, product descriptions and definitions are listed together with composition criteria (Appendix C).

The EU is encouraging the development of harmonised analytical methods to permit the verification of compliance with the quality specifications for different types of honeys. Among the compositional criteria prescribed in the existing EU honey directive are requirements relating to sugar content, moisture content, water-insoluble content, electrical conductivity, free acid, diastase activity and HMF (see Appendix C).

Honey is adulterated by the addition of other sugars, syrups or compounds which change its flavour and/or viscosity, make it cheaper to produce, or increase the fructose content in order to stave off crystallisation. The practice was common dating back to ancient times, when crystallised honey was often mixed with flour or other fillers, hiding the adulteration from buyers until the honey was liquefied. In modern times, the most common method of adulteration is the addition of clear, almost flavourless, high-fructose corn syrup which is very difficult to detect. It can be detected by isotope-ratio mass spectrometry at added levels as low as seven per cent.

VARIATIONS IN HONEY TYPES PRODUCED BY THE BEEKEEPER

The beekeeper produces a number of honey types. These include liquid, soft-set, granulated, comb honey and ling heather honey. The beekeeper has not added anything to the honey itself, but presents it in different forms to make it more saleable.

Frame of heather honey: notice the absence of pollen [Brian Nellist]

Liquid Honey

As the name implies, liquid honey is marketed in its liquid form. Such honeys are generally high in fructose.

Variations in colours of honey in light, medium and dark [Gerald Collins]

Left Chunk honey [Michael Young]   *Right* Soft-set honey [Gerald Collins]

Soft-Set Honey

A set honey with a soft texture. The beekeeper controls the rate of granulation through heating the honey and altering its physical characteristics. This honey has the texture of margarine; its colour can be pure white to dark cream.

Granulated Honey

Perfected by the beekeeper who has introduced a "seed honey" at the ratio of around 3 parts to 25 parts, it has been superseded by soft-set honey. Properly seeded granulated honey becomes hard once it is bottled and can be very difficult to remove from the container, whereas soft-set, whilst firm, is easily removed and spread.

Granulated honey [Michael Young]

Comb Honey

Comb honey is prepared in various forms. Cut-comb, as the name implies, is cut to a specific size and placed in a polycarbonate package with a transparent snap-on lid. The use of Ross Rounds™ is gaining much popularity as the bees are apt to fill the section right up to the comb wall with circular pieces of comb built within a plastic container. When drawn and completed, the beekeeper affixes a secure cover.

For section honey, the bees are encouraged to build combs within square basswood section pieces. The beekeeper packages

Top left Plain section of honey using worker-based foundation [Gerald Collins]
Top right Purpose-made comb honey perfected to a heart-shaped design
[Michael Badger]
Bottom left Ross Rounds™ in plastic section cases [Gerald Collins]
Bottom right Ross Rounds™ [Peter Schollick]

285

Cut-comb heather honey packaged for sale [Brian Nellist]

the section piece in a cardboard container. Sections are being superseded by cut-comb and Ross Rounds™.

Because of its thixotropic nature, ling heather honey is produced for bottling by pressing it from the combs. It is also produced as cut-comb, sections or Ross Rounds™.

The mead maker prefers honey provided in bulk or in small containers, rather than comb honey.

LIGHT, MEDIUM AND DARK-COLOURED HONEYS AND LING HEATHER

It is difficult to quantify the generic characteristics of honey owing to the wide variations that exist between honey types; these arise because of the many sources of forage, as well as different soils and environments which affect the plants. The largest component of nectar by far is its water content that can be as much as 80 per cent. It can be as low as 50 per cent, and in some exceptional cases in excess of 90 per cent.

Lighter Honeys
These honeys have a unique but faint bouquet (aroma) and a most delicate taste. Persons with a delicate sense of smell often say such honeys are purely sweet due to the indistinct aroma synonymous with light honeys. Mead made from such honeys is regarded by experienced wine makers as the connoisseur of meads.

Lighter honeys vary in colour from water-white to a colour similar to a good lowland malt whisky. These honeys are from

A pair of matching light honeys [Gerald Collins]

acacia, Himalayan balsam, borage, rosebay willowherb (fireweed) and white clover (Kentish white) and others. They make superb meads, both dry and sweet. Those who like sparkling meads use these honeys for champagne-type meads. Oilseed rape and charlock are light honeys but are not regarded as suitable for mead making because of their cabbage-like taste. Light honeys obtained at the back-end of the honey season are renowned for having a high water content because the bees have not been able to reduce the water content; this may arise through natural decline in the colony population of worker bees.

Medium Honeys

Such honeys are obtained from horse and sweet chestnut, sycamore, maples, lime, field beans, blackberry and many others. They have an idyllic aroma and usually have a good density. Lime

A pair of matching medium honeys [Gerald Collins]

has a minty taste and a green tinge. Blackberry is a honey full of pollen, and it also has a high tannin level. These honeys make excellent dry, sweet and dessert meads.

Darker Honeys

Such honeys make superb dry, sweet and sack dessert meads. These wines usually have high alcohol content, verging on the Sauternes-type wine varieties. Darker honeys often come from ling and bell heather and hawthorn. Proficient mead makers from the North of England and Scotland excel in making dry, sweet and sack mead from heather-based honey. Such meads are known to take up to eight years to mature.

Ling Heather Honey

Of all honeys native to the British Isles, ling heather is unique. It is thixotropic, making it the most viscous of all honeys (other than manuka), and cannot generally be extracted by centrifugal force unless the cell contents are agitated to turn the gel-like honey into a liquid form. This can be extracted using a tangential extractor. The agitation device has spring-loaded rods that are placed into the open cells of the heather comb.

Ling honey (*Calluna vulgaris*) showing its gel-like character and large air bubbles. Note the amber colour: this a near-perfect sample [Brian Nellist]

Ling heather honey is a brilliant, golden amber colour that can vary from reddish/orange to dark amber. Again, the nature of the soil influences its colour and acidity. It imparts a slightly bitter, tangy, pungent, smoky, mildly sweet taste that persists for a long time on the palate. It has a strong, distinctive, woody, warm, floral, fresh fruit aroma reminiscent of heather flowers. These attributes are dependent upon where it is grown. Pure samples crystallise slowly, if at all. Crystallisation of less than pure samples results in a smooth, light-coloured mass. The purest heather honey comes from higher moors where contamination from other floral honeys would be minimal. Like all honeys, its colour darkens through natural ageing or if it is stored in a refrigerator or deep-freeze.

A common test of ling heather by honey judges is to place an opened jar on its side to observe how quickly it will flow. A pure sample of heather honey will stay firmly in place for some time. Generally, the longer it stays in place, the purer is the sample.

OPPOSITE

Sample of pure ling heather honey, laid upon its side and demonstrating the thixotropic nature of true ling heather honey [Brian Nellist]

Bell Heather Honey

The colour of bell heather honey varies from port wine to dark brown. Its colour is influenced by the natural environment and it generally darkens and crystallises as it ages. Crystallisation is a relatively slow process and produces unmistakable large, coarse, flint-type crystals. The aroma of bell heather honey is pronounced and the flavour is strong, very often with a woody, almond taste. The soil where the plant grows often imparts a slight minty, bittersweet taste to the honey and this varies from location to location. Cross-blending of flavours arises from the intermingling of nectars obtained from the various heaths found which include *Erica cinerea*, *Erica tetralix*, the cross-leaved heath, *Erica ciliaris*, the Dorset heath, and *Erica vagans*, the Cornish heath. Bell heather is readily extracted from the comb by centrifugal extraction.

Bell honey (*Erica cinerea*): note the deep reddish-purple hue [Michael Gleeson]

GLOBAL HONEY SOURCES
FOR MEADS AND HONEY WINES

Acacia (*Robinia pseudoacacia*) This is referred to as "black locust or false acacia". It originated in the USA and has spread worldwide. Of the many acacia species, 52 are native to the Americas, 83  to Africa, Madagascar and the Mascarene Islands, 32 to Eastern Europe and Asia, and 9 to Australasia and the Pacific Islands. It is grown extensively in Bulgaria and Romania. It is not native to the UK. The honey is much favoured for light, dry meads. It is of a golden colour, excellent density and flavour. Granulates slowly.

Alfalfa or Lucerne (*Medicago sativa*) This crop was grown in wartime Britain provender for cattle, but was never a real success with farmers and growers. A member of the pea family, alfalfa is  the most cultivated forage legume in the world. It usually has the highest feeding value of all common hay crops. In the early 1960s, this crop became a boon for farmers in New Zealand (as cattle food). Beekeepers benefited from large yields of honey. The honey resembles clover, with a spicy, tangy flavour. It is a popular honey for mead making in the USA.

Apple (*Pyrus malus L*) The honey is of dubious yields for the beekeeper; it is an excellent honey in both quality and flavour that is light amber in colour.

Asparagus (*Asparagus officinalis*) The flowers yield moderate amounts of nectar in warm climates; it is a honey rarely found in the UK. It has a distinctive flavour which is amber in colour.

Avocado (*Persea americana*) A sub-tropical fruit from South-Central Mexico. Dark amber in colour, known for its velvety texture and flavour.

Basswood (*Tilia americana*) Known as the American linden tree; the honey that is often water-white colour with herbal taste.

Bell Heather (*Erica cinerea*) This honey is a port wine colour. It is referred to as the princess of honeys. It is obtained from the various heath species. In the UK, the areas of bell heather have declined since the end of the Second World War for reasons not really known. It is found on heathland throughout the UK, with moderate yields. It is harvested extensively in Lüneburg Heath, Lower Saxony, north Germany. Bell heather honey has a very fragrant flavour, releasing a highly perfumed aroma. It is a honey for sweet, sack and heavy dessert meads. It takes several years to mature.

Bird's-Foot Trefoil (*Lotus corniculatus*) Prior to the introduction of nitrogenous fertilisers, this small, clover-like plant was rampant throughout the sheep-rearing areas of the UK. The plant is well liked in Switzerland and Romania. The honey is very similar to clover honey.

Blackberry (*Rubus fruticosus*) This plant is found growing in hedgerows and cultivated on fruit farms. As a shrub it is not fussy, growing freely on any soil. As a honey, it has a high tannin content, coupled with abundant amounts of pollen that give a somewhat

hazy tinge to its medium colour. The flower is abundant in mid-July in the British Isles, producing a honey very popular with beekeepers.

Blueberry (*Vaccinium corymbosum*) This plant is common on the eastern seaboard of the USA; the honey's aroma gives off a hint of lemon; light to amber in colour.

Borage (*Borago officinalis*) Also known as starflower, this plant is grown worldwide. During the Russian pre-war five-year plans, its cultivation was compulsory as a green manure. It is grown in Eastern England and is a boon to beekeepers when it comes into flower from mid-July, yielding prodigious amounts of light yellow to straw-coloured honey. The pollen is light bluish-white; with some flowers it is almost white. Borage is grown principally for its seeds which are processed for oil.

Buckwheat (*Fagopyrum esculentum*) Until the arrival of nitrogen fertilisers, buckwheat was grown extensively worldwide. Beekeepers in Russia and the USA enjoyed the large surpluses of honey obtained from this ancient plant. Its honey is golden-to-amber, deliciously sweet and with a hint of a spicy malt or liquorice taste. Buckwheat nectar secretion is much governed by the weather; it seems to yield best in cool, moist conditions.

Charlock (*Sinapis arvensis L*) Commonly known as charlock mustard, field mustard, wild mustard or charlock, it is a member of the Brassicaceae family. It is an invasive weed which has been much

eradicated by intensive agriculture. The honey is light in colour with a mild flavour that can be detected in the finished wine.

Cherry (*Prunus cerasus*) In the same genus as the plum and the almond, the amount of surplus honey from these trees' yield is dubious in the British Isles.

Clover, White (*Trifolium*) Until the late-1950s and the advent of oilseed rape, the white clover species, Kentish white, was the most important honey-producing plant in the UK. Clover thrives on chalk

subsoils. It was grown in enormous acreages in the sheep-breeding areas of the UK. With the application of nitrogenous fertilisers, clover went into decline as a forage plant for sheep grazing. The nectar can be water-white to pale amber, giving a very bright honey. Clover honey is ideal for producing soft-set honey.

Cotton (*Gossypium hirsutum*) Cotton is one of the leading honey plants in the southern USA with the Black Prairie area of Texas regarded as the key region for its production of honey. China and India cultivate the plant, too (*Gossypium arboreum*). Its nectaries are protected from the scorching sun by its large flowers and leaves. The honey is white to extra-light amber with a good, mild flavour.

Cranberry (*Vaccinium macro-carpon*) Cranberries are an important cultivated crop in Washington and Oregon, in the north-west and Minnesota to Maine, north-east USA. Due to its

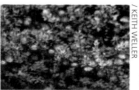

health benefits, both Chile and China grow large plantations of this berry fruit. It grows wild in some areas, but possibly of little use to the beekeeper. Cranberry honey is limited because individual cranberry bogs bloom no more than two weeks annually. The honey is medium amber in colour with a light red tint and a strong berry flavour.

Dandelion (*Taraxacum officinale*) The dandelion is common worldwide. It produces a honey that ranges from deep pale yellow in colour. It crystallises readily with a coarse grain. When fresh,  the honey has an intense aroma matching its taste and flavour, with a little bitterness at the finish. It is a honey to be avoided in mead making, as it has a pungent aroma reminiscent of horses. Beekeepers often blend dandelion honey with other honeys with milder, mellow flavours.

Field Beans (*Vicia faba*) Also known as broad beans and tick beans, field beans are of ancient origin and are grown worldwide. When in bloom, the flowers give off a very pleasant odour. The honey  light to dark amber with a mild flavour. It has a tendency to granulate quickly with a coarse grain. When the temperature and humidity are correct, field beans yield nectar prodigiously.

Fireweed (*Chamerion angustifolium*) Fireweed is a tall, perennial herb with large clusters of red-purple flowers growing dense areas on cut or burned-over timberlands throughout the USA and  Canada. No other major honey plant grows as far north; blooms from early July through late September. Fireweed honey is delicate with a smooth finish. Water-white in colour, very mild and very sweet with a sound aroma that is most unusual compared with other light-coloured honeys.

Fruit Blossom Various top fruits are useful for bees. Apple (*Malus*) and pear (*Pyrus*) are regarded as two of the four most important fruit trees the UK. Plum (*Prunus domestica*) is one of  the hardiest of trees and, for that matter, the most heavy-yielding fruit tree among the stone fruits, although the honey yields are dubious.

Gallberry (*Ilex spp*) This is an important nectar source for beekeepers in the USA. It is a thick, heavy-bodied, mild-flavoured honey which is light-coloured with a mellow flavour. It is harvested in  Florida, South Carolina and Georgia. It is a popular honey for mead making in the USA.

Goldenrod (*Solidago virgaurea var. leiocarpa*) This well-known plant features prodigious compound clusters of yellow flowers, and can be found throughout the Northern Hemisphere, especially the  USA and Canada. Goldenrod covers high prairie, pastureland and even open woods. It is the source for large quantities of amber honey with a slightly strong, almost spicy flavour that is not overly sweet.

Hawthorn (*Crataegus monogyna*) This shrub is known as "May" or "whitethorn". Its nectar yielding is often like angels' visits rare. The colour of its honey varies from amber to port wine, often with a green  tinge. It is not generally a sparkling or bright honey. The honey has a nutty, almond taste. It is said to be the prince of honeys. It is most suited for sweet, sack and dessert meads.

Himalayan Balsam (*Impatiens glandulifera*) This is a large annual plant, native to the Himalayas. It now present across much of the Northern Hemisphere and is considered to be  an invasive species in most countries of the world, owing to its questionable damaging effect to riverbanks and watercourses. The plant is outlawed in both the USA and Canada, with interstate regulations controlling its spread. The UK beekeeper can get substantial crops from this late-season flower. The honey is water-white with unattractive, brown-black cappings. The plant flowers right up to the first heavy frosts. Beekeepers often find that empty boxes of combs stored on hives in the late autumn are found to be full of sealed honey in the spring.

Horse Chestnut (*Aesculus hippocastanum*) Native to south-eastern Europe, this tree is now found worldwide. It is good bee plant, providing pollen and honey in profusion. The honey varies from amber to dark amber.

Lime (*Tilia spp*) The lime is grown throughout the world. It is known as linden in the Germanic areas of Europe, and basswood in the USA. The UK lime is still the major source of honey for beekeepers  living in an urban setting. Today, the lime tree is probably a firm favourite for surplus honey for beekeepers worldwide. However, a number of beekeepers, generally in urban areas, regard lime with some reservations because of its susceptibility to honeydew. The honey is light amber with a greenish tinge (possibly from hints of honeydew mixed in with the nectar). It has a minty taste. Its density is relatively poor compared with other honeys. After a few months, it crystallises with a fine, smooth grain. It makes nice mead that often imparts a minty taste.

Ling Heather (*Calluna vulgaris*) – a scene on the Northumberland fells
[Michael Badger]

Ling heather (*Calluna vulgaris*) This honey is quite unique. It is typically amber in colour. Its honey is thixotropic. It is found mainly in northern Great Britain, Norway and the Scandinavian countries. Ling heather is an alpine plant that has adapted to the upper moorland areas of these countries. Heather beekeepers refer to it as the "caviar of honeys". The taste is unlike any other honey. It has a very strong aroma of heather flowers with a welcomed bitter, umami all-round finish on the palate. The floral aroma is very strong and delicate.

Lucerne – See Alfalfa

Macadamia (*Macadamia integrifolia*) An exotic honey, the result of the blooms from the popular macadamia nut tree of Hawaii and Australasia; it is not readily available in quantity. Medium amber colour with a sweet aroma and delicate, nutty flavour that can impart a harsh aftertaste to meads.

Maple (*Acer spp*) The maple is found all around the Northern Hemisphere. The nectar is dark amber with characteristics identical to sycamore. The honey tastes little like butterscotch and is mildly spicy with a very unusual aroma.

WIKIMEDIA COMMONS CHRIS GUNNS

Marigold (*Calendula officinalis*) See also tagetes: it is a plant with many names (pot marigold, common marigold Scotch marigold) of the *Calendula* family Asteraceae. It is also widely found from Southern Europe to much further north in Europe, and elsewhere in warm, temperate regions of the world. It is a honey with a strong flavour from light to dark amber.

WIKIMEDIA COMMONS / BETTY CAI

Melilotus (*Melilotus spp*) Sweet clover is grown extensively worldwide, but is rarely found in the UK. The honey is a light straw colour with a greenish tinge. has a medium density, with a flavour reminiscent of mallow. The honey is sweet and bland with a very light, delicate aroma. It is known to granulate more quickly than white clover. The honey is ideally suited to mead making.

WIKIMEDIA COMMONS

Mesquite (*Prosopis alba*, white mesquite) In the south-western USA, the mesquite tree is valued for its sweet-smoky-smelling wood, principally used in barbeques and meat smokers. It produces numerous golden-coloured blooms throughout spring and summer. The honey's colour can vary from amber to water-white. The honey is reflected as earthy and aromatic with a dominating flavour that imparts itself in meads and honey wines.

WIKIMEDIA COMMONS / TUCSON HAPPENINGS

Mint (*Mentha aquatica*) As the name implies, this is water mint which is available in quantity in areas of fast-flowing streams. It has a water-white honey that is available in profusion from  mid-June to the end of July. The honey is thin but of good flavour, with a delicate bouquet.

Orange Blossom (*Citrus sinensis*) A leading honey plant in Southern Florida, Texas, Arizona and California, USA, Mexico, Spain. Orange trees bloom in March and April and produce a white  to extra-light amber honey with a pronounced aroma of orange blossoms. It has a sweet, fruity taste with a flowery perfume aftertaste that is added to meads in a true citrus flavour.

Palmetto (*Sabal adansonii*) Distributed from North Carolina to Florida, palmetto is especially abundant along the Atlantic Coast of the USA, the Yucatán Peninsula and North Africa. Trees up  60 feet tall produce whitish flowers in great compound clusters. Its honey is light amber to amber in colour with a thinner body than most honeys. Palmetto honey's taste is full-bodied and herbal in flavour with woody overtones that impart a harsh aftertaste to meads and honey wines.

Phacelia (*Phacelia tanacetifolia*) Originally a native of the south-western USA and northern Mexico, this is now found in many countries, being used as a cover crop and for green manure. It is a useful  bee plant and attracts other beneficial insects.

Pumpkin (*Cucurbita pepo*) Popular throughout the USA, its plant blossoms supply bees with a copious amounts of pollen and nectar. Pumpkin honey is amber-coloured with a spicy, complex, almost squashy flavour, ideal for melomels.

Raspberry(*Rubusidaeobatus*) Raspberries are an important commercial fruit crop, widely grown in all temperate regions of the world. The light honey has a delicate flavour. It is a favourite honey for making melomel and pyment.

Rosebay Willowherb (*Chamerion angustifolium*) This is known as fireweed in the USA and in Canada a great willowherb. It is a potash-loving annual plant that thrives areas where there have been fires. The honey is unusually pale in colour, water-white and of good density. It appears to many to be lacking in flavour, yet it does have a unique flavour, often masked by its sweetness, coupled with its fine bouquet.

Rosemary (*Rosmarinus officinalis*) Rosemary honeys from the Narbonne and Spain are famed for their fragrance that also pervades the wine. Mead made from rosemary is regarded by non-beekeeping epicures as the finest of meads. Its honey granulates to a fine, smooth, buttery texture with a light herbal taste on the palate.

Sage (*Salvia officinalis*) There are three types of sage honey commonly found across the world: black button sage, purple sage and white sage. Sage honey is rich and light with a predominantly sweet, clover-like taste with an elegant, floral aftertaste. Cherished by herbal tea drinkers with its right hint of sweetness to lemonades and teas.

Sainfoin (*Onobrychis*) While this plant was introduced to the UK in the 17th century, it is no longer grown as a crop the acreages of the past. Honeybees will forsake other nectar plants in favour

of sainfoin. It is one of the few honeys that are not generally contaminated by any other nectar. A common plant grown in the USA, Canada and Russia.

Starthistle (*Centaurea solstitialis*) An annual herb introduced from Europe's Mediterranean region, it is widespread in California and is regarded as a noxious weed that produces a white or extra-light

lemon to amber honey with a slight greenish hue, moderately sweet with a grassy, anise aroma and flavour.

Sunflower (*Helianthus annus*) A native of North America, sunflower is now distributed worldwide. It is grown for its seed oil and many other uses. The honey is amber to deep amber. The taste is very

sweet, if a little syrupy, the aroma being neutral.

Sycamore (*Acer pseudoplatanus*) This tree is not native to the UK; it is believed to have arrived in Britain by windborne seed. It propagates readily. flowers later than its near relatives, the

maples. The honey taste is mildly strong with a good density and a strange, unhoneyed aroma. The colour is variable from amber to a greenish hue which might well be honeydew.

Tagetes (*Asteraceae tagetes*) Also known as marigold; it is a member of the sunflower family native North, South and Latin America, with some species becoming naturalised  worldwide. One species, *Tagetes minuta*, is considered in many areas of the Americas as both a noxious and an invasive plant. The honey has a strong, pleasing flavour, amber in colour.

Thistle (*Cynareae*) This is a species made up of many genera, including *Carduus, Cirsium,* and *Onopordum*. Ostensibly they are weeds, but are important honey plants. It is a water-white to pale yellow  honey with a nice flavour. The thistle is the national emblem of Scotland and Lorraine, a region located in north-eastern France.

Tupelo (*Nyssa ogeche*) Tupelo honey is one of the few honeys which never granulates if pure; it is very sweet, smooth in texture, light amber colour, with complex floral flavours  of herbs and fruit. Tupelo gum trees grow in the Southern US wetlands; it blooms during April and May. Florida beekeepers place their apiaries on high platforms or even boats in these wetlands to avoid losing colonies to periodic flooding.

Wild flower is a synonymous term used in the USA that is tantamount to miscellaneous and undefined plant sources. The colour and flavour of wild flower honey can vary depending on the region in where it is produced; it is amber to dark amber in colour with mild floral overtones.

Willow (*Salix*) Willow has many genera; it is grown worldwide with many species. It is a main source of pollen for bees in spring. The honey is dark brown with a strong flavour; the yields of nectar are dubious as regards availability to the beekeeper.

A Guide to the Composition of Some Honeys by Floral Source

Honey sample	Moisture	Fructose	Glucose	Sucrose	Maltose	Higher sugars	Undetermined	pH	Free acid	Lactone	Total acid	Lactone/ free acid	Ash	Nitrogen	Diastase
Acacia	17.9	38.10	31.12	1.20	6.80	1.42	3.55	4.02	16.70	6.51	23.22	0.382	0.084	0.022	N/A
Alfalfa	16.20	39.11	33.40	2.64	6.01	0.89	2.80	3.88	20.19	10.16	30.35	0.501	0.093	0.033	17.50
Basswood	17.40	37.88	31.59	1.20	6.86	1.44	3.60	4.05	16.78	6.58	23.70	0.382	0.084	0.022	N/A
Blackberry	16.40	37.64	25.94	1.27	11.33	2.50	4.05	4.50	27.37	1.76	29.110	0.112	0.399	0.055	N/A
Blueberry	17.40	37.20	31.08	0.79	9.09	0.83	3.60	4.36	16.36	4.92	21.29	0.301	0.163	0.059	N/A
Buckwheat	18.30	35.30	29.46	0.78	7.63	2.27	4.30	3.97	35.07	6.99	42.06	0.213	0.224	0.064	38.90
Clover, white	17.90	38.36	30.71	1.03	7.32	1.56	3.20	3.84	22.95	8.71	31.66	0.366	0.156	0.046	N/A
Cranberry	17.20	35.59	1.02	1.02	8.03	2.95	7.10	4.37	23.82	6.32	30.14	0.274	0.330	0.041	N/A
Eucalyptus	17.00	39.35	32.27	1.43	6.84	0.80	2.40	4.14	18.96	7.51	26.46	0.383	0.204	0.050	21.90
Gallberry	17.10	39.85	30.25	0.72	7.71	1.22	3.20	4.20	16.19	4.46	20.65	0.269	0.163	0.028	N/A
Lime	17.40	37.88	31.59	1.20	6.86	1.44	3.60	4.05	16.78	6.58	23.70	0.382	0.084	0.022	18.1
Mint	18.80	38.84	33.33	2.10	4.93	0.96	1.00	4.01	15.90	7.85	23.75	0.494	0.123	0.019	15.00
Orange	16.70	39.26	31.83	1.87	6.50	1.33	2.50	3.67	24.23	13.21	37.35	0.540	0.082	0.030	27.80
Raspberry	17.40	34.46	28.54	0.51	8.68	3.58	3.50	4.04	33.64	5.55	39.19	0.192	0.471	0.047	N/A
Rosebay Willowherb	16.00	39.81	30.72	1.28	7.12	2.06	2.00	3.83	19.30	7.47	26.77	0.374	0.108	0.032	N/A
Tulip tree	17.60	34.65	25.85	0.69	11.57	2.96	6.60	4.45	38.28	4.71	42.99	0.121	0.460	0.076	21.77
All honeys	17.20	38.19	31.28	1.31	7.31	1.50	3.10	3.91	22.03	7.11	29.12	0.335	0.169	0.041	N/A

White, JW, "Composition of Honey". In: E Crane, Ed, Honey: A Comprehensive Survey, Heinemann, London, 1975, pp. 157-206.

OTHER SUGARY SUBSTANCES THAT BEES WILL FORAGE AND HARVEST

Honeybees are known to collect substances other than nectar: this happens in times of nectar scarcity, generally during periods of drought. Foraging bees will collect other sweet substances notably from silage clamps, the dumping of confectionery waste and honeydew. These substances contaminate and ruin a perfectly good honey.

Honeydew

Bees are attracted to and will collect honeydew, a secretion of certain plant-sucking insects, mainly aphids (Hemiptera). These insects feed on the phloem sap and extract the nutrients required. The surplus is ejected onto the surface of the plant on which they are feeding. If allowed to dry, the exudation is known as "manna". Honeydew is largely water, with up to 90 per cent of the dry matter being sugar. The sugars include the addition of complex ones such as melezitose. The aphid adds some nitrogenous matter and enzymes, and often moulds and spores. It is known that the aphids add more enzymes to honeydew and manna than are added to nectar from floral sources. High-order sugars in honeydew include melezitose, melibiose, raffinose, erlose, with additional enzymes including peptidase and proteinase.

Honeydew is a sticky, sugary, dew-like exudation found on the leaves and stems of trees and plants, especially in dry, warm conditions. There are two kinds of honeydew: one is directly obtained from plants and trees through broken plant tissue, the other is secreted by plant-sucking insects such as aphids (Hemiptera). This secretion is of a saccharine substance produced in very large amounts: honeybees will forage for it in earnest in times of nectar scarcity. Honeydew will contaminate any other honey present in the hive.

Honeydew from spruce (*Picea spp*) or Douglas fir (*Pseudotsuga menziesii*) is a dark, sweet liquid. Despite its pleasant taste, it is not

Left Note the glossy sugary solution on the pavement
[Wikimedia Commons – Dmitri Don]
Right Scolypopa australis, a species of planthopper that
secretes honeydew that is toxic to humans
[Wikimedia Commons – Richard001]

honey, and is totally unsuitable for making good mead or honey wine. If beehives are placed too far a distance from the heather plants, they will seek out honeydew from the nearby plantations. Though edible, it is not for mead making. On the whole, honeydew spoils a good honey, so forewarned is forearmed.

There is a species of planthopper in New Zealand, *Scolypopa australis*, that secretes honeydew that is toxic to humans, despite being harmless to the bees that collect it.

Confectionery Sweet Waste

In periods of nectar dearth, foraging bees are apt to search out other sources of sugar-based compounds. These compounds' constituents can vary in their attractiveness to for bees that can be as varied as molasses found on silage clamps to discarded sweet waste used by pig farmers. The contamination of honey by such harvested material sees the honey being discarded by the beekeeper.

Propolis

Propolis or bee glue is a sticky, resinous mixture honeybees forage and collect from tree buds, their sap flows, or other botanical sources. This substance should be kept away from bulk honey, as it will  alter the flavour and taste if allowed to become part of the must. The beekeeper is very careful not to allow its presence, as it can so easily contaminate a good sample of honey for mead and honey wine purposes.

HONEYS KNOWN TO BE UNSUITABLE FOR MEAD AND HONEY WINE PRODUCTION

Ragwort (*Senecio jacobaea*) Ragwort nectar produces a bitter honey; it takes a very small amount to spoil what might have been a splendid sample of honey. The common ragwort (also known as benweed, staggerweed, tansy ragwort and St James's wort) is probably the most common of the poisonous plants growing on roadsides, waste ground, pasture and agricultural land in Britain.

Scrub farmland. Ragwort (*Senecio jacobaea*), a yellow, daisy-like flower, flowers in the late summer [Michael Badger]

Manuka (*Leptospermum scoparium*) Honey is harvested from manuka myrtle trees that are found on uncultivated areas throughout New Zealand and South-Eastern Australia. Manuka honey has one

of the highest viscosities among honeys, comparable to ling heather honey. Like ling heather honey, this characteristic property is due to the presence of a protein or colloid. It is its main visually defining character, along with its typical dark cream to dark brown colour. To be labelled New Zealand manuka honey, at least 70 per cent of its pollen content must come from the tea tree (*Leptospermum scoparium*). The tea tree's honey is dark and regarded as having an unpalatable taste.

Rhododendron This is known to harbour toxic chemicals, particularly free phenols and diterpenes, that occur in significant quantities in the tissues of plants of the *Rhododendron* species.

These differ from species to species. Not all species produce them, although *Rhododendron ponticum* does. It is accepted that its nectar contains grayanotoxins that are known to be dangerous to man if eaten.

Tutu *Coriaria arborea* is one of several species called tutu. It is a common native of New Zealand. It is a highly poisonous shrub producing nectar that is toxic to man.

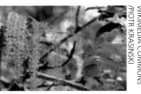

PART NINE

EXHIBITION OF MEAD AND HONEY WINES

OPPOSITE

A selection of fine Meads and Honey Wines at the 2016 National Honey Show
[Steven Turner]

EXHIBITING AND EXHIBITIONS

I am often asked why I am keen on exhibiting honey and mead. It most certainly goes back to my formative years at school, the time when competitiveness between individuals was not regarded as generating an unhealthy attitude toward competition, as it is now. I am one of the majority who feel that competition is nothing to worry about if conducted under proper conditions of fairness, ability and an even matching of those involved. My late teacher, Charles Bell, encouraged moderate competition. He recalled to me much later in life that this is good for children, but he was totally against extreme competition, as he believed that could so easily distress a child. Research tells us that temperament, culture, talent and age affect how a child handles competition. Children are not born with a competitive urge. They learn it.

Exhibitions have a beneficial effect in many ways: the standard of exhibits is constantly raised or kept at a high order; it makes the public aware of the craft; it makes for a social environment and it draws people together, something that is well worth considering at the present time.

UNDERSTANDING THE PROS AND CONS OF EXHIBITING

Firstly, as a novice exhibitor, you should understand the rules of the show. There is a saying, "Rules are meant for men, not men for rules". This should not be taken as an excuse for ignoring the rules or treating them lightly, but rather as a reminder that they are our servants or tools, and never our masters. Therefore, you have to accept them as they are. Read the show schedule carefully and prudently, highlighting the sections which are most important to the staged exhibit. Then decide which classes to enter. It is often the situation that there is only one mead class, whereby the mead may be of any variety, dry or sweet, fruit mead, etc., with the judge being someone with no real knowledge of mead or wines to boot. The larger club shows may differentiate between the mead types, or you may well have to enter the larger shows to find classes for melomels and cyser.

The biggest issue I have as an experienced exhibitor is that many judges do not make, let alone produce, mead. This means they have little "know-how" of meads and honey wines and are unlikely to be aware of substances that, in reality, should not be present, and have been "added" to enhance an exhibit. A number of non-wine-judging guild judges (NGWBJ and BJCP) do not, or are unable to, pick up on these inclusions. This puts those exhibitors who stick rigidly to the permitted additives for the mead at an unfair disadvantage. Michael Young, who makes considerable amounts of mead and honey wine, is of the opinion that the mead judges of the past were correct in their view that "a judge who does not make mead should not judge mead".

For the reasons of exactness, let us assume you are entering the UK's National Honey Show or the annual Mazer Cup International Mead Competition in the USA. Their rules are quite specific so, from the outset, you need to choose those classes suitable for your type of mead. Assuming that your mead is "pure" – that is, it has been fermented using solely honey, water, acid, tannin, yeast nutrient and yeast with no other additives whatever – it is in essence a "show mead" (see pages 53 and 63 – Permitted Additives To The "Must" For Competition And Exhibition Wines). Prohibited additives include vodka, sultanas, raisins, hops, artificial sweeteners, bananas and many others.

In selecting your meads, do not be tempted to enter poor or substandard samples. It is pointless exhibiting such meads.

DETERMINING DRY OR SWEET MEADS AND HONEY WINES

You need to determine whether the selected meads are dry or sweet. Experienced exhibitors can taste at will and determine this. The new exhibitor uses a precision hydrometer to measure the Opening Gravity (OG) and to measure the drop in Specific Gravity (SG). The hydrometer is the common tool used to measure Specific

Gravity (SG) in the United Kingdom, whilst the term "Brix" is the term used in the USA. In essence, it is a practical instrument to monitor the rate of fermentation of a must and mead that is in the various stages of becoming a finished wine. Its use affords a good sign of when fermentation is complete in dry meads and honey wines. The accepted reading usually when the SG 0.995 or 1.0 Brix is determined (although BJCP allows this to be up to 1.010). It is most important to understand that the recorded measurement is not the extent of residual sugar concentration present, but rather a sign of the likelihood that sugar is still present; it is the tasting that tells whether sugar is still present. At these low levels the hydrometer is limited to indicate a rough approximation of sugar content present. The measurement taken is much affected by the presence of other solids in the mead sample, as well as the alcohol and carbon dioxide. For this reason with little sugar in the wine, it is the presence of dissolved solids other than the sugars which play a larger and significant role in determining how high the hydrometer floats as compared to times when sugar is more abundant (for example, prior to fermentation commencing).

To be thoroughly accurate requires a Clinitest® measurement test. The Clinitest® method is based on a chemical reaction called copper reduction used for cases of diabetic control. The test consists of tablets containing copper sulphate (only one tablet is used). The tablet when added to the mead reacts with sugars present. The resultant colour change varies with the amount of sugar present within the mead sample. The test rig provides a colour chart from which the sample is compared to the colour chart provided: this simple test determines extremely accurately the residual sugar content of the sample. The procedure is to use a standard eyedropper: place 10 drops of the mead sample into a small test tube, adding one tablet. The treated wine sample will cause an immediate "boiling" reaction with accompanying colour change. By carefully observing the colour change as the reaction proceeds, avoid shaking or vibrating the test tube for 15 seconds following the boiling effect. Should the colour change rapidly from bright orange to a dark or greenish brown, the wine sample contains more than one percent residual sugar.

Undertaking a second test with a diluted mead sample is required. After the 15-second waiting period, softly agitate the test tube and compare the resultant colour of the sample to the colour chart: this will define the corresponding sugar concentration measurement.

With mead with one to five percent residual sugar, a two-drop wine sample should be diluted with eight drops of water. Then perform the test as directed above. The colour should be compared to the two-drop method colour chart; the result is then multiplied by five to determine the residual sugar concentration. For illustration purposes, if the colour change indicates 0.4 percent sugar, then the actual measurement is two percent residual sugar.

To conclude, determination of dry over sweet comes down to the physical tasting for detecting any apparent sweetness present in the tasted sample.

I have found exhibitors are confused as to the true meaning of dry. In essence the NGWBJ ruling means it is dry without any trace of sweetness. The BJCP state dry meads do not have to be bone dry. The perception of sweetness is a function of the percentage of residual sugar. It is recommended not to have reliance on the Final Gravity to determine sweetness. Consider the Original Gravity, with strength, tannin levels and, to a lesser extent, acidity, in assessing sweetness.

The United Kingdom – National Guild of Wine and Beer Judges (NGWBJ)
There is no in-between that is medium dry, i.e. having an SG of 1.001-1.005.

| Dry mead | Specific gravity (SG) 1.000 |
| Sweet mead | Specific gravity (SG) 1.06-1.020 |

The USA – Beer Judge Certification Program (BJCP) – 2015 Mead Style Guidelines

Dry mead	Specific gravity (SG) 0.990-1.010
Semi-sweet mead	Specific gravity (SG) 1.010-1.025
Sweet mead.	Specific gravity (SG) 1.025-1.050.

The mead style guide lines can be classified accordingly:

M1 – Traditional Mead

Dry Mead	Semi-Sweet Mead	Sweet Mead

M2 – Fruit Mead

Cyser	Pyment	Berry Mead	Stone Fruit Mead	Melomel

M3 – Spiced Mead

Fruit and Spice Mead	Spice, Herb or Vegetable Mead

M4 – Speciality Mead

Braggot – made with malt	Historical Mead – mead that does not fit in any other category or is from another country	Experimental Mead – as the name implies

THE CRITERIA FOR SELECTION OF AN EXHIBIT OF MEAD AND HONEY WINE FOR COMPETITION

Generally

Having studied the show schedule carefully, decide which classes you are intending to enter. If I may digress, remember this simple platitude, in that others are trying to win the classes you are entering, so leave nothing to chance: getting to the top is somewhat easy, it is staying there where the difficulty lies, as those who have tried to win previously and not succeeded will try so much more to be in the winning position.

This is where good record keeping is essential to ensure the wine you intend to select for exhibition is "pure" in the sense of its make-up in relation to the class to be exhibited.

When deciding probable entries you should never let your heart rule your head; you need to be quite ruthless in discarding those wines you know are not up to the standard – "exhibit to the standard and it will be judged to the standard". You gain nothing by exhibiting substandard wines, so don't waste the judge's time.

Reference has been made several times in the text regarding dry and sweet meads, so in choosing wines for entry ensure it is what it is supposed to be! The experienced vintner can determine the wine's character immediately: the rookie exhibitor should resort to a precision hydrometer and trial jar.

[**Note**] See page 28 – Mead and Honey Wine Judging Classifications for the UK and USA.

Dry meads should have a Specific Gravity (SG) 1.000 and less in the National Guild of Wine and Beer Judges (NGWBJ) – The USA – Beer Judge Certification Program (BJCP) – 2015 Mead Style Guidelines Specific Gravity (SG) 0.990-1.010.

Sweet meads 1.001 upwards to 1.020 (NGWBJ) – (BJCP) 1.010 upwards to 1.050.

The understanding of "dry" seems to cause many exhibitors difficulties as a good number do not grasp the true meaning of "Dry Mead" as the wine exhibit must be dry without any trace of sweetness.

Exhibit Selection for the Show Bench

1. Mead Selection
(a) Brilliantly bright: "star-bright".
(b) Free from any floating particles: any present need to be filtered out.
(c) A clean aroma and bouquet free of sulphur.
(d) An attractive colour of dark yellow or straw.
(e) Demonstrating a balance of flavour, acidity, astringency on tasting.
(f) A taste of alcohol that is definite and more pronounced in sweet meads.

(g) A good "length": the time the flavour of the mead persists on the tongue.

(h) Dry mead should be clean and fresh to the taste.

(i) Sweet mead should be clearly sweet but not overtly sweet to the point of being sickly.

(j) Sweet meads should have a more definite aroma than dry meads and a higher alcohol content.

2. Bottles and Corks

(a) The show schedule will state capacity, the size of bottle to be used, and whether it should be plain or tinted.

(b) The bottle may need to be round-shouldered with a punted base, shallow or deep-punted.

(c) The bottle should be free of indented ornamentation, lettering or fluting.

(d) The bottle should be free of scratches, chips or blemishes.

(e) Wash and clean bottles thoroughly inside, including the shoulders, rinsing in cold water.

(f) Choose the type of cork to be used, flanged or plastic. It must be free of cracks or blemishes.

3. Bottling the Mead

Mead for exhibition needs to be bottled a few days before the show. This allows it to stabilise, settle and regenerate to its full aroma that is impaired when bottling. To decant the mead from the demijohn, place the vessel on a firm base, raised at least 600 mm (2 ft) above the bottle to be filled. Obtain a metre (3 ft) of plastic tubing for the siphoning procedure. This should have a 4 mm (1/8 in) internal diameter and be thoroughly sanitised and sterilised before use.

Carefully remove the bung from the demijohn and insert one end of the tubing into the mead to one-third of the way into the liquid. At this depth, any sediment or surface matter will not have been disturbed. The siphon tube needs to be fixed in place to avoid drawing up any sediment. Gently suck on the tube to start the siphoning action and then place the tube into the base of the bottle to avoid the incorporation of any air by splashing and frothing. When the bottle is almost full, pinch the siphon tube to arrest further flow. The mead should be 12 mm (½ in) from the bottom of the cork. Cover the open neck of the bottle with a dry cloth and allow bubbles to rise to the surface and disperse, then cork. The end of the siphon tube inserted into the mouth should be sterilised immediately after use.

Once bottled, examine the contents thoroughly to identify whether any floating matter is present. This is best done with strong torchlight. If all is well, carefully clean the bottle with methylated spirits and polish it up with a dry clean cloth. Thereafter handle the bottle using a clean cloth to avoid dirty handprints on the bottle.

4. To finish off

Finally, label the bottle. Check the labels to ensure they are correct for the class you have entered, as mistakes do occur. The show rules dictate the height and position of labels. A simple template can be made by cutting a sheet of white paper to the depth prescribed in the schedule. This then fits around the bottle. The label should be placed against the top edge of the template and be centred between the bottle seams. Immaculate presentation may not get you the prize, but if a good mead, it might well get into a winning position

A labelling template used for securing competition
labels to honey jars [Michael Badger]

THE EXHIBITION AND JUDGING OF MEAD, HONEY WINE AND HONEY VINEGAR.

In my opinion, both exhibitors and mead and honey judges should have considerable experience of the many wines that come under the auspices of mead through being a producer and a continuing producer. Continuous, consistent winning at county/ state and national level will add gravitas to this theory. The aspiring exhibitor and subsequent judge should gain as much experience as possible firstly by acting as a steward to any well-respected mead judge in shows at all levels, whilst at the same time becoming a producer of these wines in quantity.

Having done this, a start might well be made at club level. With each show your confidence will increase. In addition, your ability becomes known and recognised by colleagues, on the judging front invitations coming from larger and, eventually, prestigious shows. More practice, combined with theory and more practice, makes for competency.

JUDGES KIT AND EQUIPMENT

The judge should first ensure that he has:

- a pair of white smocks, plus a hat, comfortable shoes
- the show schedule, plus pencils, paper, clipboard, black reproductive biro
- marking templates plus spare sheets
- spittoon and funnel
- clean cloths and "J" cloths, and tea and drying towels, 9-litre bucket
- at least 6 plain, colourless, clear ISO tulip-shaped bowl tasting glasses
- corkscrew and spare corks
- ruler or tape measure
- carrying case for the above equipment

- Palate refresher, plain arrowroot biscuits.

[**Note**] Some judges bring along with them a vinometer and hydrometer with trial jar – in wine circles this would create some amusement if produced by current judges, as they are regarded as items of the past: the adage, "your contemporaries might think you a fool: producing such paraphernalia will remove all doubt", comes to mind.

The preferred tasting glass should be a dishwasher-proof 215 ml (7.6 oz) ISO tulip-shaped bowl tasting glass that meets the judge's needs for swirling and nosing the mead for tasting that is dishwasher-safe.

ISO tulip-shaped bowl tasting glass
[Michael Badger]

For testing honey vinegars a smaller vessel of 120 ml (4 oz) sherry type is suitable as detailed above.

A judging kit case is recommended, too; this particular carrying case was made for me 40 years ago, it is light and contains all the needs for mead and honey wine judging.

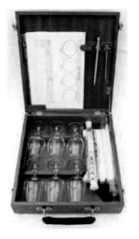

Judging kit [Michael Young]

A steward showing the correct way to hold a tasting glass by the flange to avoid heat from the hand passing through the wall of the tasting glass [Erica Osborn]

THE JUDGE'S STEWARD

Without doubt one of the most attractive aspects of judging is meeting the appointed steward allocated to you. I prefer to have a steward who "knows the ropes". It is not arrogance on my part, as I recognise that I had to start somewhere, but it is a question of pragmatism or practicality: I find that having to constantly tell your steward what is expected of them interferes with my concentration.

However, having a complete novice to assist the experienced steward is a far better option as they can converse with each other, allowing me to concentrate fully on the job in hand (see Appendix G – Mead Stewards Duties). The beginner is then free to take in what the roles and duties are in a more relaxed atmosphere, thereby gaining confidence for a future show.

I expect an experienced steward to be fully conversant with the layout of the exhibits, be totally familiar with classes and the mode of recording the awards given per exhibit: above all, he has to be numerate. The exhibitor with duplicate or triplicate entries should be known and readily identifiable at the appropriate time.

When a class has been judged, tidy up the staging, place all exhibits back into position in numerical order; ensure the correct corks are placed back into position and the results sheets are passed on to the recorders promptly.

JUDGES

The best advice I was given by Andy Andrews in my early judging forays was never take matters to chance. Getting to a show is indeed the first worry of any judging assignment – arriving late is really a poor excuse, setting off early is never a bad option or, if the show funds allow, take accommodation at a local hostelry. So many issues can quickly arise, usually out of your control, including the vehicle breaking down, traffic congestion and hold-ups. The most galling is to be given clear instructions to an unfamiliar venue or a large agricultural show to be misdirected to the wrong part of the showground as the traffic steward's knowledge of the show is generally nil. Carrying your gear from one end of a showground to another is not a good beginning to your duties.

The exhibitors are a key factor to a show's success and its continuance for year after year: without them there would be no show. Judges and their judging outcomes can dampen the enthusiasm of both new and patriotic exhibitors if they adopt a haughty or demeaning approach to the show they are engaged to judge. It should not be overlooked that the show organisers are, to resort to a cliché, "very much like the timber workers: they have to work with the timber they are given, knots and all, and do their best with what they have". The exhibitors, next to the show organisers, the stewards, are arguably the most important people he becomes involved: each in their own ways is the link between judge and the exhibitor, and once the judge picks up an entry to pass judgement the relationship begins. This becomes a direct one: he has a clear responsibility to give his best to them, helped greatly by the use of a judging template to score his marks in a fair and just way.

It is common practice to expect the judge to complete his part of judging by a set time, irrespective of the number of classes he is to officiate, let alone the number of exhibits he is to judge. The judge must be accommodated in giving them adequate time to

Gerald Moxon MBE judging at the Welsh National Honey Show
held at Royal Welsh Show 2015 [Mrs Jac Byfield]

complete; understandably, it depends upon the judge's natural speed without feeling pressured on time.

The majority of judges as they become experienced tend to speed up; however, there is a limit to how much faster a judge is expected to act without blighting the quality of their duties, as they risk letting down the exhibitors and the show and compromising their own standards of proficiency and expertise.

PRE-SHOW JUDGES BRIEFING TO ALL JUDGES

As stated earlier in the text, always arrive promptly at the show: very often there is a judges' briefing. I recommend that the show schedule is read and studied beforehand, and any queries should be raised at this briefing. I have found that it is best settled with the show officials before judging commences.

At the judging bench, I ensure that all the classes to be judged are known, and that all exhibits are visible and none are overlooked. I brief my steward on how I like to work, and I always start with dry, sweet, spices and vinegar last. You cannot do justice to judge dry meads after the palate has tasted sweet varieties first (see The Judging Procedural Process – Suggested Modus, page 327).

I work with the steward to assist him to write the respective marks "marking sheet" the list of exhibits per class; this I do firstly in pencil and when completed and checked out the marks are cast-in ink or reproductive biro.

A SUGGESTED JUDGES MARKING SHEET TEMPLATE

The judging of mead and honey wines is best undertaken by a points system. This is the points system method that I use.

Presentation	5
Clarity	10
Colour	5
Bouquet	10
Balance	10
Body	10
Flavour	50

The wide range of points for flavour allows the judge to work on the basis of that every 5 points equals 1 to 10, i.e. 1-5 = 1; 6-11 =2; and so on.

The National Guild of Wine and Bee Judges suggests that the Standard Marks for Still Wines should be as follows:

Presentation	2
Clarity	4
Colour	4
Bouquet	10
Balance, Body Flavour	30

They, of course, are a highly reputable authority, whose advice can be followed with confidence. However, like the late Harry Riches, I prefer a slightly different allocation of marks, giving more weight to Balance, Body and Flavour. Nevertheless, it would be conceited and somewhat presuming of me to suggest that my allocation of marks is a better method of allocating marks. Like Harry, we would claim that it suits our approach to the judging method. You as a judge might well adopt your own marking system: whatever system you choose to adopt, it is imperative that you stick rigidly to it, thereby ensuring consistency. As a matter of course, as a matter of checking my judging sanity, I rejudge the first four entries to make sure that my first forays into the judging are as consistent to those that I judged at the end of the class.

SOME FUNDAMENTALS

For a good number of years in the 1970s, I was fortunate to assist the late S W (Andy) Andrews who instilled in me many points of issue regarding producing and judging of meads and honey wines. Andy felt these pointers were essential for young "whippersnappers" like me to properly understand the whys and wherefores to becoming competent in mead production and a judge of wines, albeit mead or other honey wines. He quite rightly said to me that at some time I, too, will be handing down my experiences to others.

Andy was somewhat exercising a sort of dogma about becoming a master vintner in his strong belief of self-analysis in winemaking, exhibiting and judging. This he felt is so easily achieved by becoming self-analytical of all wines and meads, whether your own or others, or purchased wines from the local wine shop, more especially tasting every conceivable one available by type and variety: this I did over a number of years. My mentor emphasised the acronym "S, T, A, R" – Smell, Tastes, Analysing and Remembering…the remembering aspect allies itself to each and every instance that you come across in a new smell / odour / aroma / taste that becomes fixed in your armoury of memory for future occasions whether good, bad or indifferent. Nevertheless, should you come across a wine and its characters are somewhat alien to you, ask a fellow mead producer or judge with more experience for an opinion: I, for one, never take the attitude of "a fool for a few moments than being one for the rest of their life": I, too, had to start somewhere. Andy Andrews emphasised to me that no two wines are indistinguishable, irrespective that they may well have similar physiognomies that are probably clearly identifiable.

It may seem obvious, but obviousness can be easily forgotten especially when it comes to being in good physical condition. Judging involves high concentration, whereby tiredness and mental stress will certainly impair one's judgement if you have travelled a long distance: arrive early and have a short rest before commencing your duties. If you feel cold, take a warm drink before judging. Be aware that your body needs to be alert to enable the olfactory nerve endings to function through their close connection with the environment surrounding them.

THE JUDGING PROCEDURAL PROCESS – SUGGESTED MODUS

The Background for Judging Meads

It is essential to have regard to the background against the colour of the meads and honey wines to be judged: an essential requirement, so often overlooked:

- Red wines viewed and judged against a red background will appear light in colour
- Light golden wine under a yellow background will appear light in colour

Ideally the background should be neutral in off-white or light grey.

Sequence of Judging Meads and Honey Wines

The actual techniques and procedures firstly and above all must be systematic: the use of the judging template (see Appendix F: Mead and Honey Wine Judging Template) is core to a correct systemic approach. The following order should always be used:

- White wine before red wine
- Dry wines before sweet wine
- Wines with a low alcohol content before those known to be high in alcohol
- Heavy dessert and fortified wines
- Spiced meads and herb wines
- Composite three - bottle class types of different wines
- Honey Vinegar last of all

[Note] When judging, white and red wines should never be mixed: this equally applies to dry and sweet wines.

Whatever the size of show or status in the grade of shows, the judge should always give his best. His judging procedure, no matter what, should have the same degree of care and preparation by the excellence of judging, whether it be a club show or the Mazer Mead Competition, Colorado, or the UK's National Honey Show. Mention has been made elsewhere about the judge having a sense of proportion in his deliberations; this arises with the judge working at a club show when he may deliberate his markings to a lower standard than at the premier shows: nevertheless, he should deliver excellence by giving his best.

A concern that I have with judges (UK honey judges are a prime example) is the avoidance to reduce the degree to which a mead and honey wine judge professes his own personal opinions in the marking process: it is difficult to eliminate the personal element entirely: nevertheless, it should be encouraged to minimise this. Honey judges in the north of the UK (especially several in Yorkshire) will always give higher marks to ling heather mead over a mead whose source may well be rosemary or acacia. This is a prejudice that is wrong: each exhibit is judged on its merits, and not by personal fads of the judge.

Judging in many ways is a lonely task: he answers only to the higher officials managing the show, and it is usually to them he may seek a consultation on any points of issue.

The use of a judging marking template is a good aide-mémoire for the modus of judging.

I also believe that when you judge the first four bottles of any class you should go back to these four once you have completed the last entry in the class: by doing so, this ensures that your senses of S T A R (page 326) have kicked in in line with those that had followed the first exhibits judged.

The format to judge is as follows:

- Presentation
- Clarity
- Colour
- Bouquet
- Balance
- Body
- Flavour

Before the judging commences I ask the steward to check that all the exhibits are labelled, checked to see that they are in the correct class to be judged, and, above all, that no exhibits are overlooked. Your steward should write down all awarded marks in pencil in the first instance. As you proceed to the end of judging all the exhibits, it is quite common to find that you may have tied several exhibits with the same points. Double-check the arithmetic before proceeding further. At this stage it is my preferred method to check with the steward for duplicate or triplicate entries: these should be then judged, with the best exhibit going forward with the others being eliminated. Some judges undertake the judging of duplicate entries first… Each to his own. The judge should then look at the tied entries and rejudge them until you have an outright winner. This procedure may well throw up further tied exhibits, thereby entailing the same procedure to find the second, third, etc. This is all part of the judging procedure. The judging sheet I use is excellent for aiding the judge to a conclusion. Once the arithmetic is rechecked with all entries, the final results are cast off in black ink. The procedure of arithmetically checking the points is a very important consideration that should be double-checked once an exhibit has been judged. For my part I am more than happy to leave my judging award sheet on the show bench for all to see; understandably, it is essential that the marks add up correctly from the onset, otherwise, if a mistake is picked up, it is both embarrassing and unfortunate, as it might require a review of the whole class. I have found that the judge needs to be attired in comfortable clothing and shoes. In my own situation, being tall, I find being sat down is much easier on the back and shoulders. Most judges use plain water to cleanse their palates: I suppose I am the exception, as I prefer strong tea.

Finally, a judge needs to invoke the sixth sense of proportion when he is judging. By this I feel each show is treated upon its merits of fair-mindedness, equality and outreaching to the exhibitors whose entries make the show, as without them there would be no show. The judge should always exercise his professionalism, in that if the exhibits are worthy of entry they should be treated accordingly. The judge should always exercise caution when officiating at club shows or dealing with novice classes, as the exhibits may not be up to par as in a high-class show where the exhibits are expected to be faultless. At the smaller shows, I use these as an opportunity for encouragement to the tyro to move up a gear and take on the more experienced brethren. A faint heart never won over a fair maiden, or vice versa. Competing at the national shows is no excuse for complacency; the judge will follow the schedule to the extreme, so as an exhibitor he must not fall into the trap of "Every ass thinks himself worthy to stand with the King's horses". Once the judging is completed with awards laid out, I am more than happy to meet exhibitors to discuss their successes or failings to win with helpfulness and, where appropriate, advice.

Presentation

This involves the judge checking that the bottle, cork and its label are as specified in the show schedule. If they are at odds or not to the schedule, the judge can legitimately disqualify the entry. If in any doubt, confer with the chief steward or convenor of judges and ask them to give a ruling. Such instances might include the bottle having sloping shoulders or a screw cap end, or the show label incorrectly placed as required by the schedule or the cork not as stated, having, say, a black plastic top when the schedule requires white. It follows that exhibitors should endeavour to carry the full marks for this section.

Examine the cork and bottle for cleanliness. Should the bottle be dirty from paw marks, I give the exhibitor the benefit of the doubt, as it may have been caused by poor staging by others. Remains of gum from the label – deduct a point. Some judges are keener than others when it comes to the quality of the cork in deducting points, but if the cork is clean, that will suffice, as it is becoming difficult to obtain first-rate corks for exhibition.

THE EXHIBITORS' AND JUDGES' SENSES IN ACTION

Firstly, recognise that it is through sight, hazes, clarity and colour that you need to comprehend as an exhibitor. It is these phenomena that the judge works to in his deliberations in the judging process to reach a final decision. It is foolish behaviour as an exhibitor (if I may be permitted to say it "trying to outwit the judge" by being a head of your game, so to speak) by using ingredients or additives to enhance an exhibit, hoping that the judge will be taken-in by such malpractice.

The common chemical sense in need of explanation: this is attributed to the trigeminal nerves controlling sensations in the face and motor functions within the mouth concerning chewing, biting and swirling liquids. Trigeminal nerves have three major branches

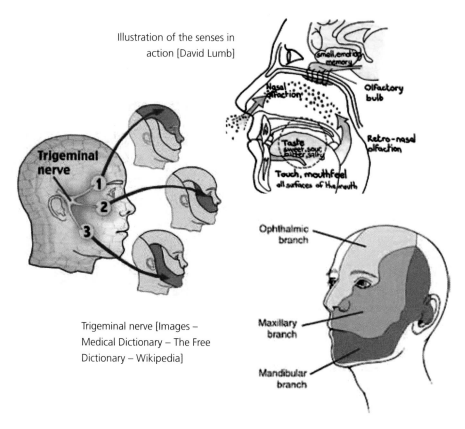

Illustration of the senses in action [David Lumb]

Trigeminal nerve [Images – Medical Dictionary – The Free Dictionary – Wikipedia]

to and from the brain: the ophthalmic nerve, the maxillary nerve, and the mandibular nerve. These all interface with the eyes, mouth and nose. These nerve endings, when stimulated, can bring on external actions including sneezing, watering of the eyes, choking and others.

The inhalation of menthol is predictable by this common sense, as it reacts quite independently from the olfactory sense organs. By taste, the apparentness of a high alcohol content in a wine, and vice versa, stimulates the nerve endings. The tactile senses come alive with the mucous membranes of the nose and mouth, as do the various areas of the tongue to both touch and tactile sensation when the wine is taken from the tasting glass, this is readily apparent with the releasing residual gas in sparkling meads and honey wines

Sight

Sight is the first of the senses to come into play in any activity. In exhibiting and judging it is a given in terms of clarity and colour. It is beyond the terms of this narrative to go into detail about interrelationships between the sensory impulses the brain has to deal with: suffice to say, the human eye is known to recognise 150+ different colours. Having said that, it is known that as we age, our colour recognition and differentiation decrease. Those amongst us who have received cataract surgery will bear witness in a relatively short time to how much sharper colours become. When the wine is first observed the procedure begins immediately with the garnering of first impressions of the visual virtues of the wine. Beginning with the wine's presentation from the bottle, its shape, colour, whether clear, green-tinted or mixed coloured, its compliance with the schedule / rules, the labelling of the bottle and, most importantly, the clarity and colour of the wine.

Hazes

Wine hazes arise from a number of sources most commonly found in young, fresh, unpolished meads and honey wines through the suspended yeast cells and other cellular matter arising from the processes of fermentation. Wines other than mead are regularly found to have a milky appearance with an accompanied yeasty "nose" and a veritable yeast flavour. However, meads and honey wines benefit from the additions of tartaric acid whose crystals may be seen at the base of the bottle, arising through the precipitation of potassium bitartrate (argol) in such situations. It is not a fault as such unless distributed when poured.

A regular haze seen in meads is the infection known as *lactobacilli*. This contaminant in its advanced stage is seen to have a silky, shimmering appearance when rotated in a strongly lit background replicating a thick, glossy, oily consistency. Only an inexperienced exhibitor would stage such an entry.

Another common haze found in melomels and fruit meads is a

pectin haze that reveals itself more readily in diffused light. The pectin haze is far from detrimental to taste, but is far from pleasing to the eye of a judge.

Clarity

It needs to be understood that clarity and colour are in essence two entirely different properties in the theme of mead and honey wines. Whilst in the opening assessment of analytical thinking, their immediate presence is somewhat thought-provoking in that they are seen concomitantly; nevertheless, they are due for and should receive separate assessment by the judge in his deliberations. Experience over time tells us that a cloudy wine is most usually flawed, much before as a judge you have formed a view tasting the liquor.

There are four accepted varying degrees of clarity:

- **Star-bright** or **Brilliant** A wine demonstrating the highest degree of clarity. The wine judges' guilds refer to such a wine as being well-polished: such a wine is said to glisten.
- **Clear** A wine that lacks the final polish of the star-bright wine: it is free of deposit or haze. Clear wines make up the majority of wines presented for exhibition.
- **Dull** or **Slightly Hazy** A wine that has a defined haze but is not cloudy.
- **Cloudy** Such a wine may have a number of reasons for its appearance that vary from a young wine that has not cleared, to spoilage organisms being present: in essence there may be several reasons for its appearance.

So an excellent exhibit will be star-bright mead that is brilliantly clear: the wine should twinkle from the punt, giving it maximum points. Sophisticated filtering devices are commonly available, giving wines a polished effect; often there may be an aftertaste to the filtered wine that may reveal itself.

To test for clarity, a quick twist to the bottle will disturb or bring into view any sediment and particles present.

A deposit in meads and honey wines is a definite fault, except those of tartrates that will not affect the wine unless disturbed whilst pouring. Nevertheless, for the purposes of exhibition in a mead and honey wine show, any deposit or haze is considered a fault; the level of deposit, if significant, is without doubt a serious fault that might well be regarded as a disqualification.

Be aware that the use of champagne yeast can and does introduce issues: the constant vibration while travelling to the show can start the mead back into fermentation. The presence of bubbles on the surface of staged mead is an indication that such fermentation may be underway. Meads that have been fermented with such a yeast type may be marked down as an experienced mead maker, and a judge will be aware that this can happen to a stable wine that has been re-energised through a change in its ambient surroundings. An obviously cloudy wine should be eliminated, and so should meads that have a visible amount of lees at the bottom of the bottle. Naturally, deeply coloured melomels, pyment, etc., may need to be decanted into a tasting glass and examined with a torch to give confidence that the mead is wholesome in looks rather than relying on looking at a bottle in bulk.

Colour

The exhibitor should be alive to oxidised mead: if staged, it is likely to be eliminated immediately. Oxidised mead is dull and lacks brightness. Comparing mead with brown malt vinegar is a simple way of identifying what an oxidised wine might look like physically. Comparing oxidised malt vinegar with an unoxidised mead and honey wine, you note the dull appearance of the malt vinegar compared to the clear brightness of the mead (see page 338).

Pleasant Odours

Pleasing and pleasant odours are few in number; the most apparent are as follows:

- **Vinous** The wine should have bouquet of a wine, rather than a smell of cordial or squash.
- **Varietal or Distinctness of the bouquet** A mead logically creates much of its smell from the basis of the honey used in the must, combined if with the fruit used as a basic ingredient, if a melomel or fruit.
- **Fruity** This often arises in a young wine as an age-related phenomenon. Both vinous and fruity aromas can be readily detected in the mead.
- **Maturity** The nature of mature mead brings out the full aroma that can be said to be polished, rounded, full and pleasant.

Unpleasant Odours

Unpleasant odours are more frequent than pleasant and reveal their presence most readily. The most familiar odours of the unpleasant nature are:

- **Hydrogen Sulphide** This a gas that is best described as the smell of rotten eggs arising through excess sulphur being generated. It often arises through incorrect additions of yeast nutrients, coupled with poor aeration during the various phases of the fermentation pathways. Vintners of experience believe that leaving the finished wine in contact with the lees (sediment) over time acerbates the problem. I am of the view that using poor or inferior yeast formulations is the real perpetrator, as fellow meadmakers have a view that certain yeast strains are inclined to produce sulphide-type odours. As discussed elsewhere in the text, I, like Ken Schramm, add nutrients to the must over a period of days, as I feel this ensures the yeast is not overwhelmed with its source of nutrition and is able to feed upon the nutrients, and its budding and growth are somewhat restrained, ensuring the vestiges of nutrients are consumed in an orderly, regulated fashion. The presence of hydrogen sulphide is a ready host to metabolising mercaptans (harmless gas) and dimethyl sulfide compounds.

- **Mousey** The main chemical compound responsible for mousey odour and off-flavour is known as 2-acetyltetra-hydropyridine (ACTPY). Its aroma is branded as being "caged mice and cracker biscuits"; its odour and taste are associated with the bacillus *lactobacilli*. The mousey flavour can be delayed as it might take over 30 seconds or more to develop on the palate; it is essential that care is taken that the judge be aware when imbibing a tainted wine that its effects are not carried over from the immediately previously tasted mead. Andy Andrews' method was to rub a little of the offending mead 'twixt the palms of the hands as the heat generated quickly releases the offending odour. Unfortunately, some vintners are unable to detect or, for that matter, distinguish this smell when it arises.

- **Yeasty** This particular odour reveals itself in the main with young, unpolished fresh mead. Fortunately it will lose the yeasty smell over time; generally it disappears with subsequent rackings and storage.

- **Mouldy** This smell comes about through poor or insufficient sterilisation mainly affecting melomel and fruit wines through spores still being active within the fruit used. In addition, poor cleanliness and sterilisation of fermentation vessels can be a culprit. Immediately after racking, demijohns should be washed and cleaned thoroughly with a strong sterilisation solution before storage for future use.

- **Oxidisation** This smell arises due the formation of excessive production of acetaldehyde through the mead being exposed

A good example of comparing oxidised malt vinegar with an
excellent sample of mead [Michael Badger]

to the air often created at each and every racking by careless
methods of allowing the mead to splash around, introducing
oxygen to the wine

Bouquet and Aroma

The smell and odour given off by the wine are referred to as the
bouquet, known as "nose" by the experts. When first opening the
bottle, allow the stale air to clear from the bottle and smell the
wine. The judge should nose the opened mead first to capture its
rebirth: should he detect the odour of ascetic acid, the exhibit is
returned to the show bench, receiving no marks for bouquet or
taste, with the words "Acetified" in the remarks column.

The bouquet should be sampled by pouring a small amount into
the tasting glass, roughly a quarter full. Holding the flange base of
the glass (not the glass barrel itself), the wine is swirled around
several times and then smelt carefully by putting the nose well
into the top of glass. The tapering of the glass assists to capture
the bouquet. The bouquet should be attractive, wholesome and
naturally attractive, free of unpleasant odour, and there must be
absolutely no indication of sulphur dioxide. The object is to seek
the odour of honey that should be emanating from the mead. The
intensity of the bouquet is critical in awarding points. The higher

The author "nosing" the bouquet - 2016 [Edward Winter]

intensity verges on the aromatic, whereas a weaker bouquet is marked down accordingly.

Melomels, pyment, cyser, metheglin and hippocras will be found to have a more marked bouquet than plain meads, whether dry or sweet, although ling heather-based meads can be an exception. Meads with a totally unattractive bouquet should not be staged, as they may not be awarded any points, possibly being eliminated further from the competition. Having nosed the mead, you should taste it immediately and suck in air by drawing it across the top of the mead. This action will take the flavours over the nasal olfactory receptors and add to the judgement of the mead.

Finally, with the mead tasted, the remaining tasks of assessing balance, body and flavour all fall into place more or less simultaneously.

The three virtues of wines (taste, aroma and colour) come into their own with smell and taste as the principal ones. The Pasteur principles of three categories of smell are, namely:

- Primary aroma of the honey or fruit
- Secondary aroma
- Tertiary odour

It has been mentioned previously that the art of memory comes into play in our reaction to bouquet / odour, as these are subjective by past experiences in the exhibiting and judging of meads and honey wines, so much so that you build up a sort of bank of smells good, bad and indifferent. Nevertheless, what is acceptable to one can be unacceptable to another.

Balance

Mead is balanced when its alcoholic strength, acidity, sweetness (residual sugar) and tannins are in harmony with each other, with no single item dominating the palate. The question of balance is a desired quality that is separate from flavour.

Body

This is a term that relates to the sensation of fullness resulting from the viscosity or density of a wine on the judge's palate. It describes the "weight" in tasting wines in which alcoholic strength and the dissolved solids present are the contributory factors that make up the "body" of the wine.

Taste, Texture and Flavour

Flavour is the most important quality of a wine. A pleasing flavour comes about through a discerning interaction of the overall sensory stimulation of the receptors at the strategic points at the back of the nose with the delicate taste buds found on the tongue. Like body and balance, flavour is assessed by tasting the wine. The tasting requires the judge to take a reasonable amount of wine into the mouth and then swill it around the mouthparts, especially the tongue. In doing so, the aroma from the mead will reach the uppermost parts of the nasal airway situated at the back of the mouth. This is necessary because the senses of taste and smell are so closely interrelated in a fairly sophisticated biological way.

The tongue is the judge's primary organ of taste for detecting sweetness, acidity, bitterness, saltiness, blandness and all the other features he needs to detect, whether good or indifferent. Physiologically, the tongue detects sweetness at the front, acidity along the edges, saltiness along the front edges, and bitterness at the rear. Interestingly, the quality of astringency is detected on the inside of the cheeks and the gums and behind the front lip. The bitterness of using too much tannin reveals itself with an off-putting drying sensation.

To appreciate sweetness, the judge's taste organs need to be up to the mark, as it is essential to be able to differentiate between a dry or sweet wine by taste to determine that exhibits have been staged in the correct class. Dry mead, as explained elsewhere, should have no detectable sweetness. The UK and the USA have differing rules regarding degrees of sweetness as mentioned elsewhere in the text (see page 27).

The acidity in mead gives it a clean, refreshing taste. Meads lacking acidity have a medicinal taste and should be marked down accordingly, to zero if appropriate. Mead lacking in acidity is said to be dull and flabby. The presence of alcohol gives a warm feeling to the back of the throat. If this feeling is excessive, a good judge will detect that the mead has been fortified with a spirit. The judge should not award a prize to any exhibit about which he has such reservations.

Having discharged the wine from the mouth into the spittoon, the final test is to see the length of time the flavour persists in the mouth. This characteristic is known as "length". The longer, the better and, when the flavour of the mead has disappeared, the mouth should feel pleasantly fresh without any hint of a disagreeable aftertaste. Quality mead is in a class of its own when the excellent combination of all the required characteristics are present, and are is in balance with each other. Quality meads should be an example of epicurean delight and not just regarded as ordinary wines.

When tasting the various wines in the judging process, there needs to be some consideration of the previously tasted sample on the judges' palates, as it can give influence on the wine currently being tasted, hence the resort to regular palate cleansing at each tasting. This is particularly relevant to a wine with a "soft nose coupled with a delicate flavour" that can often be underrated should it have been followed by a mead that encompasses a full-bodied bouquet and flavour to boot. Elsewhere it has been noted that a judge over time will garner and appreciate the aptitude to remember the many subjectable impressions arising over time in tasting and re-tasting meads and honey wines. This faculty ascends with the wines produced with differing ingredients, comprehending the good, bad and indifferent qualities and characteristics when imbibed are added to the judge's memory bank of tastes. Understandably the art of experience tells us that the more impressions one retains, the sharper the memory becomes, thereby embracing efficiency in taking less time in the wine's evaluation by giving beneficial effect in the length of time before the palate becomes fatigued and weary.

Remember the judge in his deliberations will be alive to, and alerted to, a wine that might have non-permitted additives, i.e. use of grape juice or banana juice, or sultanas / raisins in a straight mead. Such a wine is no longer a straight mead, but a melomel wine, as previously stated elsewhere in the text. In 2014 at a judging session at the Royal Welsh Show, my colleague and fellow judge Erica Osborn picked up the traces of a substance in a defined "straight mead" class that she quite rightly identified as "inconveniens aut difficile", and it was passed over. The exhibitor, following the judging, graciously acknowledged that he had used a bottle containing the dregs of an excellent melomel, not realising he had unintentionally tainted some excellent mead. This example rightly illustrates that expert judges can pick up infringements in mead exhibits.

JUDGING HONEY-BASED VINEGAR

Judging vinegar should be undertaken after all other meads and honey wines have been judged. The modern style of living has introduced a number of variants to the traditional vinegar that includes sweet varieties and fruit-based types. The schedule should give clear indicators to the exhibitor that it is either sweet or dry. The traditional vinegar should be light amber in colour. The characteristics for all honey-based vinegars should be free from any presence of any vinegar plant, sediment and cloudiness.

The vinegar should have a notable absence of acetic acid when tasted, not too acidic but pleasingly mild, smooth, emitting a delicate aroma of acid when nosed.

The judge should pour a small amount into a tulip-shaped sherry tasting glass, swirl around the glass and "nose" the liquid. The taste is best achieved by dipping the index finger into the vinegar and taste accordingly, followed by clearing the palate with water. It is inadvisable to sample vinegar in the same manner as with meads and honey wines due to the strong acetic acid taste of honey vinegar.

REMEMBER JUDGES HAVE QUIRKS, TOO!

The assessment of a mead and honey wine through its stages of judging is dependent upon (as mentioned in the text) the judge's faculties of taste and smell, as he clearly needs to undertake assessments of bouquet, flavour and balance, all of which depend upon these requirements. Individual judges' palates and noses can understandably vary, and the ages of judges are known to affect their capabilities in respect of taste and smell. These departures are evident in the judging of honey in that a first prize exhibit at one show might or perhaps achieve only a third at another or no prize at all. Albeit, there is a chance that the exhibits that took the prizes were indeed far better. Nevertheless, it happens and for this reason both exhibitors and judges should not be dismayed by such happenings.

A judge, when part of a panel in deciding awards for best exhibits and trophies, should never display blind obstinacy: above all, he should be seen to be both firm and fair about decisions made. Such a maxim will hold you in good stead due entirely to having right on your side. Nevertheless, nothing is perfect or clear-cut, as mistakes are occasionally made. Always be aware of Oliver Cromwell's utterance, "Think it possible that you may be mistaken": this thought needs to be with you when you are in full flow on the show bench, especially as a tiring judge is apt to be mistaken or to pass things which under normal situations he would have spotted or picked up: it is quite human to make mistakes; we are all fallible at times, but mistakes are not the same as incompetence.

Difficulties can arise if the exhibits are of poor quality or there are errors in staging exhibits; this often occurs in smaller events or club shows. I find that it is best to discuss the matter with the show officials before making awards, as this might cut across the grain with both exhibitors and show officials. In most situations the show may be trying its best to entice and encourage would-be exhibitors to participate. Shows at a higher grade from county to national level exhibits should be awarded on merit. There are occasions when there may only be one or two entries in a class: to which the judge should award on merit if the exhibit meets all the requirements of being a first prize winner so be it. The exhibitor at the time of submitting his entries is not to know of the lack of entries to the class, and as such should not be penalised for lack of competition. I often ask the show secretary for Highly Commended (HC) prize cards to be given for first-time exhibitors and newcomers for entries, always providing there are no obvious signs or omissions in the exhibit/s staged. I have found that such a noble gesture inspires them to continue; very often asking an "old hand" for advice gets them enthused to carry on.

After the judging is complete, the judge should stay on to answer questions from both the public and the exhibitors: as a judge you must be accessible to help and assist exhibitors as to how they may improve their chances for exhibiting in the future, or to assist them with dealing with faults that you have purposely marked them down. Such goodwill is noted and a recall to judge in the future is usually forthcoming.

PART TEN
SUGGESTED
FURTHER READING

HEATHER HONEY:
A Comprehensive Guide

Michael Badger, MBE

BeeCraft

Adam, Brother, *In Search of the Best Strains of Bees*, Hebden Bridge, Northern Bee Books (1983).
Mead Production at Buckfast Abbey, Personal Communication (1984).
Breeding the Honey Bee, Hebden Bridge, Northern Bee Books (1987).

Andrews, SW, *All About Mead*, Hebden Bridge, Northern Bee Books (1982).

Badger, MJ, *Heather Honey: A Comprehensive Guide*, Stoneleigh, Bee Craft Ltd (2016).

Chapman, N, Pollen Microscopy, Halstead, CMI Publishing Ltd (2015).

Crane, E, *Honey: A Comprehensive Survey*, London, William Heinemann Ltd (1979).
The Archaeology of Beekeeping, London, Gerald Duckworth & Co. Ltd (1983).

Dummelow, J, *The Wax Chandlers of London*, London, Phillimore (1973).

Fraser, H Malcolm, *Beekeeping in Antiquity*, London, University Press (1931; 2nd edition 1951).

Harrer, H, *Seven Years in Tibet*, London, Hart-Davis (1953).

Herrod-Hempsall, W, *Bee-keeping new and old described with pen and camera*, Volume 1, London, The British Bee Journal, (1930).
Bee-keeping new and old described with pen and camera, Volume 2, London, The British Bee Journal (1937).
Producing: Preparing: Exhibiting and Judging – Bee Produce. London, The British Bee Journal (1948).

Lyle, Sir Oliver, *The Plaistow Story*, London, UK; Tate & Lyle Ltd (1960).

Morse, R A, *Making Mead (Honey Wine)*, Kalamazoo, Michigan, USA; Wicwas1 Press (1992).

Palmer, John J., *How to Brew*, Boulder, Colorado, USA; Brewers Publications (2006).

Piatz, Steve, *The Complete Guide to Making Mead*, Minneapolis,

Minnesota, USA; Voyageur Press (2014).

Root, AL; Flottum, K; Harman, A; Shimanuki, H., *The ABC and XYZ of Bee Culture* (41st edition), Medina, Ohio, USA; A L Root Company (1879).

Schramm, K, *The Compleat Meadmaker*, Boulder, Colorado, USA; Brewers Publications (2003).

Stell, Ian, *Understanding Bee Anatomy*, London, UK; Catford Press (2012).

Vernon, Frank, *Hogs at the Honeypot*, Steventon, Basingstoke, UK; Bee Books New & Old (1981).

Waring, Adrian and Claire, *Get Started in Beekeeping* (2nd edition), London, UK; Hodder and Stoughton (2015).

Weightman, C W, *Travels with Brother Adam to Tanzania*, Personal Communication (2008).
Travels with Brother Adam to Turkey and Mount Athos Peninsula, Greece, Personal Communication (2009).

Wheler, Sir George, *A Journey into Greece*, London, T. Cadman (1682)

EPILOGUE

Kim Flottum

It is for me a signal honour to have been asked to provide the epilogue for this excellent tome, *Mead and Honey Wines: A Comprehensive Guide*.

I come from a community in northern Wisconsin that has a strong Norwegian heritage, so I was introduced to something the folks there called MEAD at a fairly young age. "Nectar of the Gods," they cried. "A Viking Drink to Die For" was the chant around campfires by their noble ancestors. I wasn't impressed.

Years later, after becoming a beekeeping scientist and a beekeeper, I was introduced again to this drink called mead. This time it was made not by an amateur ancestor of a Norwegian Viking, but by a connoisseur of honey, of yeasts, of water, of science and of taste. I was impressed.

Since then, I have dabbled in tasting meads and honeys, and I now know those I favour and, more importantly, those I do not. But since I have not been a mead maker (until now), I have not been aware of why. Now, after reading Michael's book, I do. Go back again, review the details Michael has shared on fermentation, on bottling and especially mead's worst kept secret – the honeys chosen to flavour and focus the final product. It is his attention to the details of production, of content, of, especially, the honeys to choose, of being so careful to clean, and of the virtue of patience.

The wines he discusses are as wonderful as the meads he makes and those, too, gather the attention to detail so needed to be a craftsman in this trade. I encourage you to learn the rules and follow in the footsteps of those who are confident enough to have their work examined and judged by discerning tasters. Experts in this field. Because that, friend, is the true test of your skill. Even if you think your product is already the Nectar of the Gods. So a salutation from "olde Norse ves heill, be hale, be hearty or wassail".

Kim Flottum
Editor, Bee Culture magazine
623 W Liberty St., Medina, OH 44256
330.725.6677 ext 3214
www.BeeCulture.com Twitter Facebook

APPENDICES

APPENDIX A:
MEASUREMENTS AND WEIGHTS

For purposes of the recipes given, the terms gallon and pint are *Imperial units* of measurement.

One domestic teaspoon holds the approximate weights of the following substances (unless otherwise stated, all measurements and weights are defined as "level").

Calcium carbonate (chalk or limestone)	3 g
Sodium bicarbonate (baking soda or bicarbonate of soda)	5.5 g
Granulated/cane sugar (beet sugar or sugar cane)	6 g
Citric acid	4 g
Sodium metabisulfite	6 g

A domestic teaspoon holds approximately 5 ml
A domestic dessertspoon holds approximately 10 ml
A domestic tablespoon holds approximately 15 ml
A half-pint beer mug holds approximately 16 g hops under light compression
A one-pint beer mug holds approximately 33 g hops under moderate compression

Volume

HONEY and SYRUP			MEASURING LIQUID, COOKING MEASUREMENTS		
Metric	*Imperial*	*US Cups*	*Metric*	*Imperial*	*US Cups*
45 g	1½ oz	⅛ cup	250 ml	8 fl oz	1 cup
85 g	3 oz	¼ cup	180 ml	6 fl oz	¾ cup
110 g	4 oz	⅓ cup	150 ml	5 fl oz	⅔ cup
170 g	6 oz	½ cup	120 ml	4 fl oz	½ cup
225 g	8 oz	⅔ cup	75 ml	2½ fl oz	⅓ cup
250 g	9 oz	¾ cup	60 ml	2 fl oz	¼ cup
340 g	12 oz	1 cup	30 ml	1 fl oz	⅛ cup
400 g	14 oz	1⅙ cup	15 ml	½ fl oz	1 tablespoon

Spoons (metric equivalents)
1 dessertspoon = 2 teaspoons
3 teaspoons = 1 tablespoon

Imperial		Tablespoons to US cups	
1 teaspoons	5 ml	1 tablespoon	$1/16$ cup.
2 teaspoons	10 ml	2 tablespoons	$1/8$ cup
3 teaspoons	15 ml	3 tablespoons	$3/16$ cup
4 teaspoons	20 ml	4 tablespoons	$1/4$ cup
5 teaspoons	25 ml	5 tablespoons	$1/3$ cup
6 teaspoons	30 ml	6 tablespoons	$3/8$ cup

Equivalents

1 cubic metre	33.315 cu. ft 219.98 gallons (UK) 264.18 gallons (US) 1000 litres
1 gallon (UK)	160 fl oz 1.2 gallons (US)
1 cubic foot	6.25 gallons (Imp)
1 lb./gallon (UK)	99.76 g/l (Imp/metric)

Conversions

Ounces to grams	multiply by 28.35
Pounds to kilograms	multiply by 0.454
Pints to litres	multiply by 0.568
Gallons to litres	multiply by 4.546
US gallons to litres	multiply by 3.785
Imperial gallons to US gallons	multiply by 1.2

Imperial Capacity Conversions

1 litre	0.22 gallons	1 pint	20 fl. oz
2 litres	0.44 gallons	3 pints	60 fl oz
3 litres	0.67 gallons	5 pints	100 fl oz
4.546 litres	1.00 gallons	8 pints	160 fl oz

Weight Conversions

Metric to Imperial		Imperial to Metric	
25 g	¾ oz	¹/₈ oz	3.5 g
50 g	1¾ oz	¼ oz	7.1 g
100 g	3½ oz	½ oz	14.2 g
125 g	4½ oz	1 oz	28.4 g
250 g	8¾ oz	¼ lb	113 g
500 g	1 lb ½ oz	½ lb	227 g
1 kg	2 lb 3¼ oz	1 lb	454 g
2 kg	4 lb 6½ oz	2 lb	907 g
3 kg	6 lb 9¾ oz	3 lb	1.361 kg
4 kg	8 lb 13 oz	4 lb	1.814 kg
5 kg	11 lb	5 lb	2.268 kg
10 kg	22 lb	10 lb	4.543 kg

[Note]

One US gallon equals 128 fluid ounces, or 3.7853 litres, or 0.833 Imperial gallons, while one Imperial gallon equals 160 fluid ounces, or 4.5459 litres, or 1.2 US gallons. A simple reminder is that five US gallons equal four and one-sixth Imperial gallons, and five Imperial gallons equal six US gallons.

APPENDIX B:
BLENDING MEADS AND HONEY WINES
USING THE "PEARSON SQUARE"

The Pearson Square is a simple method for a mead maker to blend wines accurately and proficiently. It's a procedure used throughout the food and drink industries due to its straightforwardness in use. The working of the Pearson Square is simplicity itself. It is a means of calculating the proper proportions required to create the right balance in the final wine. This is usually blending a high-alcohol wine with one of a low alcohol content. The resultant blend has a more reasonable alcohol level. It can also be used to blend wines that have different acidities or different degrees of sweetness. The Pearson Square is a simple method for a mead maker to blend wines. The following example illustrates its use.

SKETCH A

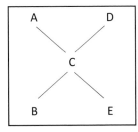

A sweet mead (A) with an ABV 15 per cent alchol is regarded as too strong for use as a social wine. To reduce its alcohol content it is blended with a mead of lower alcohol content with an ABV 10 per cent alcohol (B). The aim is to arrive at an ABV 13.5 per cent (C) as the Target ABV.

By using the Pearson Square, letters in the diagram are replaced by numbers, followed by simple subtractions, B – C and A – C.

In our example, taking the absolute values of the results:

SKETCH B

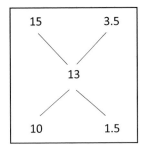

Pearson Square
[Michael Badger]

[B - C] = 3.50
[A - C] = 1.50
[D + E] = 5.00

A = 15
B = 10
C = 13.50
D = [B – C] = 3.5 parts
E = [A – C] = 1.5 parts
D + E = total 5 parts

The units for D and E are labeled as "parts". Mixing 3.5 parts of wine A with 1.5 parts of wine B will result in a final alcohol content of 13.5%.

To get these quantities into units of measurement we can calculate the percentage of each as follows, using a one gallon demijohn for the calculation:

Wine A = 3.5 / 5 parts = 0 70 per gallon

Wine B = 1.5 / 5 parts = 0 30 per gallon

Rules of using the Pearson Square

It is essential that you understand how it works. If you break these rules the Pearson Square will give you strange results.

Rule 1: The value of C must be between A and B

- If you have a 15% ABV wine and a 10% wine these two can be blended to produce a final blend, the alcohol content averages between these two concentrations.

- You cannot blend a 15% and 10% ABV wines in anticipation of 18% wine.

Rule 2: D and E are always taken as positive values

- Note the difference between A and C as well as B and C.

- Disregard and negative results and take them as positive numbers.

APPENDIX C: FERMENTATION

Honey with high water content is an ideal honey for spoiling that arises through a simple and natural reaction through the consumption of sugars in the honey by the naturally present yeasts, when the conditions are right, that is a high temperature and excess water content within the honey, then fermentation has a stable base to begin.

If the honey is kept at an ambient temperature of below 10 °C (50 °F) with the water content being below 20%, the problems of fermentation are minimal to zero.

The Process of Fermentation

The process of fermentation comes about through the consumption of the sugars by the yeasts present within the honey: the yeasts grow in size and number: the sugars are the yeasts' source of energy. The growing and multiplication of the yeasts produce many by-products, which impart flavours to the honey that blight

Honey that is fermenting: the smell of pears in addition to the physical appearance is the telltale signs [Photograph: Gerald Collins NDB]

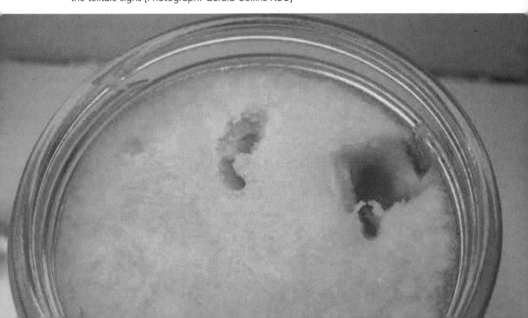

its aroma and natural flavour. These yeasts are naturally present in the nectaries of the flowers; they are picked up and carried by the bee through the nectar. It is beyond the scope of this book to explain in detail the mechanisms involved, other than to say many of these yeasts die when the inversion from nectar to honey takes place through the rise in concentration of the sugars, although some yeasts do survive. Their presence in the right conditions allows these yeasts to multiply to a point where their existence is a destructive force to the honey. Keeping the water content to below 20% minimises the risks of fermentation to zero. The concentration of the sugars is such that the yeast is inhibited from reproducing and growth does not take place. All honeys that become crystallised will find that the fluid between the crystals will become diluted by the removal of the natural solids, thereby resulting in an increased water content, which can range from 4 to 6%.

There are honeys where fermentation can be held in check by its texture, especially hard crystallised honeys, whereas fermentation will be more noticeable by soft-textured honeys.

Fermenting honey has a distinct smell reminiscent of decaying apples; the odour given off is never forgotten to beekeepers who will know when their honey is on "the turn" – that is, fermenting. Fermentation is of three kinds in crystallised honey, the first is usually created by a leaking container that permits water vapour to be taken up by the honey through its natural propensity of being hygroscopic. The process leaves on the surface of the container a very thin layer of diluted solution that is the ideal medium for fermentation to proceed. This watery layer can be removed from the surface; it has an unmistakable wine-type odour: once this has been removed, the remaining unfermented honey can be processed as normal. Care is needed to ensure that all the fermenting material is removed and that the remaining honey does not become contaminated. A second type is when the honey is warmed for processing; the fermenting honey is not obvious until it is to be poured into the bottling tank: large bubbles are seen with the unmistakable smell of fermentation becoming apparent.

The beekeeper can retain this honey for feeding purposes for the hivebees by heating it to a 95 °C-200 °F for about 3 hours. Feed back to the bees for them to reconstitute or feed to nuclei in spells of bad weather. The third type of fermentation is where the honey surface heaves like baker's dough, despite its fairly dry appearance. The smell of fermentation is it's give-away, together with the lumpy appearance. This material can by careful removal of the top 15 mm of the affected surface of the bulk honey be sufficient that the remaining honey can be processed for use.

APPENDIX D –
HYDROXYMETHYLFURFURAL (HMF)

HMF is matter produced by the chemical breakdown of fructose in the presence of "free" acids, a development that occurs in honey all the time: its rate of production is largely dependent upon the temperature to which the honey is subjected to at any given time. Therefore the higher the temperature, the faster the HMF will be produced; conversely the longer the honey is stored before it is used, the greater the quantity of HMF it will contain. That notwithstanding, the amount produced is a small quantity that is relatively insignificant, and it is completely harmless to the consumer.

Current legislation within the EU requires that the maximum content should not exceed 40 mg/kg (under 20 mg/kg) under EC Directive 1974 (74/409/EEC), and in the United Kingdom only, 80 mg/kg (under 20 mg/kg) under UK Honey Regulations 1976. The figures in brackets are the levels recommended for processors in the UK only. The UK has a special derogation from EU law allowing it to import honey at 80 mg/kg HMF. All other EU countries have to abide by the 40 mg/kg limit. The USA does not have specific honey legislation and sets no legal limits for HMF or diastase activity, the quality being guaranteed by the importers.

Yeasts are inhibited from developing in a temperature of below 10 °C (50 °F) and above 27 °C (80 °F): therefore fermentation can be kept at bay with confidence whether stored in bulk (honey stores better in bulk) or in jars under these conditions. At the lower temperature, hydroxymethylfurfural (HMF) is produced at a very slow rate.

Beekeepers may be ignorant of HMF and its effects on bulk-stored honey; however, with normal and careful handling of honeys the amount of HMF will not exceed permitted levels. Trading Standards officials are known to check honeys regularly at retail outlets: it is essential that beekeepers are made aware of HMF and how its presence can be kept at normalised levels by storing and processing it carefully.

APPENDIX E:
SOME KNOWN MEADS AND HONEY
WINES FROM AROUND THE WORLD

Type	Description	Country
Acerglyn	Mead made with honey and maple syrup	USA and Canada
Aguamie	Mead believed to be made from the maguey plant of Mexico and Latin America	Spain and Hispanic areas of South America
Balché (also known as pitarilla)	Mead produced from the bark of *Lonchocarpus violaceus* (balché tree) consumed in antiquity and to the present day by the Yucatec Maya peoples	Mexico, parts of upper central/Latin America
Bee pee	Lemon melomel mead using the lees of a different melomel mead	USA and Canada
Bilbemel	Mead made with blueberries, blueberry juice. Sometimes used for varietal mead using blueberry blossom honey	USA and Canada
Black Mead	A name sometimes given to the blend of honey and blackcurrants	UK
Bochet (also known as brochet)	Mead where the honey is caramelised or burned separately before adding the water. Yields toffee, caramel, chocolate and toasted marshmallow flavours.	USA and Canada
Bochetomel	Mead where the honey is caramelised or burned separately before adding the water. Yields toffee, caramel, chocolate and toasted marshmallow flavours, with fruit such as elderberries, black raspberries and blackberries added	USA and Canada
Boswell	A variation of metheglin with the addition of both claret and Curaçao and brandy spirit, served hot with a sprinkling of nutmeg on the surface of the liquor.	England
Braggot	Also known as bracket or brackett. Originally brewed with honey and hops, later with honey and malt, with or without hops added.	Welsh origin (bragawd)

Capsicumel	Mead flavoured with chilli peppers; peppers may be hot or mild	Mexico
Caudle	An admixture of mead and ale much valued in England from the Middle Ages	England
Chouchen	A kind of mead normally containing 14 per cent alcohol by volume. Traditionally, buckwheat honey is used and this imparts chouchen's strong colour and pronounced flavour	Brittany, France
Clarre	See Mulsum	Rome, Italy
Clionomel	Believed to be an ancient liquor of mead used as a medicine comprising mead with egg whites	None specifically identified
Cyser	Mead made from apples or apple juice. In the UK it was a commonly made drink regarded as superior to cider. Produced by cottager-type beekeepers from medieval to present times. Also known as cyster.	UK and USA
Czwórniak	Mead made using three units of water for each unit of honey	Poland
Dandaghare	Mead from Nepal, combining honey with Himalayan herbs and spices. It has been produced since 1972 in the city of Pokhara	Nepal
Dwójniak	Polish mead, using equal amounts of water and honey	Poland
Elderberry	Mead made with elderberries and honey; there are many variations to the traditional recipe	UK
Elderberry Danish Mead	Classic grape wine base mixed with the unique taste of elderberries	Cornwall, UK
Elderberry Negus	A variation of melomel with the addition of spirits. A drink concocted by Colonel Francis Negus, MP, from an original drink made with port wine in the early 18th century	UK
Frankenmel	A hippocras mead of grapes and spices	None specifically identified

Gverc	Croatian mead prepared in Samobor and many other places. The word "gverc" or "gvirc" is from the German "Gewürze" and refers to various spices added to mead	Croatia
Honey Bishop	A variation of metheglin with the addition of spirits; an ancient drink in the Middle Ages	UK
Hydromel	Name derived from the Greek *hydromeli*, literally "water-honey" (see also *melikraton* and *hydromelon*). It is also the French name for mead. (See also and compare with the Catalan *hidromel* and aiguamel, Galician *aiguamel*, Portuguese *hidromel*, Italian *idromele* and Spanish *hidromiel* and *aguamiel*.) It is also used as a name for light or low-alcohol mead	Europe, especially Portugal
Idromele	A melomel-type mead	Italy
Iqhilika	A mead and beer type that has a pleasing almond aftertaste when imbibed	Eastern Cape, South Africa
Madu	Mead from India, known as Sanskrit after the prophet Sanskrit Rigveda of Ancient India. Believed to be the most ancient record of mead some 8,000 years before present.	Indian subcontinent
Meddeglyn	See Myddyglyn	Wales and UK
Medica	Slovenian and Croatian variety of mead	Slovenia and Croatia
Medovina	A honey wine from the Slovak area, commercially available in the Czech Republic and Slovakia	Central and Eastern Europe
Medovukha	Eastern Slavic variant (honey-based fermented drink)	Central and Eastern Europe
Medu	Generic term for ancient mead produced in Germany	Germany
Meis	A mead produced in former Italian Eritrea	Eritrea and the Horn of Africa

Meodu	The name given to olde English mead, referred to in literature as meade. It was originally a concoction of honey, fruit, grain and hops	England and Wales
Met	An ancient mead believed to have been consumed from the German Middle Ages	Kingdom of Germany
Mézbor	A mead from Hungary using mainly acacia honey	Hungary and former Magyar states
Midus	Mead made from honey and berry juice, infused with carnation blossoms, acorns, poplar buds, juniper berries and other herbs. Often produced as mead distillate or mead nectar, some of the varieties having as much as 75 per cent alcohol	Lithuania
Miod	A mead with many variations	Poland and East Russia
Miodemel	Polish type of mead made with hops	Poland and East Prussia
Mjød	Mead produced to a Scandinavian recipe similar to mjöd	Norway and Denmark
Mjöd	Traditional mead from Sweden with variations in the use of fruit and spices	Sweden and Scandinavia
Mõdu	A traditional fermented drink with a taste of honey and an alcohol content of 4.0 per cent	Estonia
Morat	Mead made from blended honey and mulberries	Middle East and USA
Mulsum	Mulsum is not regarded as true mead; it is unfermented honey blended with a high-alcohol wine	Rome, Italy
Myddyglyn	A mead of Welsh origin that is laced with spices. Also known as meddeglyn.	Wales and the Borders

Myod	Traditional Russian mead, historically available in three major varieties: • aged mead ("мёд ставленный"): a mixture of honey and water or berry juices, subject to a very slow (12-50 years) anaerobic fermentation in airtight vessels, in a process similar to traditional balsamic vinegar, creating a rich, complex and high-priced product • drinking mead ("мёд питный"): a kind of honey wine from diluted honey by traditional fermentation • boiled mead ("мёд варёный"): a drink closer to beer, brewed from boiled wort of diluted honey and herbs. Very similar to modern medovukha	Russia
Nabidh	Of Arabic origin. Nabeez (Nabidh) was known to be a favoured drink of the prophet Muhammad. It is produced by steeping very ripe grapes and raisins in water and imbibing the liquor	Arabian Territories
Omphacomel	Mead that blends honey with verjuice (a highly acidic juice made by pressing unripe grapes); could therefore be considered a variety of pyment. From the Greek *omphakomeli*, literally "unripe-grape-honey"	Greece
Oxymel	Historic mead recipe, blending honey with wine vinegar. From the Greek *oxymeli*, literally "vinegar-honey" (also *oxymelikraton*)	Greece
Pitarrilla	Drink made from a fermented mixture of wild honey, balché tree bark and fresh water	Mayan, Central America
Półtorak	Polish grape mead, made using two units of honey for each unit of water	Poland
Rhodomel	Honey, rose hips, rose petals or rose attar and water. From the Greek *rhodomeli*, literally "rose-honey"	Eastern Europe, Greece and Middle East
Rubamel	A specific type of melomel made with raspberries	Romania

Sima	Quick-fermented low-alcoholic Finnish variety seasoned with lemon and associated with the festival of Vappu	Finland and Sweden
Tej/Mes	An Ethiopian and Eritrean mead, fermented with wild yeasts and the addition of gesho. Recipes vary from family to family	North-East Africa
Tella/Suwa	A style of beer; with the inclusion of honey some recipes are similar to braggot	Ethiopia and Eritrea
Thalassiomel	Known to be of Ancient Greek origin using thyme honey and sea water (thalassiomel) with the addition of egg white; regarded as a medicament for the relief of gout	Greece
Trójniak	Polish mead, made using two units of water for each unit of honey	Poland
Weirdome	A concoction of honey using rainwater with additions of herbs and spices and other unspecified flavourings on the lines of hippocras and grains. Used by UK farm workers in the 18th century to steep "flicks" of bacon and hams prior to cooking	Unknown
White mead	A mead that is coloured white with herbs, fruit or, sometimes, egg whites	Unknown
Ydromel	A mead made in the extensive areas of thyme found in Greece	Greece
Yeyin dvash	Mead from varied flora throughout the traditional Holy Land	Israel and Palestinian territories

APPENDIX F: MEAD AND HONEY WINE JUDGING TEMPLATE

GREAT YORKSHIRE SHOW - 2014	DRY MEAD	ENTERED	ENTRIES STAGED.	JUDGE:
STEWARD: Erica M. Osborn	CLASS NO. 39	16	16	Andrew Gibb

ENTRY NO	PRESENTATION (5) 1 2 3 4 5 Cork, Bottle, Label	CLARITY (10) 1 2 3 4 5 6 7 8 9 10 Oxidised, Cloudy, Dull, Bright, Star Bright	COLOUR (5) 1 2 3 4 5 Pale Straw & Upwards	BOUQUET (10) 1 2 3 4 5 6 7 8 9 10 Poor to Perfect	BALANCE (10) 1 2 3 4 5 6 7 8 9 10 Rough to Smooth	BODY (10) 1 2 3 4 5 6 7 8 9 10 Strength of Legs on the Glass	FLAVOUR (50) 5 10 15 20 25 30 35 40 45 50 Light Meads - Delicate to Finesse Sweet - Sack Meads - Medium to Strong	TOTAL (100)
413								
414								
415								
416								
417								
418								
419								
420								
421								
422								
423								
424								
425								
426								
427								
428								

APPENDIX G:
MEAD STEWARDS' DUTIES

The most rewarding way to learn more about showing meads and honey wines, especially once you've started to make them yourself, is to become a steward to a series of qualified and experienced mead judges. For a major show there are a number of protocols to be observed: some of these are itemised below as an aide-mémoire as suggested by Peter Lewis, Chief Honey Steward, Great Yorkshire Show, Harrogate, England:

Preparation

• Read, study and understand the show schedule in advance of the show. Make sure that you have a copy to hand during the judging on show day.

• Know the individual class specifications and the show's rules and regulations; in particular make sure that you are aware of, and conversant with, their local interpretation and application, highlighting with marker pen the important clauses to be observed.

• Often you will be the reference interface link as the judge might not always be fully familiar with each / every show's precise idiosyncrasies, and / or may request clarification(s): here your tact and diplomacy in conveying your knowledge of the show schedule can determine the ultimate success of the show's adjudged results, and eventually its repute and standing. Do not be afraid to ask the senior steward or the show secretary if you are unclear on any point.

• Be aware that in staging mead exhibits, "travelling" may have stimulated fermentation activity (a common phenomenon with Champagne yeasts). Check that stoppers are firmly in place and do *avoid* standing bottles on display in direct sunlight.

Prior to Commencement of Judging

- Arrive in good time for the show briefing. It's generally good practice for the steward to 'meet and greet' their assigned judge on arrival by being there themselves in advance. Be prepared to assist with carrying their judging kit.
- Preferably avoid any use of aftershaves, perfumes or strong-smelling deodorants when acting as a steward. Consumption of garlic, powerful spices, etc. is similarly best avoided from the meal eaten immediately prior to stewarding.
- Wear comfortable shoes and be dressed appropriately.
- For stewarding, *look the part*: a clean, white coat, pressed and ironed, rather than creased and crumpled from being left in a bag since the last show, creates a much better impression that inspires confidence.
- Have a pencil, pencil eraser and ink pen for marking the score sheet records and results slips. A clipboard is useful for keeping all the paperwork together, providing a firm writing surface.
- Ensure that your hands are clean before judging commences. Wear light cotton gloves when handling bottled exhibits e.g. when staging, or moving them to / from the judges' bench.
- Have clean, freshly drawn water in place for the rinse washing of wine tasting glasses as the judging proceeds.
- Ensure a bucket or container is on hand for your judge to throw away tasted mead.
- To dry the glasses clean, dry tea towels should be available (judges usually have their own. Ideally linen, not cotton. Washed rather than being brand new and unwashed).
- Make sure that the judge is well supplied with drinking water and a glass for cleansing their palate.
- Mention to the judge if this is your first time as a steward. Make sure you understand and agree what is wanted and expected of you, and that you understand the judge's needs.
- Ascertain from the judge their preferred way of working.

Whilst Engaged in Judging

- Ensure that you identify all the exhibits to be judged for your section of the competition.
- Flag any duplicates to your judge immediately at the start of judging a class. Make sure you know the number of entries per class, and are aware of any that have not been staged to avoid accidental oversight, for example.
- If you are an exhibitor with exhibits staged, ensure you tell the judge before the actual judging of the respective class (or classes) commences. You should certainly not indicate which exhibit is yours specifically, but make it clear whether you might just perhaps have, shall we tactfully say, "a vested interest".
- Pay particular attention to matching the glass and mead sample to the respective bottle throughout the judging process. Some judges like to move the exhibits around as they physically rank them in relative order of merit during consideration. Concentration is required.
- After a glass has been used, having first checked that the judge is indeed finished with that sample, empty and rinse wash it promptly before standing it to drain upside down.
- If you wish to taste and sample the meads, ask the judge first (it is preferable to bring your own two glasses for the purpose, sampling only the very slightest amount). Remember that most exhibitors do like to have something left in the bottle at least, particularly when it's a good or even winning mead.
- Carry out all the judge's stewarding requests promptly.
- Record scores on the score sheet template in pencil as each part of the assessment is undertaken. Quick, accurate arithmetic is required for adding up total scores, only finally inked in once the judge is happy and has completed judging the class, selected / agreed the results, the winners (1st, 2nd and 3rd places), etc. Do check adding-up, that entry numbers

and results all match: failure to do so will create major issues if mistakes are made, it can create ill will, questioning the show's competence.

- Do not speak to the judge unless the questions are appertaining to the judging or your role as a steward.
- Other questions should be held over until all judging is completed. Avoid chatter.
- Do not comment on any exhibits unless specifically asked to do so.
- Under *no* circumstances mention to others any remarks the judge may make while they were undertaking their duties. Judges regard this as a breach of trust, and it might be unfair or even taken as hurtful by the exhibitor concerned.
- Some shows / judges write comments on slips for the exhibits / exhibitors. This is very much an area where *local* custom and practice prevail, and an example of where discretion is strongly recommended in your advising your judge appropriately as their steward.
- Do not allow the judge to be distracted, and certainly not interfered with, whilst judging is in progress.
- If there is a show catalogue *do not* under any circumstances at all share information on exhibits or entrants with the judge.
- Make sure that all stoppers are firmly replaced once each class is judged, and that restaging is tidily organised and orderly arranged back on the show bench, exhibit labels showing (and matching) etc.

When the Judging is Completed.

Be on hand to assist the judge with dealing with awards of trophies. Do not let the judge depart from the show area until the senior steward or show secretary gives their approval.

Should the show authorities provide lunch, be available to accompany them to the dining area.

APPENDIX H:
GLOSSARY

ABV Synonym for Alcohol by Volume – The qualitative measurement of alcohol of a wine denoted as a percentage of the total volume.

Acetification The oxidisation of alcohol to acetic acid arising through infection of the wine by acetobacter bacterial organisms.

Acid Compounds that are an essential requirement for making sound, drinkable wine. Those used are normally present in fruit (citric, malic and tartaric), but not in the required amounts to assist the maturity of the wine.

Aerate To force air or oxygen into a liquor by agitation or by gas injection.

Aerobic Refers to the presence of oxygen. An aerobic fermentation occurs in the presence of oxygen.

After-taste The number and qualities of sensitivities lingering on the palate during the moments after wine is tasted. The effects of aroma and bouquet passing through mouth and nasal passages are aroused, stimulating "aftertaste".

Ageing The process of time and the keeping of wine, albeit in bulk or bottle, as it is transformed into maturity.

AHA Synonym of American Homebrewers Association – a USA-based society of mead, beer and cider-makers for the home, domestic and non-commercial producers.

Airlock A holding trap of water or glycerine to prevent air or airborne bacteria from entering the fermentation vessel while allowing carbon dioxide produced from the products of fermentation to escape to the atmosphere. Also known as a fermentation lock.

Alcoholic Limit The term given to yeast in relation to the alcohol level that is sufficient to stop the process of fermentation.

Aldehyde An essential component in the process of fermentation as an antecedent to alcohol. The exposure of the wine to air and oxygen often results in off-flavours of a sherry perception in both taste and odour.

Alpha acid A constituent of hops. This acid contributes to the levels of bitterness. The alpha acid levels range from 3 to 16 per cent.

Alpha-amylase An enzyme known to destroy starch, thus preventing starchy wines from becoming cloudy.

Amino acids Nitrogenous composites that contribute free amino acid to the yeast during the early staged phases of the fermentation process.

Anaerobic Refers to the absence of oxygen. An anaerobic fermentation occurs without the presence of oxygen.

Aroma The odour emitted from a wine. Also known as "bouquet".

Ascorbic acid See vitamin C.

Astringency Astringency in wine is the drying, rough, gathering and puckering sensation experienced after tasting most wines. The term "smooth" describes the pleasurable feeling of a high-quality astringent sensation. Astringency is also referred to as "bite".

Atemperation A procedure of gradually regulating the yeast culture to the temperature of the *must*.

Attenuation A US term related to the extent the yeast has fermented out the available sugar into alcohol. Those yeasts with high attenuation produce the most alcohol, leaving little residual sugar in the finished mead.

Autolysis The death of the yeast cells often attributed to off-flavours and taste.

Balance When all the different components in the wine are working in harmony.

Balling A US term related to the specific gravity measurement in degrees, whereby gravity measurement is represented in percentage points of solids in a solution based on cane sugar.

Bentonite A negatively charged fining agent.

Big A US term for a wine having a pronounced aroma.

BJCP Beer Judge Certification Program. The US organisation that oversees the rules of competition for mead, ciders and beers, including the certification of judges.

Blanc French word for white, relating to grape varietal names.

Body The awareness of fullness presented by the wine when taken into the mouth or swallowed.

Bouquet The odour emitted from a wine. Also known as aroma.

Brix The sugar content of an aqueous solution as a percentage by mass.

Buffer A compound or substance that integrates changes in pH.

Campden tablets See sulphite/s.

Carbon dioxide A by-product of fermentation.

Carbonation A method of adding carbon dioxide to a finished wine by mechanical means. The BJCP cites three levels in accumulative order: still, pétillant and sparkling.

Carboy A large fermentation vessel of five gallons (Imp). It is available in both glass and plastic.

Casein A positively charged fining agent.

Cloying A term applied to wine and mead production in the USA emphasising a character of sweetness that is not readily balanced by acidity or tannins.

Colloid A substance of gelatinous origin found naturally in raw honey. Colloids act as binding agents for the naturally present aromatic compounds in raw honeys.

Cyser Mead wine produced from pure apple juice with honey, water, nutrients and acids.

DAP Diammonium phosphate (NH2) 2HPO4, a yeast nutrient added to the must to provide free nitrogen.

Demijohn One-gallon (Imp) vessel, either glass or plastic used for wine fermentation.

Diacetyl A compound which, when present, adds a specific flavour or aroma reminiscent of butterscotch.

Dry (Dryness) Having no residual sugar content in the finished wine.

Ester An aromatic substance derived from an acid and an alcohol. A most desirable compound responsible for the aromas in honey and honey wines.

Ethyl alcohol (CH3CH2OH) The alcohol created by the yeasts. Also known as ethanol.

Fermentation, primary The initial conversion of sugar and oxygen to alcohol and carbon dioxide through the metabolic activity of yeast feeding on the sugars in the must.

Fermentation, secondary A second, quieter fermentation after a first vigorous fermentation experienced with certain musts, especially when ling heather is used. Malolactic fermentation is also known as a secondary fermentation.

Fermentation lock See airlock.

Fermenter Vessel used for the process of fermentation.

Final gravity The finished or final specific gravity of wine that has accomplished its point of ethanol tolerance.

Finings The clarification of a wine by removing suspended particles.

Flabby A wine or mead is said to be flabby that is lacking in structure, specifically acids and nutrients.

Flat A term denoting the absence of effervescence. In the USA it is often denoted to as a *still mead*.

Flocculation The settlement of yeast at the bottom of the fermentation vessel. Those yeasts that clear well and completely and form well-packed sediment are said to flocculate well.

Floral US term relating to the description of aroma, bouquet and scent of honeys, beer, meads, honey and country wines.

Floral source The source of the nectar used for the production of honey.

Free amino nitrogen (FAN) The amount of nitrogen freely available to the yeast as amino compounds while present in the must. FAN is critical to the formation of a healthy developing fermentation.

Fructose Fructose, or fruit sugar, is a monosaccharide found in many plants. It is often bonded to glucose to form the disaccharide, sucrose.

Fusels A term often referred to as fusel oils and fusel alcohols comprising an admixture of several alcohols, most generically from amyl alcohol. The fusels are often perceived to be solvent-like, spicy or hot arising from higher fermentation temperature, combined with reduced pH and nutrients during the fermentation phase.

Gelatin Derived from animal tissues. It is a good fining agent for red wines. It is not usually recommended for fining white wines.

Higher alcohols Alcohols other than ethanol that may be present in a wine

Hippocras A honey wine using grape juice, honey and water to which herbs are added

Hydrometer The instrument used with a trial jar to measure specific gravity of wine or the contents of the must

Hygroscopic The absorption of free moisture from the atmosphere. Honey is by nature hygroscopic

Invertase An enzyme that catalyses the hydrolysis of sucrose. It is synthesised by bees to break down sucrose into glucose and fructose

Isinglass A substance obtained from the dried swim bladders of fish. It is a form of collagen used mainly for the clarification or fining of mead, wine and beer

Lactic acid Lactic acid fermentation is accomplished when lactic acid bacteria convert simple carbohydrates such as glucose, sucrose or galactose to lactic acid

Lees Sediment in the base of a fermentation vessel

Legs The amount of trail the mead leaves on the face of a tasting glass when tipped at an angle. The longer the trail "legs", the better the sign of the present level of pertained alcohol within the mead sample. A physical sign used by mead judges

Length A term used in the analysis of a wine by the vintner and the wine judge: it is the length of time the flavour of tasted wine persists in the mouth. The longer the flavour is present, the better the wine.

Malolactic fermentation The conversion of stronger malic acid present in wine by lactic acid bacteria to weaker lactic acid and carbon dioxide. This is often referred to as a secondary fermentation

Melomel Mead produced from fruit or fruit juice, other than grape or apple, plus honey, water, acids and nutrients. Includes the addition of certain fruits to aid the fermentation

Metheglin Pyment mead flavoured with spices

Mouthfeel The instantaneous impression of mead when taken into the mouth and swallowed. The mouthfeel is generally predisposed by the residual sugar, the alcohol content, body, acidity levels and flavour

Must The unfermented or fermenting mixture and blends of honey, water, acids, nutrients and other substances that lead to the finished wine following fermentation.

Nectar A sugar-rich liquid produced by plants in glands called nectaries, either within or outside the flowers.

Original gravity (OG) The gravity of a must at the onset of pitching the yeast.

Oxidation The process whereby oxygen combines with other compounds that can and do influence both taste and natural colour of mead and honey wines.

Pectin A polysaccharide used as a gelling agent.

Pectolase or Pectinase A compound used in wines with high levels of pectin. It degrades pectin, thus increasing the amount of free-flowing juice.

Péttilant A term used in the USA to define a judiciously sparkling mead between *still and sparkling*.

pH A numeric scale used to specify the acidity or basicity (alkalinity) of an aqueous solution. The scale ranges from 1 to 14. A value of 7 characterises a neutral solution (the value of 7 embodies a neutral solution: pure water has a pH of approximately 7). Below 7 signifies an acidic solution: those greater than 7 are alkaline.

Phenols Found in wine as natural phenol and polyphenols, affecting the taste, colour and mouthfeel.

Pitching Adding yeast to the must.

Poise The unit of dynamic viscosity in the centimetre-gram-second system of units.

Potassium sorbate Commonly known as a wine stabiliser. Used to finish fermentation or, in conjunction with metabisulfite, prevent it recurring.

Potential alcohol The percentage of alcohol that will be produced should all the sugar in the must be converted. Potential alcohol will not be achieved if fermentation stops before all the sugar is spent. For calculation purposes a reading of the opening gravity (OG) must be taken before fermentations begins.

ppm Parts per million.

Pyment Mead produced from pure grape juice, often known as white mead.

Rack or racking The mechanism for transferring the must or fermented wine from one vessel to another by siphonic action.

Reagent A substance used to cause a chemical reaction.

Refractometer An optical instrument used to determine the sugar content of solution. A conversion table is required to compensate for a true reading due to the presence of alcohol.

Residual sugar The amount of sugar remaining in a wine after fermentation is completed.

Rohamet P A multi-active enzyme that breaks down the skin of fruit.

Saccharomyces cerevisiae A species of yeast believed to have been isolated originally from the skin of grapes.

Sack mead Heavy sweet meads generally served as dessert wines

Specific gravity The ratio of the density of any substance to the density of some other substance taken as standard, water being the standard for liquids and solids and hydrogen or air being the standard for gases.

Starter bottle A small vessel used to create mini-fermentations by the addition of a yeast starter; a liquid mixture of nutrients and sugars.

Structure A term related to the combination of tannins and acidity within the constitution of the mead or honey wine.

Stuck fermentation A fermentation that stops well before all the available sugar in the wine has been converted to alcohol and carbon dioxide.

Sulphite/s Commonly introduced to arrest fermentation. May also be added to wine as a preservative to prevent spoilage and oxidation. Commonly used in the USA. Sulphites also protect the wine against detrimental oxidative and enzymatic browning.

Sulphur dioxide (SO2) The most widely used additive in winemaking. Used to inhibit or kill unwanted yeasts and bacteria and to protect wine from oxidation.

Sweetness A taste feature that defines the presence of residual sugar or honey present in mead wine.

Tannin A phenolic compound found in oak, cider apple skins and grape skins. Added to wine to give it bite.

Tartaric acid A white crystalline organic acid occurring naturally in many plants, most notably in grapes. Its salt, potassium bitartrate (cream of tartar), develops naturally in the process of winemaking.

Tartness A term associated with high levels of acidity. Tartness or acidity is detected by mouth tasting. An expression used in the USA is "mouth-watering sensation".

Tea An aromatic drink made from *Camellia sinensis*. Used as a substitute for tannin.

Thiamine See vitamin B1.

Titratable acidity (TA) The total of the acid in fruit juice or the must. It is determined as a percentage of tartaric acid by titration with sodium hydroxide using a phenolphthalein indicator.

Vanillin A compound adding aroma and flavour to wine during its ageing process. A desirable component for bouquet and aftertaste.

Vinometer A device for measuring the alcohol content of wine after fermentation.

Vintner A mead maker or honey wine maker. Generically, a purveyor of wines, beers and spirits.

Vitamin B1 Thiamine. Aids the yeast in its reproductive phase.

Vitamin C Ascorbic acid. An antioxidant that assists the yeast in its reproduction.

Yeast A single-celled micro-organism that converts sugar in the must to alcohol and carbon dioxide.

Yeast nutrient Compound added to the must to provide nitrogen for yeast growth.

Yeast starter The process of growth for producing additional yeast cells within a contained controlled environment.

THE AUTHOR

Michael J Badger MBE has been a mead and honey wine vintner for over fifty years. He has been a keeper of honey bees man and boy, whose beekeeping experience extends to over sixty-five years.

He has been involved with the National Honey Show (NHS) since 1972, whilst he qualified as a Senior BBKA Honey Judge in 1984. For 43 years he was an active honey steward at the Great Yorkshire Show, being the Chief Honey Steward responsible for the annual section competition from 1986 until 2015.

He was Chairman of the Yorkshire Beekeepers' Association in 1983 and again in 2000; Chairman and President of the British Beekeepers' Association 1999-2002, and he is an Honorary Member of both the British and the Yorkshire Beekeepers' Associations. Michael's acknowledged contribution to beekeeping is immense: he was instrumental in the establishment of the British Beekeepers' Associations headquarters (the National Beekeeping Centre) at Stoneleigh Park in 2000, the Yorkshire Beekeepers' Associations Normanby Pavilion and the Hives and Honey Pavilion at the Great Yorkshire Showground, Harrogate officially opened by HRH the Duchess of Wessex in 2014.

He was Chairman of *BeeCraft* Limited, a Patron of the charity Bees Abroad, and is a Court Assistant and Liveryman of the Worshipful Company of Wax Chandlers in the City of London. Outside beekeeping his interests include a 725 hectare livestock farm managed on the principals of "Pasture for Life", a conventional grass fed beef fattening farming enterprise in Dorset, together with heavy horses and livestock breeding. Michael is married to Hilary; he has two daughters and a son, plus two grandchildren. Previous publications (in addition to papers, articles and newsletters) include his acclaimed book on *Heather Honey* (2016). In 2003 he was awarded the Member of the British Empire (MBE) for services to beekeeping.

Peter Lewis